CAN I GET A WITNESS?

CAN I GET A WITNESS?

*Prophetic Religious Voices
of African American Women*

An Anthology

Edited by
MARCIA Y. RIGGS

With Biographical Sketches and Selected Bibliography by
BARBARA HOLMES

ORBIS BOOKS

Maryknoll, New York 10545

The Catholic Foreign Mission Society of America (Maryknoll) recruits and trains people for overseas missionary service. Through Orbis Books, Maryknoll aims to foster the international dialogue that is essential to mission. The books published, however, reflect the opinions of their authors and are not meant to represent the official position of the society.

Published by Orbis Books, Maryknoll, NY 10545-0308
Manufactured in the United States of America

Library of Congress Cataloging-in-Publication Data

Can I get a witness? : prophetic religious voices of African American
   women : an anthology / edited by Marcia Y. Riggs : with biographical
   sketches and selected bibliography by Barbara Holmes.
       p.   cm.
   Includes bibliographical references.
   ISBN 1-57075-113-7 (alk. paper)
   1. Afro-American women—Religious life.   2. Race relations—
Religious aspects—Christianity.   I. Riggs, Marcia.
BR563.N4C35   1997
277.3'0092'396073—dc21   96-29584
                                                                          CIP

CONTENTS

PREFACE AND ACKNOWLEDGMENTS

Preachers in the black church often urge worshippers to respond to the Word by asking, "Can I get a witness?" As I collected and listened to the voices of the women gathered in this volume, they became an enduring yes to the preacher's question and to the quest for sources which comprise black women's religious tradition. The compilation of these sources is thus a way to document a distinctive tradition and to make available for others some of the sources within that tradition from which many contemporary womanist religious scholars retrieve our insights and receive our inspiration. As sources of scholarly insights and devotional inspiration, the voices of these women confirm the power of our words to bear witness to the power and presence of the incarnate Word.

This volume is dedicated to faithful mothers of the tradition, such as my own grandmother, Helen Spurgeon, thus acknowledging that the tradition would die if it were not embodied through the lives and work of ordinary women in church and society who nurture others into the tradition as well as do the work of justice. I also acknowledge the foresight of Robert Ellsberg at Orbis Books to perceive the need for this volume and to persist with me in completing a project which has taken longer than I would have imagined, and the work of student assistants, Barbara Holmes and David Murad, who were definitely companions in the struggle to bring this volume to completion.

INTRODUCTION

In recent years, a number of anthologies of primary sources documenting the lives and words of historic and contemporary black women have been compiled. Among those anthologies most frequently cited and used are: *Black Women in White America: A Documentary History*, edited by Gerda Lerner (1972); *Black Women in Nineteenth-Century American Life: Their Words, Their Thoughts, Their Feelings*, edited by Bert James Loewenberg and Ruth Bogin (1976); *We are Your Sisters: Black Women in the Nineteenth Century*, edited by Dorothy Sterling (1984); and most recently, *Words of Fire: An Anthology of African-American Feminist Thought*, edited by Beverly Guy-Sheftall (1995). Each of these anthologies has provided us with important primary source accounts by black women of their private and public lives from the slavery era through the contemporary period.

This anthology builds on these previous works as I chronicle black women's lives as faithful witnesses to the prophetic dimensions of the Gospel using significant sociohistorical moments (slavery, emancipation, urbanization) and movements (e.g., the Great Awakenings, abolition, temperance, suffrage, women's clubs, women's missionary efforts) as implicit principles of selection for this volume. Unlike those previous anthologies,[1] this volume has a single focus, African American women and religion, or more specifically, the reconstruction and retrieval of a prophetic religious tradition of African American women. This tradition includes the experiences and writings of African American women who were involved formally and informally with religious institutions and social reform movements of past and present times. Also, as a work of reconstruction and retrieval, this book seeks to document that tradition as predecessor to current womanist religious scholarship.

This volume intends to suggest that the prophetic religious voices of African American women constitute a distinctive tradition within African American religious history and experience. Tradition here refers to a worldview[2] which can be discerned over time through the writings of African American women who interpret the relevance of their spiritual experiences and belief systems for the church, community, and society. Documenting this tradition continues revisionist scholarship in one of the most important areas of the African American experience. As Cheryl Townsend Gilkes explains it:

> The importance of religion in the African-American experience cannot be overstated. Religion can be seen as both worldview and

human organization, and from both perspectives, women have been at the center. The African-American religious experience, especially as it has been actualized by women, combines African sensibilities, New World experiences, Western Christianity, and an activist orientation toward injustice and racial oppression. As a worldview it encompasses mythic, experiential, doctrinal, ethical, ritual, and social dimensions and transcends specific organizational or denominational forms.[3]

This volume thus documents the prophetic religious tradition of African American women as a worldview, seeking to be inclusive of known and less well-known women whose "testimony" (life and words) express the central elements of what I have described elsewhere as the socio-religious ethical tradition of black women.[4] The features of this tradition are:

> an evaluation of the relation between economics and justice in American society; the recognition of an interrelationship between oppression of Blacks in American society and other people of color; an awareness of a connection between the oppression of blacks and women in terms of misuse of power to subvert justice; and an acknowledgment of distinctive aspects of oppression for black women; a sense of racial obligation and duty; and belief in both the justice of God and justice for blacks as a command of God.[5]

The voices of African American women speaking out of this socio-religious ethical tradition may also be described as prophetic in at least three senses. First, like biblical prophets, the women relate faith and history; they were individuals who brought "faith out of the temple or sanctuary to the marketplace of human affairs where history was in process; history—the present and immediate future viewed in light of the past."[6] Also, these women, like biblical prophets, were "sensitive to evil, felt fiercely, recognized that any injustice has major consequences, agonized, evoked responsibility, were impatient with excuses, disdained pretense and self-pity, and envisioned a transformative end."[7] Accordingly, it would seem that African American women speaking out of their socio-religious tradition create

> . . . a destabilizing presence, so that the system is not equated with reality, so that alternatives are thinkable, so that the absolute claims of the system can be criticized.[8]

Second, the women's voices are consistent with a black prophetic tradition rooted in a relationship between religion and radicalism found in the "prophetic wing of the black church."[9] This tradition is in evidence from the slavery era through the contemporary civil rights era and is earmarked by (1) reappropriation of the revolutionary language of the Declaration of Independence and the Constitution; (2) espousal of providential agency; (3) a theology of national redemption emphasizing social transformation through moral reform; (4) a critique of the practice of democracy in the United States while yet asserting a "mutual dependency between church and state" —the former, being the agent of Christian love and the latter, the agent of social justice.[10]

Third, the voices of these women express a prophetic hermeneutic which seems inextricably bound up with their conversion into Christianity and appropriation of biblical traditions to judge their reality. In the words of Frances Smith Foster, an expert in the literary productions of African American women:

> Defying the laws and customs that imposed silence upon them, African American women testified to their personal experiences and perceptions and to those they shared with their communities. Those who converted to Christianity (and virtually every extant text was written by a professed Christian) took seriously the biblical injunction, to "write the vision, and make it plain" (Hab. 2:2). They used the Word as both a tool and a weapon to correct, to create and to confirm their visions of life as it was and as it could become.[11]

Therefore, the prophetic voices of the African American women in this volume are voices which are confessional, sermonic, political, and poetic—all witnesses to their God as one who created, redeemed, and sustained them and who creates, redeems, and sustains us for the work of liberation.

The volume has three parts. Part One focuses upon the calls of African American women to be God's prophetic witnesses. Part Two illustrates that self-criticism is part of the African American woman's prophetic hermeneutic as these women make claims upon the African American community to be accountable and responsible. Part Three demonstrates African American women's prophetic witness as a call for social transformation of society as a whole. Each selection is preceded by a short biographical sketch and followed by a list of bibliographic sources which offer points of departure for further reading and research. Other than the assumption that these selections are representative of an African American woman's prophetic religious tradition, there is no attempt to direct your reading of the document; rather, each woman's ideas are yours to interpret.

Finally, the selection of the voices for this volume was guided by my own archival research regarding women involved in the black women's club movement during the late nineteenth and early twentieth centuries and the women included in volumes such as the following: Hallie Quinn

Brown's *Homespun Heroines and Other Women of Distinction* (Books for Libraries Press, 1971, [1926]); Benjamin G. Brawley's *Women of Achievement* (Women's American Baptist Home Mission Society, 1919); Monroe A. Majors's *Noted Negro Women: Their Triumphs and Activities* (1983 reprint ed., Books for Libraries Press, 1971); Mrs. N. F. Mossell's *The Work of the Afro-American Woman* (Philadelphia: George S. Ferguson, 1894; reprint, Books for Libraries Press, 1971; Oxford University Press, 1988); *African American Women: A Biographical Dictionary*, edited by Dorothy C. Salem (Garland Publishing, 1993); and *Black Women in America: An Historical Encyclopedia*, edited by Darlene Clark Hine (Carlson Publishing, Inc., 1993). I was not, however, bound by the categorization of the editors of the biographical or encyclopedic volumes because their understanding of women in religion tended to confine them narrowly to those involved with institutional churches or other religious movements. Instead, my basic criterion for including a woman is that her life and writing exhibit the features of the tradition as delineated above.

Notes

[1] The anthology edited by Beverly Guy-Sheftall is an exception. She compiles documents which she characterizes as demonstrating "the evolution of feminist consciousness among African American women."

[2] See Charles L. Kammer III, *Ethics and Liberation: An Introduction* (Maryknoll: Orbis Books, 1988), 20-23. Kammer characterizes a worldview as a comprehensive framework which gives a general coherence to our lives as actors; it may exclude any conception of God but does include some general presumption about the final principles and powers that underlie the existence of both natural and human history; it includes presumptions about human nature, the nature of the world in which we live and human society; it is largely a product of the societies and communities in which we live; it contains varying mixtures of rational and affective elements; we cannot definitively state the truth or falsity of it, but assess its adequacy by referring it to another worldview, by testing its parts for internal consistency, or by seeing whether it provides an adequate description of our experience; the adoption of a worldview is an act of faith, i.e. we risk our own lives and those of others in committing ourselves to a particular worldview.

[3] Cheryl Townsend Gilkes, "Religion," in *Black Women in America: An Historical Encyclopedia*, ed. Darlene Clark Hine (Brooklyn, NY: Carlson Publishing, Inc., 1993), 967.

[4] Marcia Y. Riggs, "The Socio-Religious Ethical Tradition of Black Women: Implications for the Black Church's Role in Black Liberation," *Union Seminary Quarterly Review* 43 (1989):119-132.

[5] Ibid., 126. See also Gilkes, 970. Gilkes asserts, "African-American women have been the principal agents of a distinctive Afro-Christian tradition. There are four basic pillars of this tradition—preaching, prayer, music, and testimony."

[6]James A. Sanders, *Torah and Canon* (Philadelphia: Fortress Press, 1972), 55.

[7]Abraham J. Heschel, *The Prophets: An Introduction,* Volume I (New York: Harper and Row Publishers, 1962), 3-10.

[8]Walter Brueggemann, "The Prophet as a Destabilizing Presence," in *A Social Reading of the Old Testament*, ed. Patrick D. Miller (Minneapolis: Fortress Press, 1994), 223.

[9]See Gayraud S. Wilmore, *Black Religion and Black Radicalism* (Maryknoll: Orbis Books, 1983).

[10]Derek Q. Reeves, "Beyond the River Jordan: An Essay on the Continuity of the Black Prophetic Tradition," *The Journal of Religious Thought* 2/47 (Winter-Spring, 1990-1991): 43-51.

[11]Frances Smith Foster, *Written by Herself: Literary Production by African American Women, 1746-1892* (Bloomington: Indiana University Press, 1993), 1-2.

Part I

HEARING AND ANSWERING GOD'S CALL TO PROPHETIC WITNESS

"Who Are the Witnesses?"

ELIZABETH
(1766-1867)

Born a slave in 1766, Elizabeth had only a first name, but her identity was not in her name, it was in her faith in God. She was the preaching contemporary of Jarena Lee and Zilpha Elaw and experienced similar visionary experiences, which empowered her to resist the forces of oppression in the church and a racially divided society. Ordained by God and sustained by the Holy Spirit, she exhorted and preached the gospel under the most adverse conditions.

"Not by the Commission of Men's Hands"[1]

I was born in Maryland in the year 1766. My parents were slaves. Both my father and mother were religious people, and belonged to the Methodist Society. It was my father's practice to read in the Bible aloud to his children every sabbath morning. At these seasons, when I was but five years old, I often felt the overshadowing of the Lord's Spirit, without at all understanding what it meant; and these incomes and influences continued to attend me until I was eleven years old, particularly when I was alone, by which I was preserved from doing anything that I thought was wrong. . . .

After this time, finding as my mother said, I had none in the world to look to but God, I betook myself to prayer, and in every lonely place I found an altar. I mourned sore like a dove and chattered forth my sorrow, moaning in the corners of the field, and under the fences.

I continued in this state for about six months, feeling as though my head were waters, and I could do nothing but weep. I lost my appetite, and not being able to take enough food to sustain nature, I became so weak I had but little strength to work; still I was required to do all my duty. One evening, after the duties of the day were ended, I thought I could not live over the night, so threw myself on a bench, expecting to die, and without

---

[1]Bert James Loewenberg and Ruth Bogin, eds., *Black Women in Nineteenth-Century American Life: Their Words, Their Thoughts, Their Feelings* (University Park: The Pennsylvania State University Press, 1976, 127; 128-129; 133. It is reported that when Elizabeth was challenged by state officials in Virginia as to her authority to preach and threatened with imprisonment, she replied: "Not by the commission of men's hands: if the Lord has ordained me, I need nothing better."

being prepared to meet my Maker; and my spirit cried within me, must I die in this state, and be banished from Thy presence forever? I own I am a sinner in Thy sight, and not fit to live where thou art. Still it was my fervent desire that the Lord would pardon me. Just at this season, I saw with my spiritual eye, an awful gulf of misery. As I thought I was about to plunge into it, I heard a voice saying, "rise up and pray," which strengthened me. I fell on my knees and prayed the best I could the Lord's prayer. Knowing no more to say, I halted, but continued on my knees. My spirit was then taught to pray, "Lord have mercy on me—Christ save me." Immediately there appeared a director, clothed in white raiment. I thought he took me by the hand and said, "come with me." He led me down a long journey to a fiery gulf, and left me standing upon the brink of this awful pit. I began to scream for mercy, thinking I was about to sink to endless ruin. Although I prayed and wrestled with all my might, it seemed in vain. Still I felt all the while that I was sustained by some invisible power. At this solemn moment, I thought I saw a hand from which hung, as it were, a silver of hair, and a voice told me that all the hope I had of being saved was no more than a hair; still, pray and it will be sufficient. I then renewed my struggle, crying for mercy and salvation, until I found that every cry raised me higher and higher, and my head was quite above the fiery pillars. Then I thought I was permitted to look straight forward and saw the Saviour standing with his hand stretched out to receive me. An indescribably glorious light was in Him, and He said, "peace, peace, come unto me." At this moment I felt that my sins were forgiven me, and the time of my deliverance was at hand. I sprang forward and fell at his feet, giving Him all the thanks and highest praises, crying, Thou hast redeemed me—Thou hast redeemed me to thyself. I felt filled with light and love. At this moment I thought my former guide took me again by the hand and led me upward, till I came to the celestial world and to heaven's door, which I saw was open, and while I stood there, a power surrounded me which drew me in, and I saw millions of glorified spirits in white robes. After I had this view, I thought I heard a voice saying, "Art thou willing to be saved?" I said, "Yes, Lord." Again I was asked, "Art thou willing to be saved in my way?" I stood speechless until he asked me again, "Art thou willing to be saved in my way?" Then I heard a whispering voice say, "If thou art not saved in the Lord's way, thou canst not be saved at all;" at which I exclaimed, "Yes Lord, in thy own way." Immediately a light fell upon my head, and I was filled with light and I was shown the world lying in wickedness, and was told I must go there, and call the people to repentance, for the day of the Lord was at hand; and this message was as a heavy yoke upon me, so that I wept bitterly at the thought of what I should have to pass through. While I wept, I heard a voice say, "weep not, some will laugh at thee, some will scoff at thee, and the dogs will bark at thee, but while thou doest my will, I will be with thee to the ends of the earth."

I was at this time not yet thirteen years old. The next day, when I had come to myself, I felt like a new creature in Christ, and all my desire was to see the Savior. . . .

I felt very unworthy and small, notwithstanding the Lord had shown himself with great power, insomuch that conjecturers and critics were constrained to join in praise to his great name; for truly we had times of refreshing from the presence of the Lord. At one of the meetings, a vast number of the white inhabitants of the place, and many colored people, attended—many no doubt from curiosity to hear what the old colored woman had to say. One, a great scripturian, fixed himself behind the door with pen and ink, in order to take down the discourse in short-hand; but the Almighty Being anointed me with such a portion of his Spirit, that he cast away his paper and pen, and heard the discourse with patience, and was much affected, for the Lord wrought powerfully on his heart. After meeting, he came forward and offered me his hand, with solemnity on his countenance, and handed me something to pay for my conveyance home.

I returned, much strengthened by the Lord's power, to go on to the fulfillment of his work, although I was again pressed by the authorities of the church to which I belonged, for imprudency; and so much condemned, that I was sorely tempted by the enemy to turn aside into the wilderness. I was so embarrassed and encompassed, I wondered within myself whether all that were called to be a mouth-piece for the Lord suffered such deep wading as I experienced.

I now found I had to travel still more extensively in the work of the ministry, and I applied to the Lord for direction. I was often invited to go hither and thither, but felt that I must wait for the dictates of his Spirit.

At a meeting which I held in Maryland, I was led to speak from the passage, "Woe to the rebellious city," &c. After the meeting, the people came where I was, to take me before the squire; but the Lord delivered me from their hands.

—*Elizabeth*

Bibliography

Loewenberg, Bert James and Ruth Bogin. *Black Women in Nineteenth-Century American Life*. Unversity Park: The Pennsylvania State University Press, 1976.

Old Elizabeth. "Memoir of Old Elizabeth." In *Six Women's Slave Narratives*. Edited by Henry Louis Gates, Jr. New York: Oxford University Press, 1988.

———. *Elizabeth, A Colored Minister of the Gospel, Born in Slavery*. Philadelphia: Quaker Meeting House, 1889.

Williams, Delores S. "Visions, Inner Voices, Apparitions, and Defiance in Nineteenth-Century Black Women's Narratives." *Women's Studies Quarterly* (1993):87-89.

Jarena Lee
(1783-?)

In 1809, she was the first black woman to request the right to preach in an African Methodist Episcopal (A.M.E.) Church. Although the initial request was denied, she continued her ministry as an itinerant preacher who challenged the status quo. She also published two autobiographies during her lifetime, despite the lack of a formal education. Ultimately her gifts of ministry were sanctioned and acclaimed by the A.M.E. Church and all who were privileged to hear her preach.

"My Call to Preach the Gospel"[2]

Between four and five years after my sanctification, on a certain time, an impressive silence fell upon me, and I stood as if some one was about to speak to me, yet I had no such thought in my heart. But to my utter surprise there seemed to sound a voice which I thought I distinctly heard, and most certainly understood, which said to me, "Go preach the Gospel!" I immediately replied aloud, "No one will believe me." Again I listened, and again the same voice seemed to say, "Preach the Gospel; I will put words in your mouth, and will turn your enemies to become your friends."

At first I supposed that Satan had spoken to me, for I had read that he could transform himself into an angel of light, for the purpose of deception. Immediately I went into a secret place, and called upon the Lord to know if he had called me to preach, and whether I was deceived or not; when there appeared to my view the form and figure of a pulpit, with a Bible lying thereon, the back of which was presented to me as plainly as if it had been a literal fact.

In consequence of this, my mind became so exercised that during the night following, I took a text, and preached in my sleep. I thought there stood before me a great multitude, while I expounded to them the things of religion. So violent were my exertions, and so loud were my exclamations, that I awoke from the sound of my own voice, which also awoke the family of the house where I resided. Two days after, I went to see the preacher in charge of the African Society, who was the Rev. Richard Allen,

---

[2]"The Life and Religious Experience of Jarena Lee" as found in William L. Andrews, ed., *Sisters of the Spirit* (Bloomington: Indiana University Press, 1986), 35-37.

. . . to tell him that I felt it my duty to preach the gospel. But as I drew near the street in which his house was, which was in the city of Philadelphia, my courage began to fail me; so terrible did the cross appear, it seemed that I should not be able to bear it. Previous to my setting out to go to see him, so agitated was my mind, that my appetite for my daily food failed me entirely. Several times on my way there, I turned back again; but as often I felt my strength again renewed, and I soon found that the nearer I approached to the house of the minister, the less was my fear. Accordingly, as soon as I came to the door, my fears subsided, the cross was removed, all things appeared pleasant—I was tranquil.

I now told him, that the Lord had revealed it to me, that I must preach the gospel. He replied by asking, in what sphere I wished to move in? I said, among the Methodists. He then replied, that a Mrs. Cook, a Methodist lady, had also some time before requested the same privilege; who it was believed, had done much good in the way of exhortation, and holding prayer meetings; and who had been permitted to do so by the verbal license of the preacher in charge at the time. But as to women preaching, he said that our Discipline knew nothing at all about it—that it did not call for women preachers. This I was glad to hear, because it removed the fear of the cross—but not no sooner did this feeling cross my mind, than I found that a love of souls had in a measure departed from me; that holy energy which burned within me, as a fire, began to be smothered. This I soon perceived.

O how careful ought we to be, lest through our by-laws of church government and discipline, we bring into disrepute even the world of life. For as unseemly as it may appear nowadays for a woman to preach, it should be remembered that nothing is impossible with God. And why should it be thought impossible, heterodox, or improper, for a woman to preach? seeing the Saviour died for the woman as well as the man.

If a man may preach, because the Saviour died for him, why not the woman? seeing he died for her also. Is he not a whole Saviour, instead of a half one? as those who hold it wrong for a woman to preach, would seem to make it appear.

Did not Mary *first* preach the risen Saviour, and is not the doctrine of the resurrection the very climax of Christianity—hangs not all our hope on this, as argued by St. Paul? Then did not Mary, a woman, preach the gospel? for she preached the resurrection of the crucified Son of God.

But some will say, that Mary did not expound the Scripture, therefore, she did not preach, in the proper sense of the term. To this I reply, it may be that the term *preach*, in those primitive times, did not mean exactly what it is now *made* to mean; perhaps it was a great deal more simple then, than it is now:—if it were not, the unlearned fishermen could not have preached the gospel at all, as they had not learning.

To this it may be replied, by those who are determined not to believe that it is right for a woman to preach, that the disciples, though they were fishermen, and ignorant of letters too, were inspired so to do. To which I would reply, that though they were inspired, yet that inspiration did not save them from showing their ignorance of letters, and of man's widsom; this the multitude soon found out, by listening to the remarks of the envious Jewish priests. If then, to preach the gospel, by the gift of heaven, comes by inspiration solely, is God straitened (sic); must he take the man exclusively? May he not, did he not, and can he not inspire a female to preach the simple story of the birth, life, death, and resurrection of our Lord, and accompany it too, with power to the sinner's heart. As for me, I am fully persuaded that the Lord called me to labour according to what I have received, in his vineyard. If he has not, how could he consistently bear testimony in favour of my poor labours, in awakening and converting sinners?

In my wanderings up and down among men, preaching according to my ability, I have frequently found families who told me that they had not for several years been to a meeting, and yet, while listening to hear what God would say by his poor coloured female instrument, have believed with trembling—tears rolling down their cheeks, the signs of contrition and repentance towards God. I firmly believe that I have sown seed, in the name of the Lord, which shall appear with its increase at the great day of accounts, when Christ shall come to make up his jewels.

"The Subject of My Call to Preach Renewed"[3]

It was now eight years since I had made application to be permitted to preach the gospel, during which time I had only been allowed to exhort, and even this privilege but seldom. This subject now was renewed afresh in my mind; it was as a fire shut up in my bones. About thirteen months passed on, while under this renewed impression. During this time, I had solicited of the Rev. Bishop Richard Allen, who at time had become Bishop of the African Episcopal Methodists in America, to be permitted the liberty of holding prayer meetings in my own hired house, and of exhorting as I found liberty, which was granted me. By this means, my mind was relieved, as the house was soon filled when the hour appointed for prayer had arrived. . . .

But to return to the subject of my call to preach. Soon after this, . . . the Rev. Richard Williams was to preach at Bethel Church, where I with others were assembled. He entered the pulpit, gave out the hymn, which was sung, and then addressed the throne of grace; took his text, passed through the exordium, and commenced to expound it. The text he took is in Jonah, 2d chap. 9th verse,—"Salvation is of the Lord." But as he proceeded to explain, he seemed to have lost the spirit; when in the same instant, I

---

[3]Andrews, *Sisters of the Spirit*, 42, 44-46.

sprang, as by an altogether supernatural impulse, to my feet, when I was aided from above to give an exhortation on the very text which my brother Williams had taken.

I told them that I was like Jonah; for it has been then nearly eight years since the Lord had called me to preach his gospel to the fallen sons and daughters of Adam's race, but that I had lingered like him, and delayed to go at the bidding of the Lord, and warn those who are as deeply guilty as were the people of Ninevah.

During the exhortation, God made manifest his power in a manner sufficient to show the world that I was called to labour according to my ability, and the grace given unto me, in the vineyard of the good husbandman.

I now sat down, scarcely knowing what I had done, being frightened. I imagined, that for this indecorum, as I feared it might be called, I should be expelled from the church. But instead of this, the Bishop rose up in the assembly, and related that I had called upon him eight years before, asking to be permitted to preach, and that he had put me off; but that he now as much believed that I was called to that work, as any of the preachers present. These remarks greatly strengthened me, so that my fears of having given an offence, and made myself liable as an offender, subsided, giving place to a sweet serenity, a holy job of a peculiar kind, untasted in my bosom until then.

The next Sabbath day, while sitting under the word of the gospel, I felt moved to attempt to speak to the people in a public manner, but I could not bring my mind to attempt it in the church. I said, Lord, anywhere but here. Accordingly, there was a house not far off which was pointed out to me, to this I went. It was the house of a sister belonging to the same society with myself. Her name was Anderson. I told her I had come to hold a meeting in her house, if she would call to her neighbours. With this request she immediately complied. My congregration consisted of but five persons. I commenced by reading and singing a hymn, when I dropped to my knees by the side of a table to pray. When I arose I found my hand resting on the Bible, which I had not noticed till that moment. It now occurred to me to take a text. I opened the Scripture, as it happened, at the 141st Psalm, fixing my eye on the 3d verse, which reads: "Set a watch, O Lord, before my mouth, keep the door of my lips." My sermon, such as it was, I applied wholly to myself, and added an exhortation. Two of my congregation wept much, as the fruit of my labour this time. In closing I said to the few, that if any one would open a door, I would hold a meeting the next sixth-day evening; when one answered that her house was at my service. Accordingly I went, and God made manifest his power among the people. Some wept, while others shouted for joy. One whole seat of females, by the power of God, as the rushing of a wind, were all bowed to the floor at once, and screamed out. Also a sick man and woman in one house, the Lord convicted them both; one lived, and the other died. God wrought a judgment—some were well at night, and died in the morning.

At this place I continued to hold meetings about six months. During that time I kept house with my little son, who was very sickly. About this time I had a call to preach at a place about thirty miles distant, among the Methodists, with whom I remained one week, and during the whole time, not a thought of my little son came into my mind; it was hid from me, lest I should have diverted from the work I had to, to look after my son. Here by the instrumentality of a poor coloured woman, the Lord poured forth his spirit among the people. Though, as I was told, there were lawyers, doctors, and magistrates present, to hear me speak, yet there was mourning and crying among sinners, for the Lord scattered fire among them of his own kindling. The Lord gave his handmaiden power to speak for his great name, for he arrested the hearts of the people, and caused a shaking amongst the multitude, for God was in the midst.

—Jarena Lee

Bibliography

Andrews, William L., ed. *Sisters of the Spirit: Three Black Women's Autobiographies of the Nineteenth Century.* Bloomington: Indiana University Press, 1986.

Burrow, Rufus. "Sexism in the Black Community and the Black Church." *Journal of the Interdenominational Theological Center.* Spring, 1986.

Cummings, Lorine L. "A Womanist Response to the Afrocentric Idea: Jarena Lee, Womanist Preacher." In *Living the Intersection: Womanism and Afrocentrism in Theology.* Edited by Cheryl J. Sanders. Minneapolis: Fortress Press, 1995.

Dodson, Jualynne. "Nineteenth-Century A.M.E. Preaching Women." In *Women in New Worlds.* Edited by Hillah F. Thomas and Rosemary Skinner Keller. Nashville: Abingdon Press, 1981.

Lee, Jarena. *The Life and Religious Experiences of Jarena Lee.* Philadelphia: The Author, 1836.

———. *Religious Experience and Journal of Mrs. Jarena Lee.* Philadelphia: The Author, 1849.

Payne, Daniel A. *History of the African Methodist Episcopal Church.* Nashville: AME Sunday-School Union, 1891.

Walker, Clarence E. *A Rock in a Weary Land: The African Methodist Episcopal Church During the Civil War and Reconstruction.* Baton Rouge: Louisiana State University Press, 1982.

Wesley, Charles H. *Richard Allen.* Washington, D.C.: Associated Publishers, 1935.

Wills, David W. "Womanhood and Domesticity in the A.M.E. Tradition: The Influence of Daniel Alexander Payne." In *Black Apostles at Home and Abroad.* Edited by David W. Wills and Richard Newman. Boston: G.K. Hall, 1982.

ZILPHA ELAW
(c. 1790)

Zilpha's intense visionary experiences led to her conversion and call to ministry. She preached about a freedom through spiritual endeavor and mystical union with the Divine that transcended the oppressive social order. This freedom in the Spirit empowered evangelist Elaw to challenge the forces of injustice. She was also the nondenominational preaching partner of Jarena Lee, and one can hardly imagine a more spiritually dynamic duo.

"Conversion and Call"[4]

In the year 1817, I attended an American camp-meeting. Oh, how I should like our dear English friends to witness some of our delightful camp-meetings, which are held in the groves of the United States. There many thousands assemble in the open air, and beneath the overspreading bowers, to own and worship our common Lord, the Proprietor of the Universe; there all arise and sing the solemn praises of the King of majesty and glory. It is like heaven descended upon an earthly soil, when all unite to "Praise God, from whom all blessings flow."

The hardest hearts are melted into tenderness; the driest eyes overflow with tears, and the loftiest spirits bow down: the Creator's works are gazed upon, and His near presence felt around.

In order to form a camp-meeting, when the place and time of meeting has been extensively published, each family takes its own tent, and all things necessary for lodgings, with seats, provisions and servants; and with wagons and other vehicles repair to the destined spot, which is generally some wildly rural and wooded retreat in the back grounds of the interiors: hundreds of families, and thousands of persons, are seen pressing to the place from all quarters; the meeting usually continues for a week or more: a large circular inclosure of brushwood is formed; immediately inside of which the tents are pitched, and the space in the center is appropriated to the worship of God, the minister's stand being on one

---

[4]"Memoirs of the Life, Religious Experience, Ministerial Travels, and Labours of Mrs. Zilpha Elaw, An American Female of Colour; Together with Some Account of the Great Religious Revivals in America [Written by Herself] (1846)" as found in Andrews, *Sisters of the Spirit*, 64-67.

side, and generally on somewhat rising ground. It is a scaffold constructed of boards, and surrounded with a fence of rails.

In the space before the platform, seats are placed sufficient to seat four or five thousand persons; and at night the woods are illuminated; there are generally four large mounds of earth constructed and on them large piles of pine knots are collected and ignited, which make a wonderful blaze and burn a long time; there are also candles and lamps hung about in the trees, together with a light in every tent, the minister's stand is brilliantly lighted up; so that the illumination attendant upon a camp-meeting, is a magnificently solemn scene. The worship commences in the morning before the sunrise; the watchmen proceed round the inclosure, blowing with trumpets to awaken every inhabitant of this City of the Lord; they then proceed again round the camp, to summon the inmates of every tent to their family devotions; after which they partake of breakfast, and are again summoned by sound of trumpet to public prayer meeting at the altar which is placed in front of the preaching stand. Many precious souls are on these occasions introduced into the liberty of the children of God; at the close of the prayer meeting the grove is teeming with life and activity; the numberless private conferences, the salutations of old friends again meeting in the flesh, the earnest inquiries of sinners, the pressing exhortations of anxious saints, the concourse of pedestrians, the arrival of horses and carriages of all descriptions render the scene portentously interesting and intensely surprising. At ten o'clock, the trumpets sound again to summon the people to public worship; the seats are all speedily filled and as perfect a silence reigns throughout the place as in a Church or Chapel; presently the high praises of God sound melodiously from this consecrated spot, and nothing seems wanting but local elevation to render the place a heaven indeed. It is like God's ancient and holy hill of Zion on her brightest festival days, when the priests conducted the processions of the people to the glorious temple of Jehovah. At the conclusion of the service, the people repair to their tents or other rendezvous to dinner; at the termination of which prayers are offered up, and hymns are sung in the tents, and in the different groups scattered over the ground; and many precious souls enter into the liberty of God's dear children. At two o'clock, a public prayer-meeting commences at the stand, and is continued till three, when the ministers preach again to the people. At six o'clock in the evening, the public services commence again as before; and at the hour of ten, the trumpet is blown as a signal for all to retire to rest; and those who are unprovided with lodgings, leave the ground. On the last morning of the camp-meeting, which is continued for a week, a solemn love feast is held; after which, all the tents are struck and everything put in readiness for departure; the ministers finally form themselves in procession and march round the encampment; the people falling into rank and following them. At length the ministers turn aside from the rank, stand still, and commence singing a solemn farewell hymn; and as the different ranks of the people march by, they shake hands with their pastors, take an affectionate fare-well of them, and pass on in procession, until the last or rear rank have taken their adieu. This farewell scene is a most moving and affecting occa-sion. Hundreds of Christians, dear to each other and beloved in the Spirit, embrace each other for the last time, and part to meet no more, until the morning of the resurrection; and many a stout-hearted sinner has been so shaken to pieces at the pathetic sight, as to fall into deep conviction of his depravity before God, which has ended in genuine repentance and saving conversion to Christ. I, for one, have great reason to thank God for the refreshing seasons of his mighty grace, which have accompanied these great meetings of his saints in the wilderness. It was at one of these meet-ings that God was pleased to separate my soul unto Himself, to sanctify me as a vessel designed for honour, made meet for the master's use. Whether I was in the body, or whether I was out of the body, on that aus-picious day, I cannot say; but this I do know, that at the conclusion of a most powerful sermon delivered by one of the ministers from the plat-form, and while the congregation were in prayer, I became so overpow-ered with the presence of God, that I sank down upon the ground, and laid there for a considerable time; and while I was thus prostrate on the earth, my spirit seemed to ascend up into the clear circle of the sun's disc; and, surrounded and engulphed in the glorious effulgence of his rays, I dis-tinctly head a voice speak unto me, which said, "Now thou art sanctified; and I will show thee what thou must do." I saw no personal appearance while in this stupendous elevation, but I discerned bodies of resplendent light; nor did I appear to be in this world at all, but immensely far above those spreading trees, beneath whose shady and verdant bowers I was then reclined. When I recovered from the trance or ecstasy into which I had fallen, the first thing I observed was, that hundreds of persons were standing around me weeping; and I clearly saw by the light of the Holy Ghost, that my heart and soul were rendered completely spotless—as clean as a sheet of white paper, and I felt as pure as if I had never sinned in all my life; a solemn stillness rested upon my soul:

"The speechless awe that dares not move,
And all the silent heaven of love."

Truly I durst not move, because God was so powerfully near to me; for the space of several hours I appeared not to be on earth, but far above all earthly things. I had not at this time offered up public prayer on the camp ground; but when the prayer meeting afterwards commenced, the Lord opened my mouth in public prayer; and while I was thus engaged, it seemed as if I heard my God rustling in the tops of the mulberry-trees. Oh, how precious was this day to my soul! I was after this very frequently requested to present my petitions to the throne of grace in the public meetings at the camp; and to my astonishment, during one of the services, an old gentleman and his wife, whose heads were blanched by the frost of time, came to me, fell upon their knees, and desired me to pray for them, as also many others whom I expect to meet in a happier world; and before the meeting at this camp closed, it was revealed to me by the Holy Spirit, that like another Phoebe, or the matrons of the apostolic societies, I must employ myself in visiting families, and in speaking personally to the members thereof, of the salvation and eternal interests of their souls, visit the sick, and attend upon other of the errands and services of the Lord; which I afterwards cheerfully did, not confining my visits to the poor only, but extending them to the rich also, and even to those who sit in high places in the state; and the Lord was with me in the work to own and bless my labours. Like Enoch, I walked and talked with God: nor did a single cloud intervene betwixt God and my soul for many months after.

"Call to Ministry"[5]

At length the auspicious morning arrived for us to proceed on our journey to the holy mount of God; the carriage soon drove up to my door, and I bade farewell to my dear husband. We started off, and it being a delightful day, we had a very pleasant journey, and arrived on the campground in the afternoon of the same day. I was very cordially received by the dear friends, and the dear brethren in the ministry joyfully hailed my appearance on the camp ground; and I was promptly handed to a seat to take refreshments after my journey. There were thousands already assembled; but the best of all was, God was there; and much good was accomplished in the name of Jesus. Friday and Saturday were two heavenly days indeed; the mighty power of God was greatly displayed, and His ministers were like a flame of fire; so animated with godly zeal. I never saw so much godly effort and evangelic exertion displayed in all my life as on that occasion. On the Lord's-day morning, the presiding Elder stepped forth in the might of the Holy Spirit, like Joshua, when he went to meet the angelic captain of the Lord's hosts, and said, "Let this day be entirely spent in holiness to the Lord; let no table be spread; but let us abstain as much as possible from food, and see what the Lord will do for us this day; for this is the great day of battle against the old dragon and the powers of darkness." Oh! what a memorable day was this. The public prayer-meeting commenced at seven o'clock in the morning; and at half-past eight o'clock, dear Mr. Potts preached a powerful sermon, under which many souls were awakened to a concern for their eternal interests. At ten, the trumpet sounded again for preaching, and the presiding Elder preached from 2 Cor. v.20. "Now then we are ambassadors for Christ; as though God did beseech you by us; we pray you in Christ's stead, be ye reconciled to

---

[5]Andrews, *Sisters of the Spirit*, 80-82.

God." When he came to the application of his discourse, there seemed not to be one person on the spot, whose eyes were not suffused with tears; both high and low, rich and poor, white and coloured, were all melted like wax before the fire. In every part of that vast concourse, the number of which was estimated at seven thousands, there were heaving bursts of penitential emotion, with streaming eyes; and the mighty action of the Holy Spirit, and the quickening energy of God was so obvious and exhilarating, that all the sons of God shouted for joy. At the conclusion of this lively and interesting meeting, the people returned to their tents to pray with, and direct and comfort those who were in the distresses of godly sorrow. A number of persons were collected in our tent, who were in great distress, earnestly imploring the mercy of God. We engaged in fervent prayer with and for them; and a great noise being made from the mingling of so many voices, and of such various tones of sorrow and rejoicing, of despair and exultation, of prayer and praise hundreds were attracted to the place, and came round to witness the scene, and ascertain what was going forward. One of the brethren manifested some uneasiness and dissatisfaction at the eagerness with which the people came rushing into our tent; and I said to him, "Oh, never mind, my brother; let them come in and see the wonderful works of God;" and I was in the act of pressing through the crowd to open the back part of the tent, which I was just about to do, when I felt, as it were a hand, touch me on the right shoulder; and a voice said to me, "Go outside of the tent while I speak with thee." I turned myself round to see from whom the voice proceeded; but there were none near me but those of our own company; and not any of them were addressing me. I immediately went outside and stood at the door of the tent; and in an instant I began as it were involuntarily, or from an internal prompting, with a loud voice to exhort the people who yet were remaining near the preacher's stand; and in the presence of a more numerous assemblage of ministers than I had ever seen together before; as if God had called forth witnesses from heaven, and witnesses on earth, ministers and members, to witness on this day to my commission, and the qualifications He bestowed on me to preach his holy Gospel. How appropriate to me was the text which had been preached from just before, "Now, then, we are ambassadors for Christ." Our dear ministers stood gazing and listening with wonder and astonishment; and the tears flowed abundantly down their cheeks while they witnessed the wonderful works of God. After I had finished my exhortation, I sat down and closed my eyes; and there appeared a light shining round about me as well as within me, above the brightness of the sun; and out of that light, the same identical voice which had spoken to me on the bed of sickness many months before, spoke again to me on the camp ground, and said, "Now thou knowest the will of God concerning thee; thou must preach the gospel; and thou must travel far and wide." This is my commission for the work of the ministry, which I received, not from mortal man, but from the voice of an invisible and heavenly personage sent from God. Moreover, this did not occur in the night, when the dozing slumbers and imaginative dreams are prevalent, but at mid-day, between the hours of twelve and two o'clock; and my ministry was commenced in the midst of thousands who were both eye and ear witnesses of the fact. Oh, adorable Trinity! dispose me to do thy holy will in all things. This was my experience on the Lord's day on the camp ground; a day wherein the energies of the Holy Spirit were amazingly exerted, and His presence circulated; and on which, hundreds drank into, and were filled with the Spirit. It was such a day as I never witnessed either before or since. . . .

"On Racial Prejudice"[6]

After my dear husband was buried, and I had become a little settled, instead of submitting myself in all things to be led by the Spirit, I rather leaned to my own understanding, and procured a situation of servitude for my little girl, and another for myself, judging these the best means I could adopt for the liquidation of my debts; and I remained in service until my health was so impaired that I was compelled to relinquish it; nor did the blessing of my heavenly Father appear to prosper this course; for I was constantly obliged to be under medical treatment, and yet grew worse and worse. I therefore left my situation, and went back to my house, which I had still reserved in case I should want it. I then opened a school, and the Lord blessed the effort, and increased the number of my pupils, so that I soon had a nice little school; many of the [S]ociety of [F]riends came and visited it, and assisted me with books and other necessaries for it. They were also much pleased with the improvement of the children; and when any strangers came to visit Burlington, they introduced them to me; and it was gratifying to many of them to see a female of colour teaching the coloured children, whom the white people refused to admit into their seminaries and who had been suffered formerly to run about the streets for want of a teacher. The pride of a white skin is a bauble of great value with many in some parts of the United States, who readily sacrifice their intelligence to their prejudices, and possess more knowledge than wisdom. The Almighty accounts not the black races of man either in the order of nature or spiritual capacity as inferior to the white; for He bestows his Holy Spirit on, and dwells in them as readily as in persons of whiter complexion; the Ethiopian eunuch was adopted as a son and heir of God; and when Ethiopia shall stretch forth her hands unto him [Ps. 68:31], their submission and worship will be graciously accepted. This prejudice was far less prevalent in that part of the country [Pennsylvania] where I resided in my infancy; for when a child, I was not prohibited from any school on account of the colour of my skin. Oh! that men would outgrow their

---

[6]Andrews, *Sisters of the Spirit*, 85-86.

nursery prejudices and learn that "God hath made of one blood all the nations of men that dwell upon all the face of the earth." Acts xvii.26.

"Proclaiming the Gospel in the Slave States"[7]

I returned home in April, 1828, and remained there a few days. During my stay at home, I was one day exercised with devout contemplations of God, and suddenly the Spirit came upon me, and a voice addressed me, saying, "Be of good cheer, and be faithful; I will yet bring thee to England and thou shalt see London, that great city, and declare my name there." I looked round to ascertain from when and from whom the voice proceeded, but no person was near me; my surprise was so great that my very blood seemed to stagnate and chill in my veins: it was evidently the Spirit of the Lord whose I am, and whom I serve, who had spoken to me; and my soul responded to His word, saying, "The will of the Lord be done in and by me on earth, as it is by His servants in Heaven." My mind was at this time very much perplexed as to what was the will of God concerning me: I was in doubt as to what I ought to do; but, after a few days, I took my journey again to Philadelphia, with the intention of visiting the southern or slave-holding states of America; here I saw my dear daughter, and remained with my friends during some few weeks; but the confusion of my mind still continued, and whenever I opened a Bible, wherever I visited, as well as my apartment, the book of the prophet Jonah was perpetually presented before me. I mentioned to my friends the uncertainty of my mind as to what the Lord required me to do, the propriety of a voyage to England, and my repeatedly opening in the Bible at the book of Jonah; and they assured me that if it was God's will that I should then visit England, He would make it appear, and smooth the way for me in His own good time. I therefore rested upon this assurance; and while I yet abode in Philadelphia, I dreamed one night, that I saw two ships cleared out of the docks there, bound for England, and I was not on board either of them. I then concluded that the time for my journey to England had not yet come; and being now satisfied on this matter, I started off for the southern territories of the United States, where slavery is established and enforced by law. When I arrived in the slave states, Satan much worried and distressed my soul with fear of being arrested and sold for a slave, which their laws would have warranted, on account of my complexion and features. On one occasion, in particular, I had been preaching to a coloured congregation, and had exhorted them impressively to [ac]quit themselves as men approved of God, and to maintain and witness a good profession of their faith before the world, &c. I had no sooner sat down, than Satan suggested to me with such force, that the slave-holders would speedily capture me,

---

[7]Andrews, *Sisters of the Spirit*, 90-93; 97-98.

as filled me with fear and terror. I was then in a small town in one of the slave states; and the news of a coloured female preaching to the slaves had already been spread widely throughout the neighbourhood; the novelty of the thing had produced an immense excitement and the people were collecting from every quarter, to gaze at the unexampled prodigy of a coloured female preacher. I was sitting in a very conspicuous situation near the door, and I observed, with very painful emotions, the crowd outside, pointing with their fingers at me, and saying, "that's her," "that's her;" for Satan strongly set before me the prospect of an immediate arrest and consignment by sale to some slave owner. Being very much alarmed, I removed from my seat to a retired part of the room where, becoming more collected, I inquired within myself, "from whence cometh all this fear?" My faith then rallied and my confidence in the Lord returned, and I said, "get thee behind me Satan, for my Jesus hath made me free." My fears instantly forsook me, and I vacated my retired corner, and came forth before all the people again; and the presence and power of the Lord became greatly manifested in the assembly during the remainder of the service. At the earnest request of the friends, I consented to preach there again on the following Lord's-day morning, which I accordingly did. Some of the white brethren in connexion with the Methodist Society were present on that occasion; at the conclusion thereof, they introduced themselves to me, and wished me to preach for them in the afternoon; to which I agreed; and they obtained permission of the authorities to auditory; and God gave forth proofs that my ministry was from Him, in giving me many seals to it on that day; thus was I relieved from my fearful forebodings, and pursued my course with increased energy, rejoicing in the prosperity and success with which the Almighty crowned my efforts.

After this, I visited Baltimore in the State of Maryland and attended a conference of the coloured brethren, by whom I was very kindly received; a large field of labour was provided, and a great and effectual door of utterance opened to me by the Lord. After labouring there for some weeks, I proceeded to the City of Washington, the capital of the United States, and the seat of government: here also I laboured with much success; many souls obtaining the knowledge of salvation by the remission of their sins, with the gift of the Holy Spirit, through the instrumentality of so feeble an earthen vessel. I continued my travels southward into the State of Virginia, and arrived at the City of Alexandria, where the Lord rendered my labours effectual to the conversion of many from darkness to light, and from the power of Satan unto God. I abode there two months, and was an humble agent, in the Lord's hand, of arousing many of His heritage to a great revival; and the weakness and incompetency of the poor coloured female but the more displayed the excellency of the power to be of God. There were some among the great folks whom curiosity induced to attend my ministry; and this formed a topic of lively interest with many of the slave holders, who thought it surpassingly strange that a person (and a female) belonging to the same family stock with their poor debased, un-educated, coloured slaves, should come into their territories and teach the enlightened proprietors the knowledge of God; and more strange still was it to some others, when in the spirit and power of Christ, that female drew the portraits of their characters, made manifest the secrets of their hearts, and told them all things that ever they did. This was a paradox to them indeed: for they were not deficient of pastors and reverend divines, who possessed all the advantages of talents, learning, respectability and worldly influence, to aid their religious efforts; and yet the power of truth and of God was never so manifest in any of their agencies, as with the dark coloured female stranger, who had come from afar to minister amongst them. But God hath chosen the weak things of the world to confound the mighty. Divine goodness raised me and honoured me as an angel of God; yet my bodily presence continued weak; the passions, frailties and imper-fections of humanity abounded in my own consciousness; the union of such meanness and honour rendered me a riddle to myself. I became such a prodigy to this people, that I was watched wherever I went; and if I went out to tea with any of the friends, the people would flock around the house where I was; and as soon as they judged that the repast was finished, they came in and filled the house, and required me to minister to them the word of life, whether I had previously intended to preach or not. The people became increasingly earnest in their inquiries after truth; and great was the number of those who were translated out of the empire of darkness into the Kingdom of God's dear Son. . . .

My next visit was to Baltimore, and from thence I went to Annapolis, where I continued during a great part of the winter. Here, also, the Lord gave forth to the people His gracious attestations that my ministry was from Him; for my speech and my preaching were not with enticing words of man's wisdom, but in demonstration of the Spirit, and in power; it was mighty through God, to the pulling down of strongholds; and became the power of God to the salvation of many. On one Lord's-day evening in this place, I was led by the Spirit to discourse very impressively on mortality and death; so much so, that my sermon might have been well suited to a funereal occasion; I was succeeded in the pulpit by a local preacher, a coloured brother and a slave; this poor brother seemed to manifest an undue anxiety for his freedom. Certainly, freedom is preferable to bond-age, as saith the apostle Paul, 1 Cor. vii. 21; who bade the Christian breth-ren in bondage to be unconcerned about it, unless an opportunity arrived of their attaining freedom; in which case, they were to avail themselves thereof. This poor brother in bonds, however, was very impatient of sla-very, and anxiously sighed for liberty. Alas! his life and spirit, his body, his bones, and his blood, as respects this life, were legally the property of, and at the disposal of his fellow man. But his sighs were heard in heaven by Him who looseth the prisoners, and the time of his release arrived. In that same week he was taken ill, and finally fell asleep in Jesus, departing to be "where the wicked cease from troubling, and the weary are at rest. There the prisoners rest together; they hear not the voice of the oppressor; the small and great are there, and the servant is free from his master." Job iii.17-19. His interment was a remarkably afflictive occasion: his corpse was brought into the chapel during the time of service, and the wailing of the congregation grew so intense, that the officiating minister was unable to proceed with the service. The suddenness of the stroke was surprising; and the loss of their beloved minister appeared to his sorrowful flock more like a dream than a fact. Oh, the abominations of slavery! though Philemon be the proprietor, and Onesimus the slave, yet every case of slavery, however lenient its inflictions and mitigated its atrocities, indicates an oppressor, the oppressed, and the oppression. Slavery in every case, save those of parental government, criminal punishment, or the self-protecting detentions of justifiable war, if such can happen, involves a wrong, the deepest in wickedness of any included within the range of the second table.

—*Zilpha Elaw*

Bibliography

Braxton, Joanne M. *Black Women Writing Autobiography: A Tradition Within a Tradition*. Philadelphia: Temple University Press, 1989.

Elaw, Zilpha. "Memoirs of the Life, Religious Experience, Ministerial Travels and Labours of Mrs. Zilpha Elaw: An American Female of Colour." In *Sisters of the Spirit: Three Black Women's Autobiographies of the Nineteenth Century*. Edited by William L. Andrews. Bloomington: Indiana University Press, 1986.

Shockley, Ann Allen. "Zilpha Elaw." In *Afro-American Women Writers, 1746-1933: An Anthology and Critical Guide*. Boston: G.K. Hall, 1988.

SOJOURNER TRUTH [ISABELLA BAUMFREE]
(1797-1883)

We continue to resonate with the question and the woman, Sojourner Truth, who asked the question, "Arn't I a Woman?" The passage of time has not eroded the relevance of her speech because her words emanated from the heart of an oppressed people. She challenged the definition of womanhood that excluded black women as she modeled the strength and resilience of black femininity. After a dramatic conversion experience, she joined the Methodist Church, and subsequently lived and worked in several millennium and utopian-oriented religious communities. Sojourner Truth was an orator of extraordinary skill, lecturing and exhorting in opposition to slavery and for the rights of women from the depths of her faith. She was a powerhouse of a woman, a model of womanhood for the ages.

"The Lord Has Made Me a Sign"[8]

The Lord has made me a sign unto this nation, an' I go round a'testifyin', an' showin' their sins agin my people. My name was Isabella; but when I left the house of bondage, I left everything behind. I wa'n't goin' to keep nothin' of Egypt on me, an' so I went to the Lord an' asked him to give me a new name. An the Lord gave me Sojourner, because I was to travel up an' down the land, showin' the people their sins, an' bein' a sign unto them. Afterward I told the Lord I wanted another name, 'cause everybody else had two names; and the Lord gave me Truth, because I was to declare the Truth to the people. . . . I journeys round to campmeetin's, an' wherever folks is, an' I sets up my banner, an' then I sings, an' then folks always come up round me, an' then I preaches to 'em. I tells 'em about Jesus, an' I tells 'em about the sins of this people.

"Arn't I a Woman?"[9]

I want to say a few words about this matter. I am a woman's rights. I have as much muscle as any man, and can do as much work as any man. I have plowed and reaped and husked and chopped and mowed, and can any man do more than that? I have heard much about the sexes being equal. I can carry as much as any man, and can eat as much too, if I can get it. I am as strong as any man that is now. As for intellect, all I can say is, if woman have a pint, and man a quart—why can't she have her little pint full? You need not be afraid to give us our rights for fear we will take too much,—for we can't take more than our pint'll hold. The poor men seem to be all in confusion, and don't know what to do. Why children, if you have woman's rights, give it to her and you will feel better. You will have your own rights, and they won't be so much trouble. I can't read, but I can hear. I have heard the bible and have learned that Eve caused man to sin.

---

[8]Dorothy Sterling, ed., *We Are Your Sisters: Black Women in the Nineteenth Century* (New York: W. W. Norton and Company, 1984), 151.

[9]Margaret Washington, ed., *Narrative of Sojourner Truth* (New York: Vintage Books, 1993), 117-118. According to a footnote in Washington's text, this version of the popular speech by Sojourner Truth is the one recorded by the *Anti-Slavery Bugle*, June 21, 1851, and is more accurate than the remembrance of the activist Frances Gage who offered the oft-quoted "Ain't I a Woman?" account of Sojourner's address in 1851.

Well, if woman upset the world, do give her a chance to set it right side up again. The Lady has spoken about Jesus, how he never spurned woman from him, and she was right. When Lazarus died, Mary and Martha came to him with faith and love and besought him to raise their brother. And Jesus wept and Lazarus came forth. And how came Jesus into the world? Through God who created him and a woman who bore him. Man, where is your part? But the women are coming up blessed be God and a few of the men are coming up with them. But man is in a tight place, the poor slave is on him, woman is coming on him, he is surely between a hawk and a buzzard.

"Ain't I a Woman?"[10]

Well, children, where there is so much racket there must be something out of kilter. I think that 'twixt the negroes of the South and the women at the North, all talking about rights, the white men will be in a fix pretty soon. But what's all this here talking about?

That man over there says women need to be helped into carriages, and lifted over ditches, and to have the best place everywhere. Nobody ever helps me into carriages, or over mud-puddles, or gives me any best place! And ain't I a woman? Look at me! Look at my arm! I have ploughed, and planted, and gathered into barns, and no man could head me! And ain't I a woman? I could work as much and eat as much as a man—when I could get it—and bear the lash as well! And ain't I a woman? I have borne thirteen children, and seen them most all sold off to slavery, and when I cried out with my mother's grief, none but Jesus heard me! And ain't I a woman?

Then they talk about this thing in the head: what's this they call it? ["Intellect," whispered someone near.] That's it honey. What's that got to do with women's rights or negro rights? If my cup won't hold but a pint, and yours holds a quart, wouldn't you be mean not to let me have my little half-measure full?

Then that little man in black there, he says women can't have as much rights as men, because Christ wasn't a woman! Where did your Christ come from? Where did your Christ come from? From God and a woman! Man had nothing to do with Him. . . .

If the first woman God ever made was strong enough to turn the world upside down all alone, these women together ought to be able to turn it back, and get it right side up again! And now they are asking to do it, the men better let them.

---

[10]Loewenberg and Bogin, *Black Women in Nineteenth-Century American Life*, 235-236. This is an account of the previously cited speech as recorded by Mrs. Frances D. Gage, who presided over the 1851 woman's rights convention in Akron, Ohio and as found in *History of Woman's Suffrage* (1881), edited by Elizabeth Cady Stanton, Susan B. Anthony, and Matilda Joslyn Gage.

"I Suppose I am About the Only Colored Woman That Goes About to Speak for the Rights of Colored Women"[11]

Is it not good for me to come and draw forth a spirit, to see what kind of spirit people are of? I see that some of you have got the spirit of a goose, and some have got the spirit of a snake. I feel at home here. I come to you, citizens of New York, as I suppose you ought to be. I am a citizen of the state of New York; I was born in it, and I was a slave in the state of New York; and now I am a good citizen of this State. I was born here, and I can tell you I feel at home here. I've been lookin' round and watchin' things, and I know a little mite 'bout Woman's Rights, too. I come forth to speak 'bout Woman's Rights, and want to throw in my little mite, to keep the scales a-movin'. I know that it feels a kind o' hissin' and ticklin' like to see a colored woman get up and tell you about things, and Woman's Rights. We have all been thrown down so low that nobody thought we'd ever get up again; but we have been long enough trodden now; we will come up again, and now I am here.

I was a-thinkin', when I see women contendin' for their rights, I was a-thinkin' what a difference there is now, and what there was in old times. I have only a few minutes to speak; but in the old times the kings of the earth would hear a woman. There was a king in the Scriptures; and then it was the kings of the earth would kill a woman if she come into their presence; but Queen Esther come forth, for she was oppressed, and felt there was a great wrong, and she said I will die or I will bring my complaint before the king. Should the king of the United States be greater, or more crueler, or more harder? But the king, he raised up his sceptre and said: "Thy request shall be granted unto thee—to the half of my kingdom will I grant it to thee!" Then he said he would hang Haman on the gallows he had made up high. But that is not what women come forward to contend. The women want their rights as Esther. She only wanted to explain her rights. And he was so liberal that he said, "the half of my kingdom shall be granted to thee," and he did not wait for her to ask, he was so liberal with her.

Now, women do not ask half of a kingdom, but their rights, and they don't get 'em. When she comes to demand 'em, don't you hear how sons hiss their mothers like snakes, because they ask for their rights; and can they ask for anything less? The king ordered Haman to be hung on the gallows which he prepared to hang others; but I do not want any man to

---

[11]Gerda Lerner, ed., *Black Women in White America: A Documentary History* (New York: Vintage Books, 1972), 567-568. These comments were delivered at the Fourth National Woman's Rights Convention, New York City, 1853.

be killed, but I am sorry to see them so short-minded. But we'll have our rights; see if we don't; and you can't stop us from them; see if you can. You may hiss as much as you like, but it is comin'. Women don't get half as much rights as they ought to; we want more, and we will have it. Jesus says: "What I say to one, I say to all—watch!" I'm a-watchin'. God says: "Honor your father and your mother." Sons and daughters ought to behave themselves before their mothers, but they do not. I can see them a-laughin' and pointin' at their mothers up here on the stage. They hiss when an aged woman comes forth. If they'd been brought up proper they'd have known better than hissing like snakes and geese. I'm 'round watchin' these things, and I wanted to come up and say these few things to you, and I'm glad of the hearin' you give me. I wanted to tell you a mite about Woman's Rights, and so I came out and said so. I am sittin' among you to watch; and every once and a while I will come out and tell you what time of night it is.

—Sojourner Truth

Bibliography

Haraway, Donna Jeanne. "Ecce Homo, Ain't (Arn't) I a Woman, and Inappropriate/ d Others: The Human in a Post-Human Landscape." In *Feminists Theorize the Political*. 1995.

McKissack, Patricia C. and Frederick McKissack. *Sojourner Truth: Ain't I a Woman?* New York: Scholastic, 1992.

Painter, Nell Irvin. "Representing Truth: Sojourner Truth's Knowing and Becoming Known." In *This Far By Faith: Readings in African-American Women's Religious Biography*. Edited by Judith Weisenfeld & Richard Newman. New York: Routledge, 1996.

Truth, Sojourner and Olive Gilbert. *The Narrative of Sojourner Truth*. Salem, N.H.: Ayer, 1992. Reprint edition. [1878]

Washington, Margaret, ed. *Narrative of Sojourner Truth*. New York: Vintage Books, 1993.

HARRIET ROSS TUBMAN
(c. 1821-1913)

Moses made one crossing out of bondage. Harriet Tubman, the black female "Moses," made many. She was the preeminent conductor on the underground railroad. Moses had a staff; she had a pistol and several disguises, but both depended upon the delivering God. Her involvement with the Union Army and John Brown's rebellion are the fabric from which legends are woven. When Harriet Tubman invaded the house of bondage and transported its occupants to safety, she loosened the invisible and visible constraints of a captive people and dared them to be free.

"Harriet's Religious Character"[12]

Harriet's religious character I have not yet touched upon. Brought up by parents possessed of strong faith in God, she had never known the time, I imagine, when she did not trust Him, and cling to Him, with an all-abiding confidence. She seemed ever to feel the Divine Presence near, and she talked with God "as a man talketh with his friend." Hers was not the religion of a morning and evening prayer at stated times, but when she felt a need, she simply told God of it, and trusted Him to set the matter right.

"And so," she said to me, "as I lay so sick on my bed, from Christmas till March, I was always praying for poor ole master. 'Pears like I din't do nothing but pray for ole master. 'Oh, Lord, convert ole master;' 'Oh, dear Lord, change dat man's heart, and make him a Christian.' And all the time he was bringing men to look at me, and dey stood there saying what dey would give, and what dey would take, and all I could say was, 'Oh, Lord, convert ole master.' Den I heard dat as soon as I was able to move I was to be sent with my brudders, in the chain-gang to de far South. Then I changed my prayer, and I said, 'Lord, if you ain't never goint to change dat man's heart, *kill him*, Lord, and take him out of de way, so he won't do no more mischief.' Next ting I heard ole master was dead; and he died just as he had lived, a wicked, bad man. Oh, den it 'peared like I would give de world full of silver and

---

[12]Sarah Bradford, *Harrriet Tubman: The Moses of Her People* (New York: Corinth Books, 1961), 23-25.

gold, if I had it, to bring dat pore soul back, I would give *myself* ; I would give eberyting! But he was gone, I couldn't pray for him no more."

As she recovered from this long illness, a deeper religious spirit seemed to take possession of her than she had ever experienced before. She literally "prayed without ceasing." " 'Pears like, I prayed all de time," she said, "about my work, everywhere; I was always talking to de Lord. When I went to the horse-trough to wash my face, and took up de water in my hands, I said, 'Oh, Lord, wash me, make me clean.' When I took up de towel to wipe my face and hands, I cried, 'Oh, Lord, for Jesus' sake, wipe away all my sins!' When I took up de broom and began to sweep, I groaned, 'Oh, Lord, whatsoebber sin dere be in my heart, sweep it out, Lord, clear and clean'; but I pray no more for pore ole master." No words can describe the pathos of her tones as she broke into these words of earnest supplication.

"One of Two Things"[13]

One day there were scared faces seen in the Negro quarter, and hurried whispers passed from one to another. No one knew how it had come out, but some one had heard that Harriet and two of her brothers were very soon, perhaps to-day, perhaps to-morrow, to be sent far south with a gang, bought up for plantation work. Harriet was about twenty or twenty-five years old at this time, and the constantly recurring idea of escape at *some-time*, took sudden form that day, and with her usual promptitude of action she was ready to start at once.

She held a hurried consultation with her brothers, in which she so wrought upon their fears, that they expressed themselves as willing to start with her that very night, for that far North, where, could they reach it in safety, freedom awaited them. But she must first give some intimation of her purpose to the friends she was to leave behind, so that even if not understood at the time, it might be remembered afterward as her intended farewell. Slaves must not be seen talking together, and so it came about that their communication was often made by singing, and the words of their familiar hymns, telling of the heavenly journey, and the land of Canaan, while they did not attract the attention of the masters, conveyed to their brethren and sisters in bondage something more than met the ear. And so she sang, accompanying the words, when for a moment unwatched, with a meaning look to one and another:

> "When dat ar ole chariot comes,
> I'm gwine to lebe you,

---

[13]Bradford, *Harriet Tubman*, 26-29.

> I'm boun' for de promised land,
> Frien's, I'm gwine to lebe you."

Again, as she passed the doors of the different cabins, she lifted up her well-known voice; and many a dusky face appeared at door or window, with a wondering or scared expression; and thus she continued:

> "I'm sorry, frien's, to lebe you,
> Farewell! oh, farewell!
> But I'll meet you in de mornin',
> Farewell! oh, farewell!
> I'll meet you in de mornin',
> When you reach de promised land;
> On de oder side of Jordan,
> For I'm boun' for de promised land."

The brothers started with her, but the way was strange, the north was far away, and all unknown, the masters would pursue and recapture them, and their fate would be worse than ever before; and so they broke away from her, and bidding her goodbye, they hastened back to the known horrors of slavery, and the dread of that which was worse.

Harriet was now left alone, but after watching the retreating forms of her brothers, she turned her face toward the north, and fixing her eyes on the guiding star, and committing her way unto the Lord, she started again upon her long, lonely journey. Her farewell song was long remembered in the cabins, and the old mother sat and wept for her lost child. No intimation had been given her of Harriet's intention, for the old woman was of a most impulsive disposition, and her cries and lamentations would have made known to all within hearing Harriet's intended escape. And so, with only the North Star for her guide, our heroine started on the way to liberty. "For," said she, "I had reasoned dis out in my mind; there was one of two things I had a *right* to, liberty, or death; if I could not have one, I would have de oder; for no man should take me alive; I should fight for my liberty as long as my strength lasted, and when de time came for me to go, de Lord would let dem take me."

"On Reaching Free Soil"[14]

After many long and weary days of travel, she found that she had passed the magic line, which then divided the land of bondage from the land of freedom. But where were the lovely white ladies whom in her visions she had seen, who, with arms outstretched, welcomed her to their hearts and

---

[14]Bradford, *Harriet Tubman*, 30-32.

homes. All these visions proved deceitful: she was more alone than ever; but she had crossed the line; no one could take her now, and she would never call any man "Master" [any]more.

> "I looked at my hands," she said, "to see if I was de same person now I was free. Dere was such a glory ober eberything, de sun came like gold trou de trees, and ober de fields, and I felt like I was in heaven."

But then came the bitter drop in the cup of joy. She was alone, and her kindred were in slavery, and not one of them had the courage to dare what she had dared. Unless she made the effort to liberate them she would never see them [any]more, or even know their fate.

> "I knew of a man," she said, "who was sent to the State Prison for twenty-five years. All these years he was always thinking of his home, and counting by years, months, and days, the time till he should be free, and see his family and friends once more. The years roll on, the time of imprisonment is over, the man is free. He leaves the prison gates, he makes his way to his old home, but his old home is not there. The house in which he had dwelt in his childhood had been torn down, and a new one had been put up in its place; his family were gone, their very name was forgotten, there was no one to take him by the hand to welcome him back to life."
>
> "So it was wid me," said Harriet, "I had crossed de line of which I had so long been dreaming. I was free; but dere was no one to welcome [me] to de land of freedom, I was a stranger in a strange land, and my home after all was down in de old cabin quarter, wid de olde folks, and my brudders and sisters. But to dis solemn resolution I came; I was free, and dey should be free also; I would make a home for dem in the North, and de Lord helping me, I would bring dem all dere. Oh, how I prayed den, lying all alone on de cold, damp ground; 'Oh, dear Lord,' I said, 'I haint got no friend but *you*. Come to my help, Lord, for I'm in trouble!' "
>
> *—Harriet Tubman*

Bibliography

Bradford, Sarah. *Harriet Tubman: The Moses of Her People.* [1886] New York: Corinth Press, 1961.

Quarles, Benjamin. "Harriet Tubman's Unlikely Leadership." In *Black Leaders of the Nineteenth Century.* Edited by Leon Litwack and August Meier. Urbana: University of Illinois Press, 1988.

Williams, Lorraine A. "Harriet Tubman." In *Dictionary of American Negro Biography.* Edited by Rayford W. Logan and Michael R. Winston. New York: Norton, 1982.

SISTER KELLY
(c.1830)

An ex-slave who became a washerwoman in Nashville, Tennessee, after the Civil War, Sister Kelly got religion at the age of twelve. "As with most of the ex-slave conversion accounts, she testifies to an existential experience credited to the 'holy uplifting spirit' of God. This transformation of self gave Sister Kelly confidence to deal with whatever life had in store for one of God's 'little ones.'"[15]

"Proud of That 'Ole Time Religion' "[16]

Well, we used to have little singing and praying like good ole time revival; and we would take pots and put them right in the middle of the floor to keep the sound in the room; yeah, keep the white folks from meddling. Yes'm, the sound will stay right in the room after you do that. Well, we allus used these old house wash pots like you boil clothes in, you know. Just turn one down in the middle of the floor, that was sufficient.

Let me tell you how I got it. And I sho' got a good one, too; my 'ligion will stand for all time, I'm a-telling you. One Sunday morning I got up. I was just 12 years old. That morning, I commenced to crying and I just couldn't stop; seem like my heart was full of water. Well, I cried all that morning, and when we got dinner done, I went in and asked the old white woman to let me go home. That was when I was at the Brook place. I never said nothin' 'bout why I wanted to go, I just asked her to let me go. She wouldn't let me leave, o'course, 'cause I was hired out to her. You see, honey, that wasn't the Brook place; that was 'bout four miles from there where I was hired out. Well, then, seem like my heart would but sho' 'nuf. By and by something just said to me, you go but don't stay long. I went on home and cried most all the way. I couldn't help it to save my life. Well, Ole Miss Mary Brook ask me what was the matter, and I said I didn't know. You know in them times folks had little chairs sitting back in the chimney corner; and I went and set back in there and cried some more. 'Pear like to me I couldn't keep from it, and

---

[15]Milton C. Sernett, ed., *Afro-American Religious History: A Documentary Witness* (Durham: Duke University Press, 1985), 69.

[16]Ibid., 70-74.

so by and by she says to me, "Honey, time you was goin' home." I don't know what was the matter with me, but I took and got over the fence and started on down the road. Well, I walked along, and by and by I got down into a little flat place right near a pond, and 'pear like to me something said, "You never shall die a sinner." Well, I jest trembled and shook like a leaf. I know what was the matter with me then. Well, I heard that voice three times, and every time it said, "You never shall die a sinner." It seem like it was inside of me, somehow or other. I said, "What is that talking to me?" Well, chile, I got happy and I jest went up and down, jest shouting and praying and crying for dear life. I said, "Lord what was that talking to me that way?" I jest asked him like that; ooh yes, good God, I 'members it jest like it was yesterday. Something said like I'm speaking to you right now, "You better gwan, might come back and talk to you again." I stopped right still and started thinking, and seem like a clear loud voice said, "You is jest in God's hands, and you must praise and bless God all the time." Well, honey, you know I was young, and I knowed no more about it than this here rock, but I sho' felt something and I heard something, too. . . .

Well, I tell you chile, when I got up from prayer, I felt like I was brand new—I had done been washed in Jesus' blood, ooh my great and holy Father! Sometimes I gits to thinking 'bout it and I git happy. Yesirree, chile, if you wants ole sister Kelly to tell you 'bout her 'ligious 'sperience, I sho' kin tell you that, 'cause I sho' been through a great fight with the devil, I tell you, oooh praise God. I didn't know no more 'bout nothin' than this rock, but honey you asks me now, I kin tell you with the very words that God put in my mouth.

That morning, seem like Jesus said to me, "My little one, what makes you so hard to believe, when you know I am the one and only God?"—oooh blessed Jesus, there ain't but one God, honey, and that is the one I am telling you 'bout right now. Yessir, I heard him all on the inside, saying "Come unto me, oh my little one, what makes you so hard to believe when you know I am the one and only God, and there ain't but one God but me?" Seems jest like yesterday 'stid of years and years ago, and I still feels the blessed spirit jest like brand new, ain't like this here rock now, I tell you, ooh praise His holy name.

Well, I still didn't know nothin' 'bout praying, but I says "Oooh, my good and holy Father, what can I say to Thee for Thy blessings?" and he said in a voice that shook me like a storm, "Open your mouth and I will fill it with all the elements from on high." Lord, bless his holy name, I never will forget that morning when I was saved by his blood, and changed to the woman you see today. I'm sho' Sister Kelly now.

I tell you, honey, you got to be touched from the inside, and be struck by his hand like I was 'fore you feel that holy uplifting spirit.

Well, the last time the Lord spoke to me, he said, "My little one, I have carried you out of this world, and you is no more of this world, but of another world, the holy world, and they will hate you for my sake." That's the truth, ain't it? I don't fear no man but Jesus. He is my God, do you hear me? . . .

Yes, honey, you jest remember this what Sister Kelly's telling you. This ole world is mighty happy to some of you young folks, but when you is running around having yo' good time, jest remember that you got to stand before the most holy of all, God a'mighty, every deed you done, you gotta give strict account of, you got to know yourself, too, don't never fergit that. When I'm dead and gone on to take my seat beside his blessed throne, you'll 'member what ole Sister Kelly told you. . . .

After I found Jesus I didn't fool with all these youngsters' pranks. I tell you I'm sorry for you, and you young folks that don't know nothin'. You think this world is all of it, but I tell you it ain't; there's sho' a better world 'n this waiting for all those who trust the Lord, do you hear me? I'm a-telling you, you better get that ole time religion, that what you'all better do. You go to stand 'fore God for yo'self, jest like me and anybody else.

—*Sister Kelly*

Bibliography

Johnson, Clifton H., editor. *God Struck Me Dead: Voices of Ex-Slaves*. Cleveland, Ohio: The Pilgrim Press, 1993.

Sernett, Milton C., ed. *Afro-American Religious History: A Documentary History*. Durham: Duke University Press, 1985.

Unwritten History of Slavery: Autobiographical Accounts of Negro Ex-slaves. Nashville: Fisk University, 1945; reprint ed., Washington, D.C.: Microcard Editions, 1968.

VIRGINIA W. BROUGHTON

(c.1850)

Throughout the state of Tennessee, Virginia Broughton ardently advocated for the rights of women by organizing women into proactive bible study groups. In these groups, she reenvisioned biblical paradigms and raised the consciousness of black women by daring them to see themselves in sacred texts. She was a Baptist missionary and teacher who may be characterized as the forerunner for womanist biblical interpretation.

"Call to Service"[17]

In a certain city of the fair South Land of the United States of America there was born a wee little girl baby, whom her father named Virginia, in honor of the state of his nativity, which he never ceased to praise. This Negro child had the godly heritage of being well born of honorable parents who had secured their freedom at great cost.

Virginia's father was an industrious, intelligent man, who, early in life, hired his time from his master and thereby was enabled to purchase his own freedom and also that of his wife.

As freedmen they began to build up a home and rear children who could enjoy the privileges of education that only very few of our race could enjoy at that time. Before the late Civil War Virginia attended a private school, taught by Professor Daniel Watkins, and was reading in the fourth reader when the new day of freedom dawned upon the race and brought with it the glorious light of education for all who would receive it.

Fisk University was one of the first institutions of learning established for the freedmen. Virginia was enrolled among its first pupils and classified with the most advanced. After ten consecutive years of faithful study she graduated from the College Department of Fisk University, May, 1875.

Virginia has the distinction of being the first college graduate of womankind south of Mason and Dixon line. The prevailing custom in the South at that time regarding the education of women made it possible for this Negro girl to have such a distinction.

Immediately after her graduation, in answer to a telegram, she went to Memphis and there passed a creditable examination for a position in the public schools of that city. So brilliant was her success in the examination, her friends insisted that she take the principal's examination. This, however, she declined to do, as she did not wish to be a rival of her male classmate who was aspiring for that position.

For twelve years she taught in the public schools of Memphis, being promoted from time to time, until she became principal of the North Memphis school, and later assistant principal of the Kortrecht grammar school, the most advanced public school in that city for colored youth.

While teaching in the last position mentioned a stranger introduced as Miss J. P. Moore, accompanied by Miss E. B. King, called to see Virginia, and invited her to attend a missionary meeting appointed for women only. As this was an entirely new thing under the sun twenty years ago, curiosity prompted Virginia to go and ascertain what such a meeting would be.

---

[17]Virginia W. Broughton, "Twenty Year's Experience of a Missionary" [1907] in *Spiritual Narratives*, Sue Houchins, ed., The Schomburg Library of Nineteenth-Century Black Women Writers (New York: Oxford University Press, 1988), 7-14.

Miss J. P. Moore, the good woman who called the meeting, stated the object and opened the service with an appropriate devotional exercise. She at once enlisted the sympathy and promised cooperation of the women in attendance. We organized what was then called a Bible Band. The principal object of the organization was the daily study of the Bible. This organization grew and increased in numbers, influence, and spiritual strength. The work began in one of our intelligent progressive churches, in which the pastor was a strong, intellectual, devout man, well prepared to encourage and defend this new feature in the church life of our people. Soon Bible Bands were organized throughout the city of Memphis and the women of our churches took on new life. Every Monday afternoon women could be seen in all sections of the city with Bibles in their hands, going to their Bible Band meetings.

The interest became so general in this Bible Band work that Miss J.P. Moore advised the women to petition the W.B.H.M.S. for a Stationary Missionary. This was done. Miss Burdette, corresponding secretary W.B.H.M.S., came to Memphis and after thorough investigation Memphis was selected as a regular mission station, and beloved Mrs. M. Ehlers was sent as our first missionary to train our women and children to do their Lord's work more perfectly.

This Bible Band work being fairly established in Memphis, as a means of greater development, God opened a way throughout that fearless pastor, Rev. R.N. Countee, for the establishment of a Christian school, known as "The Bible and Normal Institute." Ere this school was completed a heartless assassin slew the philanthropist who was providing the means for erecting and furnishing the building.

Alas! Alas! Imagine the dilemma this blow placed our work in; school building and furnishings incomplete and a debt of several thousand dollars upon us. We can say with the song writer at this point,

> "God moves in a mysterious way
> His wonder to perform;
> He plants his footsteps in the sea,
> And rides upon the storm."

This crisis was God's way of opening the doors for women to speak in many of our churches in that section that were interested in the new Bible School. Hitherto Paul's statement, "Let your women keep silence in the churches, for it is not permitted unto them to speak," had locked and barred the doors of our churches against women speaking.

In the meantime, while God was providing the way to enter churches, He was also preparing His female servants to enter them with an effectual message from His Word, even as He prepared Peter while on the house top for meeting the committee that came to greet him in behalf of Cornelius, the Gentile, with whom he had had no dealings. Although Virginia was interested in Bible Band work she had no dream of doing missionary work, for she was teaching at a lucrative salary, and fully engaged in her home and school duties. About this time Virginia's beloved mother, the joy of her heart, was called to her home beyond the skies. This blow came like a clap of thunder in a clear sky—the deepest sorrow Virginia had ever known up to that time. The whole world seemed lone and drear to Virginia, and her greatest comfort came from the hope of soon departing this life and joining her mother in the blessed home-land of the soul. Virginia's health was poor at that time, and she felt so confident she would soon die, she resigned her position in the school and moved to another city, where she hoped her children would be cared for, should she die. Conditions and circumstances were so unsatisfactory she did not remain long in her adopted city, but soon returned to her former home. In the spring of 1887 Virginia had a very serious illness; her life was despaired of; she had selected her burial robes and made such other preparations as she deemed necessary, and with intense longing to depart she lay on her bed waiting on the Lord for the expected summons.

Husband, children and all other earthly ties and possessions were given up. By and by the Lord manifestly came, but not as she expected, to bear her ransomed spirit home, but she was overshadowed with the veritable presence of God, and made to understand thoroughly and clearly in language spoken to the soul, that God was not ready for her then, but He had a work for her to do. That marvelous experience was accompanied with renewed strength of body that continued to increase from that moment until she was able to leave her bed. Virginia's physical weakness, at that time, prohibited her from witnessing a great baptizing that she desired greatly to see, but she was given another rich spiritual blessing that more than compensated her for failing to see the baptizing. She was privileged to hear sweet heavenly music that is unlawful for man to utter, and she quietly rested, sweetly rejoicing in the Lord, as a babe lulled to rest in its mother's arms. In time her strength increased and she came to her normal condition of health. The following song was at once given her, suggestive of many of her experiences, and also as one of the ways God would direct her in her work.

SONG.

"How firm a foundation, ye saints of the Lord,
    Is laid for your faith in His excellent Word;
  What more can He say, than to you He hath said,
    You, who with Jesus, for refuge hath fled?"

This song, through all these twenty years, has not only been an inspiration for service, but its truths have been verified in the varied experiences we herein relate.

Virginia gladly began her work again in the Bible class taught by Mrs.

M. Ehlers, the stationed missionary in her home city. The first meeting she attended after her recovery was one of great joy to her; she was so full of joy she spoke twice in that meeting, and then and there won friends to the Lord's cause that have ever since proved faithful allies of hers in the great work of missions whereunto God had called her. Among those friends we would mention the two devoted sisters, Peggie and Hannah.

Mrs. Ehlers, and the other white missionaries who visited us in those early days, were not slow in discerning Virginia's adaptability and ability to help in advancing the work. They began at once to encourage her and develop her gifts by assigning her special duties to perform in the meetings. Virginia's increased zeal was also manifest in her church, and she was used in various official capacities in the local Bible Band of her church and the Sunday-school work. Bible Band meetings were held throughout the city, and Virginia was seen going here and there to these meetings whenever an opportunity was given her to encourage the work. Because of her readiness to speak and her Bible knowledge she soon came to be an important factor to help conduct the devotional services.

This great Bible Band work among our women was soon noised abroad and invitations came to us from the regions around to send out a worker that the people generally might learn of the work and share in its blessings. A certain district association met in Memphis, and Rev. Copeland, another staunch friend to woman's work, presented our Bible Band work to his associate brethren. Many of them were favorably impressed and requested that we send one of our Bible women to their churches to tell them more about the work, and organize the women of their churches. Thus, in due season, being approved by the church, Virginia was sent on her first missionary journey to the regions beyond her home city.

"A Period of Stern Opposition"[18]

The Lord permitted a few of our Bible women to grow strong under this special ministry of grace known as the Bible Band work. This strength led the women to contend for the Bible plan of church government in the discipline of members, in supporting churches, and in preaching and teaching the gospel. The common evil practices of intemperance in beer drinking, tobacco using, excessive eating and dressing, and the desecrating custom of using church houses for fairs, festivals and other worldly amusements were all strongly condemned by our Bible women, while righteousness, holiness, purity and all the kindred graces of Christianity were upheld and emphasized. Ministers and laymen, who looked with disdain upon criticism that came from a woman, all those who were jealous of the growing popularity of the woman's work, as if there was some cause of alarm

---

[18]Houchins, *Spiritual Narratives*, 34-42.

for the safety of their own positions of power and honor, all rose up in their churches, with all the influence and power of speech they could summon to oppose the woman's work and break it up if possible. The work had taken root too deeply in the hearts of our women ever to be uprooted, but we were given a good shaking and thrashing, and for a season the work seemed to stand still. The separate associational meeting was broken up, many local Bible Bands disbanded, and the good women patiently waited in silence, praying for God's will to be done. Virginia continued to hold meetings where she could find an opportunity. As God has always provided some way of escape for his servants, He provided for Virginia, for there were some preachers who never closed their churches against our work, and hence an opportunity was given for self-defense in the thickest of the fight. Brethren would come to our meetings to catch every word spoken, if thereby they might have some just cause to condemn our teaching, as being false doctrine. One minister was so desirous to destroy the work like Saul of Tarsus, he desired letters of authority that he might follow in the wake of our missionaries and destroy whatever good they might have accomplished. We praise God that just as He arrested Paul in his wild career and caused him to repent, He also stopped that minister, turned him around completely and made him one of the strongest friends to our work we have in all the land.

While in his rage, desiring to destroy our work, he came to hear Virginia speak for the expressed purpose of getting a just case against her. Virginia was totally ignorant of this scheme, but she did notice the reverend gentleman sat with his back toward her while she spoke, as if warming himself near the stove. She spoke in her usual earnest, impressive manner, and from the sequel that we will now relate, it is quite evident she spoke more wisely than she knew. When she concluded her remarks and asked those who wished to speak to express themselves, this Rev. H. arose and made a marvelous confession. He told of his purpose in coming to that meeting, as already stated, and then said that he was regarded by his church as a fluent speaker, but he was then unable to speak and only rose to make a confession. The following are his words:

"I have been washed, rinsed, starched, hung up, dried, sprinkled and ironed, and am now ready for service; not to destroy, but to do all in my power to forward this branch of God's work as zealously as I had determined to oppose it."

He had kept his word and today our woman's work has no better friend among the able ministers of the race than that brother. This minister had a brother, Frank, who lived in the town where we met him. The brother was so opposed to our work when Miss King and Virginia called to see his wife, who was specially interested in their work, he left his own house, refusing even to meet the missionary women. He went to his work, and from his own testimony, he became so troubled he could not work, but was compelled to come down to the church and hear what those women said. Suffice it to say, just as his brother was so wondrously transformed during Virginia's discourse, so was he. Great joy came to all our sisters in that place, for those two men's friendship meant much to the existence of our work there.

Another brother who opposed our work said, on a certain occasion, "I would rather take a rail and flail the life out of a woman than to hear her speak in the church." As he spoke, not knowing what he said, God forgave him, brought him to the light, and he made an open confession of his fault.

There was another brother in the Durhamville district who took special delight in harassing the weaker women in the absence of their teacher. Upon a certain occasion, when Virginia was visiting that section, the sisters reported that brother and asked Virginia to speak to him. As usual an opportunity was given the missionary to present her work to the church. All believers rejoiced as she spoke, and the enemies were silenced for the time being. In concluding her address she said: "If any one present is not convinced of the Divine authority of the woman's work, ask any question and as far as I am able I'll gladly give the Bible teaching relating to it." No one asked a single question, although the brother was present that had given the sisters of that church so much annoyance. When the service closed, however, we met the brother and rejoiced to learn that he had been won over to the cause of missions and he joined heart and hand with the Bible women to push the Lord's work on to victory. He never faltered after that day, but ever defended and supported our cause to the day of his death.

When the opposition raged fiercely, a certain minister, Bob T. by name, came to one of our churches with the expressed intention to throw Virginia out of the window. God was manifestly present that night, and raised up friends to protect her and maintain the cause she represented, that she had never known before, and no hand was raised against her. Glory be to God for his great power of deliverance, as shown on that special occasion.

In some places church houses were locked against our Bible women, and violent hands even laid upon some. Dear Sister Nancy C. said had not Sister Susan S. come to her rescue she would have been badly beaten for attempting to hold a woman's meeting in her own church.

In another vicinity Brother F.P. became so enraged he drew a gun on his wife after she had gotten in a wagon to go to one of our Bible Band meetings, and threatened to take her life if she went a step farther. Of course she was obliged to stop that time and stay home, but that man soon died; he was not permitted to live long enough to prohibit that good woman a second time from going when her missionary sisters called a meeting. This incident did much to allay the persecution throughout that section. While men opposed and Satan strove our progress to retard, God was with us and was only permitting those trials our dross to consume and our gold to refine. Those oppositions proved to be stepping stones to nobler and more extended endeavors. Virginia was soon appointed missionary by the W.B.H.M.S. Thus strengthened, she was better prepared to work than ever. She made two missionary tours through the North and East. This was a source of great strength and pleasure to her.

After such a season of conflict she needed the rest and desirable change the northern tours provided. In the great Saratoga meetings of the Northern Baptists' Anniversary, Virginia spoke twice and seemed to please the great audiences. The press complimented her addresses as being among the best delivered. All the other lady speakers were of the Caucasian race. God used her in the North to touch many hearts by singing the plantation melodies. . . .

As Virginia traveled through the rural districts during the period of opposition it was difficult at times to get any conveyance. She was never particular, riding in anything that could be secured, from a wheelbarrow to a top buggy, and often walking when nothing could be secured. About this time God moved one of her country friends to dedicate his buggy and two horses to the work of missions. So whenever this friend, whom we will call Brother Jas. T., knew Virginia was expected, conveyance was always provided. The home of that dear brother and his beloved wife ever kept its doors open to God's traveling heralds, and was accordingly blessed both temporarily and spiritually. A certain meeting was appointed in that neighborhood and these good people, Brother J.T. and his wife, expected to meet Virginia there and convey her on her journey through the country. Virginia was somewhat delayed and came to the place of meeting after the women had all gathered while they waited. Rev. Elias A., the pastor, was criticizing our work very severely, counting it a waste of time and even less than child's play. In the midst of the controversy the women observed a dust in the road which announced the near approach of some vehicle. All eyes were turned in that direction and soon the buggy that brought the missionary came in sight. With great joy the women arose, clapped their hands, and cried out in joyous exclamations. They believed that their cause would be well defended.

The work was fully explained and God used Virginia, little woman as she was, so gently, so sweetly, and so quietly that the good minister was soon led into the light of the gospel teaching regarding our work, and he quieted down as a shorn lamb, bade us go forward and assured us that he would encourage the work in his church.

Not one of all our opposers would ever enter into single combat with Virginia.

"Sanctification"[19]

About ten years after the beginning of Virginia's career as missionary the doctrine of sanctification began to agitate the Christian church greatly,

---

[19]Houchins, *Spiritual Narratives*, 79-82.

and our missionary encouraged the agitation as her own experience, and her conception of the Bible teaching of that truth led her to see the grave need of greater consecration and loyalty to Christ's cause on the part of both ministers and laity. A fresh anointing or filling of the Holy Spirit was given Virginia to give her the needed courage, wisdom and strength to contend for this truth and endure the persecutions that were sure to follow so aggressive a movement. The leading advocates of sanctification in some sections were so radical in their views on this subject that a wave of persecution spread far and wide, in some places churches were torn asunder and new churches were formed under the name of Holiness churches. Virginia bore up bravely under persecution and providentially was removed from the scene of the conflict and brought in touch with more advanced Christians, who aided her in getting a clearer idea of the Bible teaching of sanctification. Thus she was enabled to adjust much of the growing confusion in the ranks of our Bible women, who like herself desired to follow the Lord wholly and at the same time retain their membership in their respective churches. We praise God for his presence in this special time of need, and for his wonderful deliverance of our missionary from the bitterest persecution of all her experiences, which at one time seemed a direct aim at her earthly existence. Among those who prayed for her, special mention should be made of the Woodlawn Bible women, who called a special meeting at their church to pray for their leader. God heard their prayers and then and there assured them that they would see their sister again standing as usual in their church to tell the blessed story of Jesus and his love. Virginia could and did rejoice as one persecuted for righteousness' sake. That experience was a source of great spiritual strength, and although while passing through it to depart this life and be with Christ was far more preferable than life, she has lived to see God's power and wisdom in her deliverance and in prolonging her life on earth for further conflict. All glory and praise be given to the mighty God! whose might was manifestly shown in Virginia's deliverance and restoration. Many have been led into a closer walk with God, and many more have been led to see that God does call his children to a higher plane of consecrated Christian living than the nominal church member lives. God not only calls, but has promised power and assurance of victory o'er temptation to all believers who love him and keep his commandments. God wills that his children represent Him on earth, in their daily lives of useful service. To do this they must have the power and wisdom from above, that God will freely give to those who ask for them. If we know how to give good gifts to our children how much more will God give the Holy Spirit to those who ask for Him. The various helpful agencies God has provided in preachers, teachers, apostles, prophets and evangelists are all sent forth to edify and perfect his people, that they may grow unto the measure of his stature of the fullness of Christ unto a perfect man, and be no longer tossed about as children by every wind of doctrine. Eph. 4:11, 12, 13.

May we all see the importance of the constant use of the appointed means of grace, the daily study of God's word, humble, faithful prayers, songs of praise and labors of love that our spiritual development may continue to be manifestly increased. In time may we all attain unto the perfect man in Christ Jesus, who of God, is made unto us, wisdom, and righteousness, and sanctification, and redemption. I Cor. 1:30. Yes, in Christ Jesus all believers are sanctified, and according to their faith they become partakers of that grace that enables them to stand and testify to his power to save his people from their sins.

—Virginia W. Broughton

"Texts of Special Significance in Virginia's Twenty Years' Experience"[20]

We shall now give a few texts and outlines that God has enabled Virginia to use effectively:

Bible Authority for Women's Work. Text, Gen. 2:18.
(1) Woman's creation.
    (a) Made of refined material.
    (b) Man's helpmeet.
    (c) Man incomplete without woman.
(2) Marriage ordained of God.
    (a) Woman, mother of all being.
    (b) Hope of man's restoration. Gen. 3:15.
    (c) Woman's help indispensable in the home as man's comforter and the trainer of children.
(3) Woman as helpmeet in business. Illustrations: Deborah, Esther, Ruth, Lydia.
(4) Woman as helpmeet in church.
    (a) As teacher. II Kings 22:14. Acts 18:26.
    (b) As hostess to care for God's servants. II Kings 4:10. I Kings 17:15.
    (c) As missionaries. Acts 9:39. Rom. 16:1.
(5) Called of God to service. Eph. 2:1-10.
    (a) All believers one in Christ. Gal. 3:28.
    (b) All required to work according to respective gifts. I Cor. 12:7. Matt. 25:14, 15.
(6) Appeal to women to develop themselves and prepare for service.
    (a) Bought by blood of Jesus to serve. I Cor. 6:20.
    (b) Rewarded according to works. Rev. 22:12.
    (c) Developed through excess of gifts. I Tim. 4:13-15.
    (d) Growth commanded of God. 2 Pet. 3:18.

---

[20]Houchins, *Spiritual Narratives*, 130-140.

Christian Work. Text, John 9:4.

(1) Jesus' declaration.
   (a) What his work was.
   (b) Took delight in his work.
   (c) Finished his work.

(2) Individual work required.
   (a) No discharge from service.
   (b) All supplies furnished, strength, wisdom, grace. Jas. 1:5. Phil. 4:19.
   (c) Work indicated by one's natural gifts and adaptability. Illustrations: Peter, Paul, Mary, Dorcas, Lydia.

(3) Time to work specified.
   (a) Delay dangerous.
   (b) Night of death sure.
   (c) Joy comes when work is finished.

(4) Rewarded according to work. Rev. 22:12.
   (a) Faithfulness rewarded. Matt. 25:21, 23.
   (b) Love to Christ should be constraining force.

Christian Growth. Text, II Pet. 3:18.

(1) Why should I grow?
   (a) God commands it.
   (b) Growth essential to law of spiritual life as well as physical.
   (c) To have strength for service.

(2) How can I grow?
   (a) By feeding upon God's word, spiritual songs and prayer.
   (b) By living in a healthful atmosphere (having proper associates).
   (c) By active service.

(3) For what purpose should I grow?
   (a) God's glory.
   (b) Good of humanity.
   (c) Personal edification and usefulness.

"Call to Service." Text, John 11:28.

(1) Jesus calls a woman.
   (a) A prepared woman. Lu. 10:39.
   (b) She loved Jesus supremely. Mark 14:3.
   (c) She anointed Jesus for his burial.

(2) An imperative need.
   (a) Women in trouble. John 11:1
   (b) Send for Jesus.
   (c) Required to move stones. John 11:39.
   (d) Divine power manifest to do what man could not do. John 11:42-44.

(3) Effect upon Mary and Martha.
   (a) Martha served without complaining.
   (b) Mary expressed her love by her precious gift.

(c) Many Jews believed.

(4) Application to women of this age.

    (a) Troubled about many things.

    (b) Opportunities of service. Jesus' means of help.

    (c) Women should seize every opportunity given for their development.

    (d) Results already obtained from efforts of awakened womanhood.

Victory of the Cross. Texts, Rev. 11:15, Heb. 1:13.

(1) All power given to Jesus.

    (a) Conquest assured. Ps. 2:8.

    (b) Everything already subject to Jesus. Heb. 2:8.

    Illustrations from mineral kingdom. Is. 14:16.

    Vegetable kingdom. Mark 11:20.

    In animal kingdom Bible gives illustrations from tiniest insects to king of the beasts, showing all things created are subject to God.

(2) Gospel dispensation.

    (a) Man's opportunity to share in the glory here after to be manifest.

    (b) Christ's service man's highest privilege.

    (c) Man called to put on the whole armor of God for the conflict. Eph. 6:10-19.

(3) Soldiers of Christ fight with assurance of victory. I Cor. 9:26.

    (a) Our captain a victor. John 16:33.

    (b) Through faith we too shall conquer.

    (c) Faith the victory that overcomes the world. I John 5:4.

(4) They that overcome will reign with Jesus. Rev. 2:26; 3:21.

"Power of Holy Spirit." Text, Acts 1:8.

(1) Promised to all believers. Acts 2:4.

    (a) Sent on day of Pentecost. Acts 2:4.

    (b) Disciples waited for evidence of Holy Spirit before they began their work after the resurrection. Acts 1:14.

    (c) Not alone for Apostles but for all believers. Acts 2:39.

(2) Holy Spirit given on condition.

    (a) Surrender of self. Gal. 2:20.

    (b) Willingness to serve. John 7:17.

    (c) Obedience to commandments. John 14:15, 16.

(3) Holy Spirit manifest.

    (a) In consecrated living. Gal. 2:20.

    (b) In effective service. Is. 6:6-8.

    (c) In developing Christian character. Acts 3:8-13.

    (d) In producing fruits of the Spirit. Gal. 5:22, 23.

(4) Christian life a failure without the Holy Spirit.

    (a) Man unable to overcome temptation without aid of Holy Spirit. I Cor. 10:13.

    (b) Salt without savor good for nothing. Matt. 5:13.

(c) God's will revealed by Holy Spirit. I Cor. 2:10.

(5) Plea to Christians to seek the Holy Spirit's power.

    (a) God willing to give. Lu. 11:13.

    (b) Can't please God without Holy Spirit's power. Rom. 8:8.

    (c) Carnal mind not subject to God's law. Rom. 8:7.

    (d) Walk in Spirit and you will not fulfill the lust of the flesh. Gal. 5:16.

An Open Door. Text, I Cor. 16:9.

(1) Paul's opportunity.

    (a) To preach to Gentiles. Acts 14:27.

    (b) He entered heartily upon his work.

    (c) Opposition met and overcome. Acts 14:19, 26.

(2) Applied to Negro women.

    (a) Opportunities or open doors to serve great. Race to uplift. Beginning in the home.

    (b) Professions and schools of all kinds open to women.

    (c) Responsibilities in proportion to opportunities.

    (d) Woman's Christian organizations great means of development.

(3) Appeal to use given opportunities.

    (a) Present results spurs to greater effort.

    (b) Some results mentioned. Rescue homes, orphanages, homes for aged, reforms in home life, kindergartens, temperance societies, and charitable organizations of all kinds have begun to be established and fostered since women have begun to enter the doors of usefulness open to them.

    (c) The gospel is being encouraged and sent to the ends of the earth through the generous support of good women.

    (d) Negro women have evidently come to the kingdom for such a time as this. Esther 4:14. Negro men's hearts are failing before the ruthless hand of oppression and persecution of all kinds and if our nation is encouraged and saved from the fiery furnace through which it now passes Negro women like Esther of old must take the case to the King of kings and by her prayers and tears plead for their deliverance.

    (e) In the encouragement given these sisters in black by their more favored white Christian sisters the light begins to dawn and we are nerved for the fray.

    (f) Enter the open doors for the judge of all the earth will do right.

Praise. Text, Ps. 150:6.

(1) God is a jealous God.

    (a) He desires manifest expressions of love. Illustration, Lu. 19:40.

    (b) Praise evidence of a conscience void of offense. Ps. 51:12, 13.

    (c) A sad countenance not a good inducement to lead sinners to Christ.

(2) Praise is comely for the upright. Ps. 33:1; 147:1.

(a) God has done so much for them. Ps. 138:8.

(b) Hope for future so bright. I Cor. 15:57.

(c) God is pleased to have his people praise him. Ex. 20:3.

(d) Praise Him, for his mighty acts; his excellent greatness; his boundless love; his tender mercies. Ps. 136.

(3) How shall we praise Him?

(a) With a life of cheerful service.

(b) In songs of praise, words of testimony and fervent prayers of thanksgiving.

(c) With stringed instruments and all other kinds of musical instruments. Ps. 150.

Then shall the earth yield her increase and God, even our God, shall bless us.

O praise the Lord, all ye nations, praise him all ye people.

For his merciful kindness is great toward us and the truth of the Lord endureth forever. Praise ye the Lord. Ps. 117.

Bibliography

Broughton, Virginia W. *Twenty Years' Experience of a Missionary* in *Spiritual Narratives* (with an Introduction by Sue E. Houchins). New York: Oxford University Press, 1988.

Part II

BEING A PROPHET WITNESS IN THE AFRICAN AMERICAN COMMUNITY

"Why Do You Witness?"

Maria W. Stewart
(1803-1879)

Born in New England, she was a school teacher and political activist who defied the social conventions of her day by engaging in public political debates usually reserved for men. Although her public speaking venture was brief, she published several articles and speeches. Maria Stewart exhorted her listeners to strive for economic and communal independence from the majority culture; hers was a quest toward generational empowerment.

An Address Delivered Before the Afric-American Female Intelligence Society of America (1832)[1]

The frowns of the world shall never discourage me, nor its smiles flatter me; for with the help of God, I am resolved to withstand the fiery darts of the devil, and the assaults of wicked men. The righteous are as bold as a lion, but the wicked fleeth when no man pursueth. I fear neither men nor devils; for the God in whom I trust is able to deliver me from the rage and malice of my enemies, and from them that rise up against me.

The only motive that has prompted me to raise my voice in your behalf, my friends, is because I have discovered that religion is held in low repute among some of us; and purely to promote the cause of Christ, and the good of souls, in the hope that others more experienced, more able and talented than myself, might go forward and do likewise. I expect to render a strict, a solemn, and an awful account to God for the motives that have prompted me to exertion, and for those with which I shall address you this evening.

What I have to say concerns the whole of us as Christians and as a people; and if you will be so kind as to give me a hearing this once, you shall receive the incense of a grateful heart.

The day is coming, my friends, and I rejoice in that day, when the secrets of all hearts shall be manifested before saints and angels, men and devils. It will be a great day of joy and rejoicing to the humble followers of Christ, but a day of terror and dismay to hypocrites and unbelievers. Of that day and hour knoweth no man, no, not even the angels in heaven, but

[1]Marilyn Richardson, ed., *Maria W. Stewart, America's First Black Woman Political Writer* (Bloomington: Indiana University Press, 1987), 50-55.

the Father only [Matthew 24:36]. The dead that are in Christ shall be raised first. Blessed is he that shall have a part in the first resurrection. Ah, methinks I hear the finally impenitent crying, "Rocks and mountains! fall upon us, and hide us from the wrath of the Lamb, and from him that sitteth upon the throne [Revelation 6:16]!"

> High on a cloud our God shall come
> Bright thrones prepare his way;
> Thunder and darkness, fire and storm
> Lead on the dreadful day.

Christ shall descend in the clouds of heaven, surrounded by ten thousand of his saints and angels, and it shall be very tempestuous round about him, and before him shall be gathered all nations, and kindred, and tongues and people; and every knee shall bow, and every tongue confess [Romans 14:11]; they also that pierced him shall look upon him, and mourn. Then shall the King separate the righteous from the wicked, as a shepherd divideth the sheep from the goats, and shall place the righteous on his right hand, and the wicked upon his left [Matthew 25:32, 33]. Then, says Christ, shall be weeping and wailing, and gnashing of teeth, when ye shall see Abraham and the prophets, sitting in the kingdom of heaven, and ye yourselves thrust out. Then shall the righteous shine forth in the kingdom of their Father as the sun.

He that hath ears to hear, let him hear [Matthew 13:9]. The poor despised followers of Christ will not then regret their sufferings here, they shall be carried by angels into Abraham's bosom, and shall be comforted; and the Lord God shall wipe away their tears. You will then be convinced before assembled multitudes, whether they strove to promote the cause of Christ, or whether they sought for gain or applause, "Strive to enter in at the strait gate; for many, I say unto you, shall seek to enter it, and shall not be able [Luke 13:24]. For except your righteousness shall exceed the righteousness of the Scribes and Pharisees, ye shall in no wise enter into the Kingdom of heaven [Matthew 5:20]."

Ah, methinks I see this people lying in wickedness; and as the Lord liveth, and as your souls live, were it not for the few righteous that are to be found among us, we should become as Sodom, and like unto Gomorrah. Christians have too long slumbered and slept; sinners stumbled into hell, and still are stumbling, for the want of Christian exertion; and the devil is going about like a roaring lion, seeking whom he may devour. And I make bold to say, that many who profess the name of Christ at the present day, live so widely different from what becometh the Gospel of our Lord Jesus Christ, that they cannot and they dare not reason to the world upon righteousness and judgment to come.

Be not offended because I tell you the truth; for I believe that God has fired my soul with a holy zeal for his cause. It was God alone who inspired my heart to publish the meditations thereof; and it was done with pure motives of love to your souls, in the hope that Christians might examine themselves, and sinners become pricked in their hearts. It is the word of God, though men and devils may oppose it. It is the word of God; and little did I think that any of the professed followers of Christ would have frowned upon me, and discouraged and hindered its progress.

Ah, my friends, I am speaking as one who expects to give account at the bar of God; I am speaking as a dying mortal to dying mortals. I fear there are many who have named the name of Jesus at the present day, that strain at a gnat and swallow a camel; they neither enter in to the kingdom of heaven themselves, nor suffer others to enter in. They would pull the motes out of their brother's eye, when they have a beam in their own eye [Matthew 7:3]. And were our blessed Lord and Saviour, Jesus Christ, upon the earth, I believe he would say of many that are called by his name, "O, ye hypocrites, ye generation of vipers, how can you escape the damnation of hell [Matthew 23:33]." I have enlisted in the holy warfare, and Jesus is my captain; and the Lord's battle I mean to fight, until my voice expires in death. I expect to be hated of all men, and persecuted even unto death, for righteousness and the truth's sake.

A few remarks upon moral subjects, and I close. I am a strong advocate for the cause of God and for the cause of freedom. I am not your enemy, but a friend both to you and to your children. Suffer me, then, to express my sentiments but this once, however severe they may appear to be, and then hereafter let me sink into oblivion, and let my name die in forgetfulness.

Had the ministers of the gospel shunned the very appearance of evil; had they faithfully discharged their duty, whether we would have heard them or not; we should have been a very different people from what we now are; but they have kept the truth as it were, hid from our eyes, and have cried, "Peace, Peace!" when there was no peace; they have plastered us with untempered mortar, and have been as it were blind leaders of the blind.

It appears to me that there are no people under the heavens so unkind and so unfeeling towards their own, as are the descendants of fallen Africa. I have been something of a traveller in my day; and the general cry among the people is, "Our own color are our greatest opposers;" and even the whites say that we are greater enemies towards each other, than they are towards us. Shall we be a hissing and a reproach among the nations of the earth any longer? Shall they laugh us to scorn forever? We might become a highly respectable people; respectable we now consider ourselves, but we might become a highly distinguished and intelligent people. And how? In convincing the world, by our own efforts, however feeble, that nothing is wanting on our part but opportunity. Without these efforts, we shall never be a people, nor our descendants after us.

But God has said, that Ethiopia shall stretch forth her hands unto him.

True, but God uses means to bring about his purposes; and unless the rising generation manifest a different temper and disposition towards each other from what we have manifested, the generation following will never be an enlightened people. We this day are considered as one of the most degraded races upon the face of the earth. It is useless for us any longer to sit with our hands folded, reproaching the whites; for that will never elevate us. All the nations of the earth have distinguished themselves, and have shown forth a noble and gallant spirit. Look at the suffering Greeks! Their proud souls revolted at the idea of serving a tyrannical nation, who were no better than themselves, and perhaps not so good. They made a mighty effort and arose; their souls were knit together in the holy bonds of love and union; they were united, and came off victorious. Look at the French in the late revolution! Nor traitors among them, to expose their plans to the crowned heads of Europe! "Liberty or Death!" was their cry. And the Haytians [sic], though they have not yet been acknowledged as a nation, yet their firmness of character, and independence of spirit have been greatly admired, and high [sic] applauded. Look at the Poles, a feeble people! They rose against three hundred thousand mighty men of Russia; and though they did not gain the conquest, yet they obtained the name of gallant Poles. And even the wild Indians of the forest are more united than ourselves. Insult one of them, and you insult a thousand. They also have contended for their rights and privileges, and are held in higher repute than we are.

And why is it, my friends, that we are despised above all the nations upon the earth? Is it merely because our skins are tinged with a sable hue? No, nor will I ever believe that it is. What then is it? Oh, it is because that we and our fathers have dealt treacherously with one another, and because many of us now possess that envious and malicious disposition, that we had rather die than see each other rise an inch above a beggar. No gentle methods are used to promote love and friendship among us, but much is done to destroy it. Shall we be a hissing and a reproach among the nations of the earth any longer? Shall they laugh us to scorn forever?

Ingratitude is one of the worst passions that reigns in the human breast; it is this that cuts the tender fibres of the soul; for it is impossible for us to love those who are ungrateful towards us. "Behold," says that wise man, Solomon, counting one by one, "a man have I found in a thousand, but a woman among all those have I not found."

I have sometimes thought, that God had almost departed from among us. And why? Because Christ has said, if we say we love the Father, and hate our brother, we are liars, and the truth is not in us; and certainly if we were the true followers of Christ, I think we could not show such a disposition towards each other as we do: for God is all love.

A lady of high distinction among us, observed to me that I might never expect your homage. God forbid! I ask it not. But I beseech you to deal with gentleness and godly sincerity towards me; and there is not one of you, my dear friends, who has given me a cup of cold water in the name of the Lord, or soothed the sorrows of my wounded heart, but God will bless you, not only you, but your children for it. Cruel indeed, are those that indulge such an opinion respecting me as that.

Finally, I have exerted myself both for your temporal and eternal welfare, as far as I am able; and my soul has been so discouraged within me, that I have almost been induced to exclaim, "Would to God that my tongue hereafter might cleave to the roof of my mouth, and become silent forever!" And then I have felt that the Christian has no time to be idle, and I must be active, knowing that the night of death cometh, in which no man can work; and my mind has become raised to such an extent, that I will willingly die for the cause that I have espoused; for I cannot die in a more glorious cause than in the defence (sic) of God and his laws.

O woman, woman! Upon you I call; for upon your exertions almost entirely depends whether the rising generation shall be anything more than we have been or not. O woman, woman! Your example is powerful, your influence great; it extends over your husbands and your children, and throughout the circle of your acquaintance. Then let me exhort you to cultivate among yourselves a spirit of Christian love and unity having charity one for another, without which all our goodness is as sounding brass, and a tinkling cymbal [I Corinthians 13:1]. And, O, my God, I beseech thee to grant that the nations of the earth may hiss at us no longer! O suffer them not to laugh us to scorn forever!

—*Maria W. Stewart*

Bibliography

Giddings, Paula. *When and Where I Enter: The Impact of Black Women on Race and Sex in America.* New York: Bantam Books. Pp. 49-54.

Loewenberg, Bert J. and Ruth Bogin. *Black Women in Nineteenth-Century American Life: Their Words, Their Feelings, Their Thoughts.* University Park: The Pennsylvania State University Press, 1976. Pp. 183-200.

Martin, Clarice J. "Biblical Theodicy and Black Women's Spiritual Autobiography: 'The Miry Bog, the Desolate Pit, a New Song in My Mouth,' " in *A Troubling in My Soul.* Maryknoll: Orbis Books, 1993.

Porter, Dorothy B. "The Organized Education Activities of Negro Literary Societies, 1828-46." *Journal of Negro Education.* 5 (October 1936):555-576.

Richardson, Marilyn. *Maria Stewart: America's First Black Woman Political Writer.* Bloomington: Indiana University Press, 1987.

Riggs, Marcia Y. "Ethics for Living a Dream Deferred." *Drew Gateway.* 59(1989):3-22.

Julia A. J. Foote
(1823-1900)

She was an independent woman whose call to ministry as a missionary and itinerant evangelist in the African Methodist Episcopal Zion (A.M.E.Z.) Church set her at odds with the prevailing assumptions about the place of black women in church and society. In 1894, she became the first black woman ordained a deacon, and the second to be ordained an elder.

Like many of the itinerant evangelists, her ministry began with a dramatic conversion story. After being "slain in the Spirit" for several hours, she claimed the call and launched her ministry. Mrs. Foote knew that she had been ordained by God, and she would consequently never accept misguided human constraints.

"My Call to Preach"[2]

For months I had been moved upon to exhort and pray with the people, in my visits from house to house; and in meetings my whole soul seemed drawn out for the salvation of souls. The love of Christ in me was not limited. Some of my mistaken friends said I was too forward, but a desire to work for the Master, and to promote the glory of his kingdom in the salvation of souls, was food to my poor soul.

When called of God, on a particular occasion, to a definite work, I said, "No, Lord, not me." Day by day I was more impressed that God would have me work in his vineyard. I thought it could not be that I was called to preach—I, so weak and ignorant. Still, I knew all things were possible with God, even to confounding the wise by the foolish things of this earth. Yet in me there was a shrinking.

I took all my doubts and fears to the Lord in prayer, when, what seemed to be an angel, made his appearance. In his hand was a scroll, on which were these words: "Thee have I chosen to preach my Gospel without delay." The moment my eyes saw it, it appeared to be printed on my heart. The angel was gone in an instant, and I, in agony, cried out, "Lord, I cannot do it!" It was eleven o'clock in the morning, yet everything grew dark as night. The darkness was so great that I feared to stir.

---

[2]"A Brand Plucked from the Fire: An Autobiographical Sketch by Mrs. Julia A. J. Foote" in William L. Andrews, ed., *Sisters of the Spirit* (Bloomington: Indiana University Press), 200-201.

At last "Mam" Riley entered. As she did so, the room grew lighter, and I arose from my knees. My heart was so heavy I scarce could speak. Dear "Mam" Riley saw my distress, and soon left me.

From that day my appetite failed me and sleep fled from my eyes. I seemed as one tormented. I prayed, but felt no better. I belonged to a band of sisters whom I love dearly, and to them I partially opened my mind. One of them seemed to understand my case at once, and advised me to do as God had bid me, or I would never be happy here or hereafter. But it seemed too hard—I could not give up and obey.

One night as I lay weeping and beseeching the dear Lord to remove this burden from me, there appeared the same angel that came to me before, and on his breast were these words: "You are lost unless you obey God's righteous commands." I saw the writing, and that was enough. I covered my head and awoke my husband, who had returned a few days before. He asked me why I trembled so, but I had not power to answer him. I remained in that condition until morning, when I tried to arise and go about my usual duties, but was too ill. Then my husband called a physician, who prescribed medicine, but did me no good.

I had always been opposed to the preaching of women, and had spoken against it, though, I acknowledge, without foundation. This rose before me like a mountain, and when I thought of the difficulties they had to encounter, both from professors and non-professors, I shrank back and cried, "Lord, I cannot go!"

The trouble my heavenly Father has had to keep me out of the fire that is never quenched, he alone knoweth. My husband and friends said I would die or go crazy if something favorable did not take place soon. I expected to die and be lost, knowing I had been enlightened and had tasted the heavenly gift. I read again and again the sixth chapter of Hebrews.

"Heavenly Visitations Again"[3]

Nearly two months from the time I first saw the angel, I said that I would do anything or go anywhere for God, if it were made plain to me. He took me at my word, and sent the angel again with this message: "You have I chosen to go in my name and warn the people of their sins." I bowed my head and said, "I will go, Lord."

That moment I felt a joy and peace I had not known for months. But strange as it may appear, it is not the less true, that, ere one hour had passed, I began to reason thus: "I am elected to preach the Gospel without the requisite qualifications, and besides, my parents and friends will forsake me and turn against me; and I regret that I made a promise." At that instant all the joy and peace I had felt left me, and I thought I was standing

---

[3]Andrews, *Sisters of the Spirit*, 202-204.

on the brink of hell, and heard the devil say: "Let her go! Let her go! I will catch her." Reader, can you imagine how I felt? If you were ever snatched from the mouth of hell, you can, in part, realize my feelings.

I continued in this state for some time, when, on a Sabbath evening—ah! that memorable Sabbath evening—while engaged in fervent prayer, the same supernatural presence came to me once more and took me by the hand. At that moment I became lost to everything in this world. The angel led me to a place where there was a large tree, the branches of which seemed to extend either way beyond sight. Beneath it sat, as I thought, God the Father, the Son, and the Holy Spirit, besides many others, whom I thought were angels. I was led before them: they looked me over from head to foot, but said nothing. Finally, the Father said to me: "Before these people make your choice, whether you will obey me or go from this place to eternal misery and pain." I answered not a word. He then took me by the hand to lead me, as I thought, to hell, when I cried out, "I will obey thee, Lord!" He then pointed my hand in different directions, and asked if I would go there. I replied, "Yes, Lord." He then led me, all the others following, till we came to a place where there was a great quantity of water, which looked like silver, where we made a halt. My hand was given to Christ, who led me into the water and stripped me of my clothing, which at once vanished from sight. Christ then appeared to wash me, the water feeling quite warm.

During this operation, all the others stood on the bank, looking on in profound silence. When the washing was ended, the sweetest music I had ever heard greeted my ears. We walked to the shore, where an angel stood with a clean, white robe, which the Father at once put on me. In an instant I appeared to be changed into an angel. The whole company looked at me with delight, and began to make a noise which I called shouting. We all marched back with music. When we reached the tree to which the angel first led me, it hung full of fruit, which I had not seen before. The Holy Ghost plucked some and gave me, and the rest helped themselves. We sat down and ate of the fruit, which had a taste like nothing I had ever tasted before. When we had finished, we all arose and gave another shout. Then God the Father said to me: "You are now prepared, and must go where I have commanded you." I replied, "If I go, they will not believe me." Christ then appeared to write something with a golden pen and golden ink, upon golden paper. Then he rolled it up, and said to me: "Put this in your bosom, and, wherever you go, show it, and they will know that I have sent you to proclaim salvation to all." He then put it into my bosom, and they all went with me to a bright, shining gate, singing and shouting. Here they embraced me, and I found myself once more on earth.

When I came to myself, I found that several friends had been with me all night, and my husband had called a physician, but he had not been able to do anything for me. He ordered those around me to keep very quiet, or to go home. He returned in the morning, when I told him, in part, my story. He seemed amazed, but made no answer, and left me.

Several friends were in, during the day. While talking to them, I would, without thinking, put my hand into my bosom, to show them my letter of authority. But I soon found, as my friends told me, it was in my heart, and was to be shown in my life, instead of in my hand. Among others, my minister, Jehial [Jehiel] C. Beman, came to see me. He looked very coldly upon me and said: "I guess you will find your mistake before you are many months older." He was a scholar, and a fine speaker; and the sneering, indifferent way in which he addressed me, said most plainly: "You don't know anything." I replied: "My gifts are very small, I know, but I can no longer be shaken by what you or any one else may think or say."

"Public Effort—Excommunication"[4]

From this time the opposition to my lifework commenced, instigated by the minister, Mr. Beman. Many in the church were anxious to have me preach in the hall, where our meetings were held at that time, and were not a little astonished at the minister's cool treatment of me. At length two of the trustees got some of the older sisters to call on the minster and ask him to let me preach. His answer was: "No; she can't preach her holiness stuff here, and I am astonished that you should ask it of me." The sisters said he seemed to be in quite a rage, although he said he was not angry.

There being no meeting of the society on Monday evening, a brother in the church opened his house to me, that I might preach, which displeased Mr. Beman very much. He appointed a committee to wait upon the brother and sister who had opened their doors to me, to tell them they must not allow any more meetings of that kind, and that they must abide by the rules of the church, making them believe they would be excommunicated if they disobeyed him. I happened to be present at this interview, and the committee remonstrated with me for the course I had taken. I told them my business was with the Lord, and wherever I found a door opened I intended to go in and work for my Master.

There was another meeting appointed at the same place, which I, of course, attended; after which the meetings were stopped for that time, though I held many more there after these people had withdrawn from Mr. Beman's church.

I then held meetings in my own house; whereat the minster told the members that if they attended them he would deal with them, for they were breaking the rules of the church. When he found that I continued the meetings, and that the Lord was blessing my feeble efforts, he sent a committee of two to ask me if I considered myself a member of his church. I

---

[4]Andrews, *Sisters of the Spirit*, 205-207.

told them I did, and should continue to do so until I had done something worthy of dismemberment.

At this, Mr. Beman sent another committee with a note, asking me to meet him with the Committee, which I did. He asked me a number of questions, nearly all of which I have forgotten. One, however, I do remember: he asked if I was willing to comply with rules of the discipline. To this I answered: "Not if the discipline prohibits me from doing what God has bidden me to do; I fear God more than man." Similar questions were asked and answered in the same manner. The committee said what they wished to say, and then told me I could go home. When I reached the door, I turned and said: "I now shake off the dust of my feet as witness against you [Mark 6:11; Luke 9:5]. See to it that this meeting does not rise in judgment against you."

The next evening, one of the committee came to me and told me that I was no longer a member of the church, because I had violated the rules of the discipline by preaching.

When this action became known, the people wondered how any one could be excommunicated for trying to do good. I did not say much, and my friends simply said I had done nothing but hold meetings. Others, anxious to know the particulars, asked the minister what the trouble was. He told them he had given me the privilege of speaking or preaching as long as I chose, but that he could not give me the right to use the pulpit, and that I was not satisfied with any other place. Also, that I had appointed meeting on the evening of his meetings, which was a thing no member had a right to do. For these reasons he said he had turned me out of the church.

Now, if the people who repeated this to me told the truth—and I have no doubt but they did—Mr. Beman told an actual falsehood. I had never asked for his pulpit, but had told him and others, repeatedly, that I did not care where I stood—any corner of the hall would do. To which Mr. Beman had answered: "You cannot have any place in the hall." Then I said: "I'll preach in a private house." He answered me: "No, not in this place; I am stationed over all Boston." He was determined I should not preach in the city of Boston. To cover up his deceptive, unrighteous course toward me, he told the above falsehoods.

From his statements, many erroneous stories concerning me gained credence with a large number of people. At that time, I thought it my duty as well as privilege to address a letter to the Conference, which I took to them in person, stating all the facts. At the same time I told them it was not in the power of Mr. Beman, or any one else, to truthfully bring anything against my moral or religious character—that my only offence was in trying to preach the Gospel of Christ—and that I cherished no ill feelings toward Mr. Beman or anyone else, but that I desired the Conference to give the case an impartial hearing, and then give me a written statement expressive of their opinion. I also said I considered myself a member of the Conference, and should do so until they said I was not, and gave me their reasons, that I might let the world know what my offence had been.

My letter was slightly noticed, and then thrown under the table. Why should they notice it? It was only the grievance of a woman, and there was no justice meted out to women in those days. Even ministers of Christ did not feel that women had any rights which they were bound to respect.

"Women in the Gospel"[5]

Thirty years ago there could scarcely a person be found, in the churches, to sympathize with anyone who talked of Holiness. But, in my simplicity, I did think that a body of Christian minsters would understand my case and judge righteously. I was, however, disappointed.

It is no little thing to feel that every man's hand is against us, and ours against every man, as seemed to be the case with me at this time; yet how precious, if Jesus but be with us. In this severe trial I had constant access to God, and a clear consciousness that he heard me; yet I did not seem to have that plenitude of the Spirit that I had before. I realized most keenly that the closer the communion that may have existed, the keener the suffering of the slightest departure from God. Unbroken communion can only be retained by a constant application of the blood which cleanseth.

Though I did not wish to pain anyone, neither could I please anyone only as I was led by the Holy Spirit. I was sure, as never before, that the best men were liable to err, and that the only safe way was to fall on Christ, even though censure and reproach fell upon me for obeying his voice. Man's opinion weighed nothing with me, for my commission was from heaven, and my reward was with the Most High.

I could not believe that it was short-lived impulse or spasmodic influence that impelled me to preach. I read that on the day of Pentecost was the Scripture fulfilled as found in Joel ii.28,29; and it certainly will not be denied that women as well as men were at that time filled with the Holy Ghost, because it is expressly stated that women were among those who continued in prayer and supplication, waiting for the fulfillment of the promise. Women and men are classed together, and if the power to preach the Gospel is short-lived and spasmodic in the case of women, it must be equally so in that of men; and if women have lost the gift of prophecy, so have men.

We are sometimes told that if a woman pretends to a Divine call, and thereon grounds the right to plead the cause of a crucified Redeemer in public, she will be believed when she shows credentials from heaven; that is, when she works a miracle. If it be necessary to prove one's right to preach the Gospel, I ask of my brethren to show me their credentials, or I can not believe in the propriety of their ministry.

But the Bible puts an end to this strife when it says: "There is neither

---

[5]Andrews, *Sisters of the Spirit*, 208-209.

male nor female in Christ Jesus" [Gal. 3:28]. Philip had four daughters that prophesied, or preached. Paul called Priscilla, as well as Aquila, his "helper," or, as in the Greek, his "fellow-laborer." Rom. xv. 3; 2 Cor. viii.23; Phil. ii.5; 1 Thess. iii.2. The same word, which, in our common translation, is now rendered a "servant of the church," in speaking of Phoebe (Rom. xvi.1.), is rendered "minister" when applied to Tychicus. Eph. vi.21. When Paul said, "Help those women who labor with me in the Gospel," he certainly meant that they did more than to pour out tea. In the eleventh chapter of First Corinthians Paul gives directions, to men and women, how they should appear when they prophesy or pray in public assemblies; and he defines prophesying to be speaking to edification, exhortation and comfort.

I may further remark that the conduct of holy women is recorded in Scripture as an example to others of their sex. And in the early ages of Christianity many women were happy and glorious in martyrdom. How nobly, how heroically, too, in later ages, have women suffered persecution and death for the name of the Lord Jesus.

In looking over these facts, I could see not miracle wrought for those women more than in myself.

Though opposed, I went forth laboring for God, and he owned and blessed my labors, and has done so wherever I have been until this day. And while I walk obediently, I know he will, though hell may rage and vent its spite.

—*Julia A. J. Foote*

Bibliography

Andrews, William L., ed. *Sisters of the Spirit: Three Black Women's Autobiographies of the Nineteenth Century*. Bloomington: Indiana University Press, 1986.

Foote, Mrs. Julia A. J. "A Brand Plucked From the Fire: An Autobiographical Sketch" [1886] in *Spiritual Narratives*. New York: Oxford University Press, 1988.

Loewenberg, Bert James and Ruth Bogin. *Black Women in Nineteenth-Century American Life*. University Park: The Pennsylvania State University Press, 1976.

Walls, William J. *The African Methodist Episcopal Zion Church: Reality of the Black Church*. Charlotte: A.M.E. Zion Publishing House, 1974.

FRANCES ELLEN WATKINS HARPER
(1825-1911)

Frances Ellen Watkins Harper was a nineteenth-century teacher, novelist, poet, and public speaker. Although her works spoke to all Americans about the need for justice and equality, she admonished African Americans to become of sound moral character and to exhibit moral courage. Her novel, Iola Leroy or Shadows Uplifted *(1892), is a classic example of Harper's keen critical analysis of the plight of African Americans during the Reconstruction period. Most importantly, though, the insights in this novel and Harper's other writings continue to offer us moral, social, economic, and political directives for becoming a liberated people.*

"Our Greatest Want"[6]

Leading ideas impress themselves upon communities and countries. A thought is evolved and thrown out among the masses; they receive it and it becomes interwoven with their mental and moral life—the thought be good the receivers are benefited, and helped onward to the truer life; if it is not, the reception of the idea is a detriment.

A few earnest thinkers and workers infuse into the mind of Great Britain a sentiment of human brotherhood. The hue and cry of opposition is raised against it. Avarice and cupidity oppose it, but the great heart of the people throbs for it. A healthy public opinion dashes and surges against the British throne, the idea gains ground and progresses till hundreds of thousands of men, women and children arise, redeemed from bondage, and freed from chains, and the nation gains moral power by the act. Visions of dominion, proud dreams of conquest fill the soul of Napoleon Bonaparte, and he infuses them into the mind of France, and the peace of Europe is invaded. His bloodstained armies dazzled and misled, follow him through carnage and blood, to shake earth's proudest kingdoms to their base, and the march of a true progression is stayed by a river of blood.

In America, where public opinion exerts such a sway, a leading is success. The politician who chooses for his candidate not the best man but the most available one. —The money getter, who virtually says let me

---

[6]*The Anglo-African*, 1(May 1859)5:160.

make money, though I coin it from blood and extract it from tears.— The minister, who stoops from his high position to the slave power, and in a word all who barter principle for expediency, the true and right for the available and convenient, are worshipers at the shrine of success. And we, or at least some of us, upon whose faculties the rust of centuries has lain, are beginning to awake and worship at the same altar, and bow to the idols.

The idea, if I understand it aright, that is interweaving itself with our thoughts, is that the greatest need of our people at present is money, and that as money is a symbol of power, the possession of it will gain for us the rights which power and prejudice now deny us.—And it may be true that the richer we are the nearer we are to social and political equality; but somehow, (and I may not fully comprehend the idea,) it does not seem to me that money, as little as we possess of it, is our greatest want. Neither do I think that the possession of intelligence and talent is our greatest want. If I understand our greatest wants aright, they strike deeper than any want that gold or knowledge can supply. We want more soul, a higher cultivation of all our spiritual faculties. We need more unselfishness, earnestness and integrity. Our greatest need is not gold or silver, talent or genius, but true men and true women. We have millions of our race in the prison house of slavery, but have we yet a single Moses in freedom. And if we had, who among us would be led by him?

I like the character of Moses. He is the first disunionist we read of in the Jewish scriptures. The magnificence of Pharaoh's throne loomed up before his vision, its oriental splendors glittered before his eyes; but he turned from them all and chose rather to suffer with the enslaved, than rejoice with the free. He would have no union with the slave power of Egypt. When we have a race of men whom this blood stained government cannot tempt or flatter, who would sternly refuse every office in the nation's gift, from a president down to a tide-waiter, until she shook her hands from complicity in the guilt of cradle plundering and man stealing, then for us the foundations of an historic character will have been laid. We need men and women whose hearts are the homes of a high and lofty enthusiasm, and a noble devotion to the cause of emancipation, who are ready and willing to lay time, talent and money on the altar of universal freedom. We have money among us, but how much of it is spent to bring deliverance to our captive brethren? Are our wealthiest men the most liberal sustainers of the anti-slavery enterprise? Or does the bare fact of their having money, really help mound public opinion and reverse its sentiments? We need what money cannot buy and what affluence is too beggarly to purchase. Earnest, self-sacrificing souls that will stamp themselves not only on the present but the future. Let us not then defer all our noble opportunities till we get rich. And here I am, not aiming to enlist a fanatical crusade against the desire for riches, but I do protest against chaining down the soul, with its Heaven endowed faculties and God-given attributes, to the one idea of getting money as stepping into power or even gaining our rights in common with others. The respect that is only bought by gold is not worth much. It is no honor to shake hands politically with men who whip women and steal babies. If this government has no call for our services, no aim for your children, we have the greater need of them to build up a true manhood and womanhood for ourselves. The important lesson we should learn and be able to teach, is how to make every gift, whether gold or talent, fortune or genius, subserve the cause of crushed humanity and carry out the greatest idea of the present age, the glorious idea of human brotherhood.

—Frances E. W. Harper

Bibliography

Boyd, Melba Joyce. *Discarded Legacy: Politics and Poetics in the Life of Frances E. W. Harper (1825-1911)*. Detroit: Wayne State University Press, 1994.

Brown, Hallie Q. *Homespun Heroines and Other Women of Distinction*. Xenia, Ohio: Aldine Publishing Co., 1926.

Burrow, Rufus. "Sexism in the Black Community and the Black Church." *Journal of the Interdenominational Theological Center*. 13(Spring 1986):317-322.

Davis, Arthur P. and J. Saunders Redding, eds. *Cavalcade: Negro American Writing from 1760 to the Present*. Boston: Houghton Mifflin, 1971.

Foster, Frances Smith, ed. *A Brighter Coming Day: A Frances Ellen Watkins Harper Reader*. New York: Feminist Press, 1990.

———. *Minnie's Sacrifice, Sowing and Reaping, Trial and Triump: Three Rediscovered Novels*. Boston: Beacon Press, 1994.

Harper, Frances E. W. *Iola Leroy* [1892]. Boston: Beacon Press, 1987.

Hill, Patricia Liggins. "Frances Watkins Harper's Moses (A story of the Nile): Apologue of the Emancipation Struggle." *AME Zion Quarterly Review*. 95/4(January 1984):11-19.

Sherman, Joan R. *Invisible Poets: Afro-Americans of the Nineteenth Century*. Second Edition. Urbana: University of Illinois Press, 1989.

Shockley, Ann Allen. *Afro-American Women Writers: 1746-1933*. Boston: G.K. Hall, 1988.

IDA B. WELLS-BARNETT
(1862-1931)

Wells-Barnett is known for her courageous drive to end lynching in this nation. Wells-Barnett's criticism also extended to the black community when she thought that the community was not exhibiting the moral courage or developing the needed leadership to be a force for justice. She offered particularly strong critiques of institutional religion and black religious and political leaders—the driving forces of the African American community. As one of the interpreters of her life and work indicates, Wells-Barnett had a prophetic voice whereby "[s]he was an excellent agent for agitation and through this allowed others with the skills of prophetic voice and pastoral voice to mobilize Black folk for social change."[7]

"The Requisites of True Leadership"
By Miss Ida B. Wells, Editor of *Free Speech*,
Memphis, Tenn.[8]

Mr. President:—I do not know how the subject which has been given me is to harmonize with aims of this Association, unless it be that it recognizes that the race whose youth we are engaged in teaching is without the one great essential of elevation and progress—True Leadership—and that from the schools and colleges here represented must come the true leaders of the people.

Humanity in all ages has been a disorganized mass of power until driven by some great molecular force into cohesion in church and State—human Solar System which some human sun draws with centripetal force towards itself—a gigantic body requiring a head to complete its symmetry of figure and direct its movement.

Indeed all organized effort betokens leadership, and upon the world's leadership the seal of history has set the stamp, and by that seal we know that leadership is true or false in proportion as it has been true to God, humanity and self.

The world is familiar with the history of the race whose youth we represent, and it is therefore not necessary to rehearse how we became a ship suddenly cut loose from its mooring and borne far out upon life's ocean by the tempest of war without a rudder, chart or compass; whose crew have largely been unscrupulous politicians, and ministers and teachers of limited education.

Brushing aside the cobwebs of self-complacency and the veil of sentiment about what this race of ours has already accomplished, the plain naked truth confronts us that except in education centers, and then largely in individual cases, the masses of the people are making too little progress in the things which make a nation strong and great, namely: Education, Character, Wealth and Unity; and that the proscription, injustice and out-

---

[7]Emilie M. Townes, *Womanist Justice, Womanist Hope* (Atlanta: Scholars Press, 1993), 205.

[8]*Journal of the Proceedings of the American Association of Educators of Colored Youth: The Session of 1891, Held in Nashville, Tenn., December 29th to 31st, 1891* (Winston, NC: Stewarts Printing House, 1892), 73-79.

rage of which we complain is due to this condition of affairs; that if we would slay the Hydra-headed monster prejudice there must be earnest, persistent efforts along these lines.

The Negro is the backbone of the South; his labor has cleared the forest, trained the swamps, tilled the soil, built the railroads and dotted the wildernesses with cities. He is the preferred laborer of the section of the country and he needs to be taught how to utilize that power for his own benefit. He needs to be taught also that he holds the solution of the problem in his own hand, and that solution lies in saving his money that with it he may educate himself and children, buy a home, and go into business and build for himself individually and collectively, a good character. If we travel abroad with our eyes open we know that the better class of our people are yet a handful as compared with the thousands who yet grope in darkness; waste their money, squander their time, and undermine health—many knowing nothing of race pride and others caring not even when they know. They need to be taught that it is absolutely necessary to save money, combine their earnings and enter the commercial and financial world if they would have employment for their sons and daughters after education.

For the dissemination of these truths among the thousands are needed true leaders who themselves possess an intelligent grasp of the situation, and consecration to the work. It is a work in which all members of the race so fitted should engage: for until this leaven is thoroughly mixed among the masses and they have risen in the scale, the most intellectual, refined and wealthy among us must suffer proscription and be deprived many advantages because of race connection. Withdrawing one's self from one's race does not hasten the glad and happy time when this class shall be in the majority, and ignorance, poverty and immorality, the minority.

The individual suffers because of the general race condition. Too well is it known that we are representatives of a race possessing no collective power or strength in commerce, politics, intellect or character; and our treatment, however unjust or unchristian, is but an expression of scorn and contempt that such a condition obtains among us.

Truly it is a condition tangible and real, and not a theory which confronts us. Yet how few of our hundreds of graduates with all their learning have gone into the world with a true conception of the work before them.

Their aspirations were high to do valiant work for the race; but they lacked the strength which comes from knowledge of the situation, and too often, like the seed which fell among thorns these aspirations are choked by worldly cares and disappointments, or wither away under the fierce sun of persecution.

They go forth armed with their diplomas, honestly believing that armour invincible and that their talents will batter down the walls of prejudice and secure individual recognition and employment. They find in reality that it does not lift them above general race conditions—that the race is not financially, politically nor intellectually able to help either itself or him and that he must battle with and for his people. Too often he fails to realize the promise of his young manhood, becomes discouraged, gives up the struggle in disgust and rusts away his life as a drone in the hive, or else confines himself to selfish pursuits caring naught save for his individual welfare. Neither his home nor school life prepared him for life in its reality—for the real leadership expected of him, and his ignorance of these things, however great his knowledge of classics and abstract sciences, causes him to fall by the wayside.

The united training of its youth by the home, school and State, in patriotism, fortitude and frugality made one nation so celebrated that the name of Spartan has become a synonym for heroism and endurance. Rome easily commanded the world because her youth, trained from the cradle as soldiers, presented a front of matchless discipline to the combined armies of the world.

A race situated as peculiarly as our own, along with its book-learning, calls for instruction for its youth (who are our embryo leaders) adapted to its peculiar needs, and training which will meet existing and not imaginary conditions. They should not only go out from these institutions with trained intellects, skilled hands, refined tastes, noble aspirations of the civilizing and christianizing influences thrown around them in these schools, but they should be taught in some concrete systematic way that the masses of his people are literally "children of a larger growth" who are just learning the rudiments of self-government and to whom, by reason of his superior intelligence, he is to be a leader; that they are poverty stricken, ignorant and superstitious and the whole race suffers from proscription and injustice because of it and that it requires his active, honest, earnest leadership to bring them to the required standard. Send them forth as missionaries; even as the teachers of the North came South to teach us, we must go forth to others.

The main requisites of such leadership are first, devotion to principle or courage of conviction. No great reform in the world's history has ever been successful or far-reaching in its influence without an earnest, steadfast devotion which so takes hold of its leaders that they willingly brave the world's censure—aye, even death itself in its defense. So perished the Apostles and counted the world well lost,—the sacrifice of life glorious; so died the early Christian in Rome's amphitheater and at her stakes until, as has been said of Thomas Crammer, that his death at the stake lighted a torch which has shone round the world; so Leonidas and his immortal three hundred gave up their lives in defense of country. Owen Lovejoy died in defense of the freedom of the press, and brave old John Brown's blood was shed at Harper's Ferry in advocacy of liberty, of whom his son truly says: "He gave noble life for a mighty sentiment." Their deaths were not in vain; they not only wrote their names in the highest niche in the temple of fame but added impetus to the cause of liberty and Christianity which shall roll on gathering new strength while time shall last, and men are left to exclaim, "As Christ died to make men holy, so they died to make men free."

This devotion to principle does not always call for life, but it always means sacrifice of some kind. No man does great things without great sacrifice. Said Lady Henry Somerset in a sermon at Tremont Temple in Boston, recently: "If I were asked to summarize that which I believe condensed the whole secret of every great leader's history, I would go straight to these words, for in them I find the whole inspiration of every life that has been called to lead humanity—self-sacrifice, suffering and pain. Right through the ages this principle has come down to us, even from the time when it was breathed in the old legend, which tells how Curtius leaped into the dark chasm which closed on the flashing form of horse and rider, and we realize that the divine in the human heart, struggling in the twilight of the world, had grasped, as it must always grasp—as it did when Father Damien went to the Leper Island—the sublime, God-given principle that one must die—nay, better, one must be *willing* to die for the people.

When the great light of the beacon fire of Calvary illuminated that black darkness around, it seemed for a time but to kindle the flames of the fagots on which the martyrs died; but that light lit the great heathen world of Rome, and dispelled the darkness of mythology, until the temples of Jupiter and Venus rang out with the glorious Te Deums with the worship of Jesus Christ.

No cause was ever victorious against evil for which men and women have not lived and suffered and died, and the secret of true power for sacrifice has been that they dared to look beyond the paltry, visible surroundings of that cause."

It was this devotion to principle which dragged William Lloyd Garrison through the streets of Boston at the heels of a howling mob. No one is a true leader who to save himself in position fears to speak in defence of right no matter what its apparent cost.

He does not know that all the forces of nature are friends to the friend of God. And his is a base motive who cannot trust these forces to sustain him—which as servants of the Most High are more unerring than weak human foresight. The spirit of earnest devotion in pulpit, school-room, and work-shop is absolutely necessary in leading the people to elevation.

Perseverance is the next great element entering into true leadership. "No man having put his hand to the plow and looking back is fit for the kingdom of God," or capable of true leadership. Patient, persistent, intelligent effort brings all things to pass, as shown by the success of the abolition movement, temperance and other reforms, which were scoffed and jeered in the outset. It is this which has given us the cable, steam engine, electric motors, cotton gin, sewing machine and other inventions in the material world, the result of tireless persistent activity. And this constant effort will wear away the barriers which impede race progress.

I will denominate self-control as the third requisite of true leadership,

"Better is he that ruleth his spirit than he that taketh a city." Only the man who holds the forces of his physical, intellectual and moral nature in subjection to a firm and intelligent will, can ever hope to lead or control others. A pure example is better than much preaching. There is no stronger illustration of the truths we would teach, the paths we would have mankind follow than that our own lives represent the standards of sobriety, virtue and honor and stand a silent yet forceful exponent for all we would have the race become; that self-control which restrains from hasty or intemperate action, degrading habits or immoral practices.

The greatest test of character is the ability to stand prosperity. In moments of success which come to earnest devoted souls, comes also the temptation to use power and influence for selfish ambition or turning aside from the paths of virtue.

Charles Stewart Parnell, the most magnificent leader of modern times, met the English Parliament on its own grounds and steadily, persistently and by their own methods forced concessions and won more splendid victories in the cause of home rule than ever before. He united Ireland, kept the British lion at bay and aroused the admiration of the civilized world for his matchless leadership. In an evil hour he forgot to be true to himself and exert in his own behalf the moral strength, the possession of which he had given such splendid evidence, and he went down in the wreck occasioned by one grave instance of his lack of self-control, and not all his former prestige and power could restore him; and the cause for which he fought so grandly, and had brought so near to victory has been indefinitely retarded.

Our would-be leaders need especially to cultivate and practice self-control.

And while devotion to principle or courage of conviction, perseverance and patience, and self-control are the predominating requisites of true leadership, over and above them all—embodying the truest leadership—is a deep abiding love for humanity.

It is this which inspires devotion to principle; ennobles perseverance; gives the divine patience and tenderness so necessary in dealing with ignorance, superstition and envy; and strengthens and encourages self-control. The world has never witnessed a sublimer example of love for humanity than that of our blessed Savior whose life on earth was spent in doing good. We cannot hope to equal the infinite love, tenderness and patience with which He taught and served fallen humanity, but we can approximate it. Only in proportion as we do so is our leadership true. The reward of such love is expressed in the following beautiful poem:

> "Abou Ben Adhem (may his tribe increase)
> Awoke one night from a dream of peace,
> And saw, within the moonlight in his room,
> Making it rich, and like a lily in bloom,
> An angel writing in a book of gold:—

Exceeding peace had Ben Adhem bold,
And to the presence in the room he said:
'What writest thou?'—The vision raised its head,
And with a look made all of sweet accord,
Answer'd, 'The names of those who love the Lord.'
'And is mine one?' said Abou. 'Nay, not so,'
Replied the angel. Abou spoke more low
But cheerily still; and said 'I pray thee then
"Write me as one that loves his fellow men." '
The angel wrote, and vanished. The next night
It came again with a great awakening light,
And show'd the names whom love of God had
bless'd
And lo! Ben Adhem's name led all the rest."

—Ida B. Wells-Barnett

Bibliography

Duster, Alfreda M., ed. *Crusade for Justice: The Autobiography of Ida B. Wells*. Chicago: University of Chicago Press, 1970.

Holt, Thomas C. "The Lonely Warrior: Ida B. Wells-Barnett and the Struggle for Black Leadership." In *Black Leaders of the Twentieth Century*. Edited by John Hope Franklin and August Meier. Urbana: University of Illinois Press, 1982.

Lerner, Gerda. "Early Community Work of Black Club Women." *Journal of Negro History*. 59(April 1954):158-167.

Neverdon-Morton, Cynthia. *Afro-American Women of the South and the Advancement of the Race, 1895-1925*. Knoxville: University of Tennessee Press, 1989.

Ochiai, Akiko. "Ida B. Wells and Her Crusade for Justice: An African American Woman's Testimonial Autobiography." *Soundings* 75(Summer-Fall, 1992):365-381.

Sterling, Dorothy. *Black Foremothers: Three Lives*. Old Westbury, N.Y.: Feminist Press, 1979.

Thompson, Mildred. *Ida B. Wells-Barnett: An Exploratory Study of an American Black Woman, 1893-1930*. Vol. 16 of *Black Women in United States History*. Edited by Darlene Clark-Hine. Brooklyn: Carlson Publishing Co., 1990.

Townes, Emilie M. "Because God Gave Her Vision: The Religious Impulse of Ida B. Wells-Barnett." In *Spirituality and Social Responsibility*. Edited by Rosemary Keller. Nashville: Abingdon Press, 1993.

———. "Ida B. Wells-Barnett: An Afro-American Prophet." *Christian Century* 106(March 15, 1989):285-286.

———. *Womanist Justice, Womanist Hope*. Atlanta: Scholars Press, 1993.

Tucker, David M. "Miss Ida B. Wells and Memphis Lynching." *Phylon* 32(Summer 1971).

Mary Eliza Church Terrell
(1863-1954)

As the first president of the National Association of Colored Women, Mary Church Terrell guided a movement which was formed to support and uplift black women as well as to address the economic and social concerns of the entire black community. Appropriately described as a "genteel militant,"[9] Terrell was a role model for the African American community as she (fluent in three languages) addressed foreign assemblies as well as confronted the status quo in court and on the streets in the United States, e.g. participating in the first sit-ins and boycotts to integrate restaurants in Washington, D.C. Mary Church Terrell was an insightful leader who led both through moral suasion and civil disobedience.

"The Duty of the National Association of Colored Women"[10]

The National Association of Colored Women had at its second convention every reason to rejoice and be exceedingly glad. From its birth in July 1896, till the present moment its growth has been steady and its march ever onward and upward to the goal of its ambition.

An infant of but three years is this organization, over which I have had the honor to preside, ever since it first saw the light of day in the Capital of the Nation, and yet in those short years it has accomplished a vast amount of good. So tenderly has this child of the organized womanhood of the race been nurtured, and so wisely ministered unto by all who have watched prayerfully and waited patiently for its development, that it comes before you to-day a child hale, hearty and strong, of which its fond mothers have every reason to be proud.

As individuals, colored women have always been ambitious for their race. From the day when shackles first fell from their fettered limbs till now, they have often single-handed and alone, struggled against the most desperate and discouraging odds, in order to secure for their loved ones and themselves that culture of the head and heart for which they hungered and thirsted so long in vain. But it dawned upon them finally, that

---

[9]Sharon Harley, "Mary Church Terrell: Genteel Militant" in Leon Litwack and August Meier, eds., *Black Leaders of the Nineteenth Century*, (Urbana: University of Illinois Press, 1988), 307-321.

[10]*AME Church Review* 16/3(January 1900):340-354.

individuals working alone, or scattered here and there in small companies, might be ever so honest in purpose, so indefatigable in labor, so conscientious about methods, and so wise in projecting plans, yet they would accomplish little, compared with the possible achievement of many individuals, all banded together throughout the entire land, with heads and hearts fixed on the same high purpose and hands joined in united strength. As a result of a general realization of this fact, the National Association of Colored Women was born.

Though we are young in years, and have been unable to put into execution some plans on which we had built high hopes, the fruits of organized effort are already apparent to all. If in the short space of three years the National Association had done nothing but give an impressive object lesson in the necessity for, and the efficacy of, organization, it would have proved its reason for existence and its right to live; but, seriously handicapped though we have been, both because of the lack of experience and lack of funds, our efforts have for the most part been crowned with success.

In the kindergartens established by some of our organization, children have been cultivated and trained. A sanatorium with a training school for nurses has been set on such a firm foundation in a Southern city, and has given such abundant proof of its utility and necessity, that the municipal government has voted it an annual appropriation of several hundred dollars. To our poor benighted sisters in the black belt of Alabama we have gone, and have been both a help and a comfort to these women, through the darkness of whose ignorance of everything that makes life sweet or worth the living, no ray of light would have penetrated but for us. We have taught them the A, B, C of living, by showing them how to make their huts more habitable and decent with the small means at their command, and how to care for themselves and their families more in accordance with the laws of health. Plans for aiding the indigent, orphaned and aged have been projected and in some instances have been carried to a successful execution. Mother's meetings have been generally held and sewing classes formed. Abuses like lynching, the convict lease system and the Jim Crow laws have been discussed with a view of doing something to remedy these evils. In Chicago, magnificent work has been done by the Illinois Federation of Colored Women's Clubs through whose instrumentality schools have been visited, truant children looked after, parents and teachers urged to co-operate with each other, public institutions investigated, rescue and reform work engaged in to reclaim unfortunate women and tempted girls, garments cut, made and distributed to the needy poor. In short, what our hands have found to do, that we have cheerfully done. It is not, therefore, because I feel that the National Association of Colored Women has been derelict, or has failed, that I shall discuss its duty to our race, but because I wish to emphasize some special lines of work in which it is already engaging, but to which I would pledge its more hearty support.

The more closely I study the relation of this Association to the race, the more clearly defined becomes its duty to the children.

Believing in the saving grace of the kindergarten for our little ones, at our first convention, as one may remember, I urged with all the earnestness that I could command, that the Association should consider the establishment of kindergartens as the special mission it is called upon to fulfill. The importance of engaging extensively in this effort to uplift the children, particularly those to whom the opportunity of learning by contact what is true and good and beautiful could come through no other source, grows on me more and more every day. Through the kindergarten alone, which teaches its lessons in the most impressionable years of childhood, shall we be able to save countless thousands of our little ones who are going to destruction before our very eyes. To some the task of establishing kindergartens may seem too herculean for the Association to undertake, because of the great expense involved. Be that as it may, we shall never accomplish the good it is in our power to do, nor shall we discharge our obligation to the race, until we engage in this work in those sections at least where it is most needed.

In many cities and towns the kindergarten has already been incorporated in the public school system. Here it may not be necessary for the Association to work. But wherever the conditions are such that our children are deprived of the training which they can receive from the kindergarten alone, deprived of that training which from the very nature of the case, they so sorely need, there the Association should establish these schools, from which so much benefit to our little ones will accrue.

Side by side in importance with the kindergarten stands the day nursery, a charity of which there is an imperative need among us. Thousands of our wage-earning mothers with large families dependent upon them for support are obliged to leave their infants all day to be cared for either by young brothers and sisters, who know nothing about it, or by some good-natured neighbor, who promises much, but who does little. Some of these infants are locked alone in a room from the time the mother leaves in the morning until she returns at night; their suffering is, of course, unspeakable. Not long ago, I read in a southern newspaper that an infant thus locked alone in a room all day, while its mother went to wash, had cried itself to death. Recently I have had under direct observation a day nursery, established for infants of working women, and I have been shocked at some of the miserable little specimens of humanity brought in by mothers, who had been obliged to board them out with either careless or heartless people. In one instance the hands and legs of a poor little mite of only fourteen months had been terribly drawn and twisted with rheumatism contracted by sleeping in a cold room with no fire during the severe winter, while the family with whom it boarded enjoyed comfortable quarters overhead. And so I might go on enumerating cases, showing how terrible is the suffering of infants of working women, who have no one with whom to leave them, while they earn their daily bread. Establishing day nurseries is clearly a practical charity, of the need of which there is abundant proof in every community where our women may be found.

What a vast amount of good would be accomplished, if by every branch of the Association, a home we provided for the infants of working women, who no matter how tender may be their affection for their little ones, are forced by stern necessity to neglect them all day themselves, and at best, can only entrust them to others, from whom, in the majority of cases, they do not receive the proper care. It would not only save the life, and preserve the health of many a poor little one, but it would speak eloquently of our interest in our sisters, whose lot is harder than our own, but to whom we should give unmistakable proof of our regard, our sympathy, and our willingness to render any assistance in our power. When one thinks of the slaughter of the innocents which is occurring with pitiless persistency every day, and reflects upon how many are maimed for life through neglect, how many there are whose intellects are clouded because of the treatment received during their helpless infancy, establishing day nurseries can seem neither unnecessary nor far-fetched, but must appeal directly to us all. No great amount is required to establish a day nursery, and part of the money necessary for its maintenance might be secured by charging each of the mothers who take advantage of it a small sum. In no other way could the investment of the same amount of money bring such large and blessed returns.

To each and every branch of the Association, then, I recommend the establishment of a day nursery, as a means through which it can render one of the greatest services possible to humanity and the race.

For the sake of argument, let us suppose that absolute lack of means prevents an organization from establishing either a kindergarten or a day nursery. Even under such circumstances a part of its obligation to the children may be discharged.

For no organization is so poor both in mental resources and in money that it cannot form a children's club, through which we can do a vast amount of good. Lessons may be taught and rules of conduct impressed, while the children of a neighborhood are gathered together for amusement and play, as in no other way. Both by telling and reading stories, teaching kindness to animals, politeness to elders, pity for the unfortunate and weak, seeds may be sown in youthful minds, which in after years will spring up and bear fruit, some an hundred fold. What a revolution we should work, for instance, if the children of today were taught that they are responsible for their thoughts, that they can learn to control them, that an impure life is the result of impure thoughts, that crime is conceived in thought before it is executed in deed. No organization of the Association should feel entirely satisfied with its work, unless some of its energy, or some of its brain, or some of its money is used in the name, and for the sake of the children, either by establishing a day nursery, a kindergarten, or forming a children's club, which last is possible to all.

Let us remember that we are banded together to do good, to work most vigorously and conscientiously upon that which will redound most to the welfare and progress of the race. If that be true, I recommend to you, I plead to you, for the children, for those who will soon represent us, for those by whom as a race we shall soon stand or fall in the estimation of the world, for those upon whom the hope of every people must necessarily be built. As an Association, let us devote ourselves enthusiastically, conscientiously, to the children, with their warm little hearts, their susceptible little minds, their malleable, pliable characters. Through the children of today, we must build the foundation of the next generation upon such a rock of integrity, morality, and strength, both of body and mind, that the floods of proscription, prejudice, and persecution may descend upon it in torrents, and yet it will not be moved. We hear a great deal about the race problem, and how to solve it. This theory, that and the other, may be advanced, but the real solution of the race problem, both so far as we, who are oppressed and those who oppress us are concerned, lies in the children.

Let no one suppose that I would have a large organization like ours a body of one idea, with no thought, plan or purpose except that which centers about children. I am an optimist, because I see how we are broadening and deepening out into the various channels of generosity and beneficence, which indicates what a high state of civilization we have already reached. Homes for the orphaned and aged must be established; sanatoriums, hospitals, and training schools for nurses founded; unfortunate women and tempted girls encircled by the loving arms of those who would woo them back to the path of rectitude and virtue; classes formed for cultivating the mind; schools of domestic science opened in every city and village in which our women and girls may be found. All this is our duty, all this is an obligation, which we should discharge as soon as our means will permit. But in connection with such work let us not neglect, let us not forget, the children, remembering that when we love and protect the little ones, we follow in the footsteps of Him, who when He wished to paint the most beautiful picture of Beulah land it is possible for the human mind to conceive, pointed to the children and said—"Of such is the kingdom of heaven."

It is frequently charged against the more favored among us who have been blessed with advantages of education and moral training superior to those enjoyed by the majority, that they hold themselves too much aloof from the less fortunate of their people. Without discussing the reasons for such a condition of things, it must be patent to the most careless observer that the more intelligent and influential among us do exert themselves as much as they should to uplift those beneath them, as it is plainly their duty to do.

It has been suggested, and very appropriately, I think, that this Association should take as its motto—*Lifting as we climb.* In no way could we live up to such a sentiment better than by coming into closer touch with masses of our women, by whom whether we will or not, the world will always judge the womanhood of the race. Even though we wish to shun them, and hold ourselves entirely aloof from them, we cannot escape the consequences of their acts. So, that, if the call of duty were disregarded altogether, policy and self-preservation would demand that we do go among the lowly, the illiterate, and even the vicious to whom we are bound by the ties of race and sex, and put forth every possible effort to uplift and re-claim them.

It is useless to talk about elevating the race if we do not come into closer touch with the masses of our women, through whom we may cor-rect many of the evils which militate so seriously against us, and inaugu-rate the reforms without which, as a race, we cannot hope to succeed. It is often difficult, I know, to persuade people who need help most to avail themselves of the assistance offered by those who wish to lift them to a higher plane. If it were possible for us to send out a national organizer, whose duty it would be to form clubs throughout the length and breadth of the land, it would be no easy matter, I am sure, to persuade some of our women to join them, even though they know that by so doing they would receive just that kind of instruction and counsel which they so greatly need. This fault is not peculiar to our women alone but is common to the whole human race. Difficult though it be for us to uplift some of our women, many of whose practices in their own homes and in the service of their employers rise like a great barrier to our progress, we should neverthe-less work unceasingly to this end until we win their confidence so that they will accept our aid.

Through such clubs as I have just mentioned, the attention of our women might be called to the alarming rapidity with which they are losing ground in the world of labor—a fact patent to all who observe and read the signs of the times. So many families are supported entirely by our women, that if this movement to withhold employment from them continues to grow, we shall soon be confronted by a condition of things serious and disas-trous indeed. It is clearly the duty of this, the only organized body of col-ored women in the country, to study the labor question, not only as it affects the women, but also as it affects the men. When those who for-merly employed colored women as domestics, but who refuse to do so now, are asked why they have established what is equivalent to a boycott against us, they invariably tell us that colored women are now neither skilled in the trades nor reliable as working women. While we know that in the majority of cases colored women are employed because of the cruel, unreasonable prejudice which rages so violently against them, there is just enough truth in the charge of poor workmanship and unreliability to make us wince when it is preferred.

To stem this tide of popular disfavor against us should be the desire and determination of every colored woman in the country who has the interest of her race at heart. It is we, the National Association, who must point out to our women how fatal it will be to their highest, best interest, and to the highest, best interests of their children, if they do not build up a reputation for reliability and proficiency, by establishing schools of domestic science as soon as our means will permit; and it is the duty of this Association to raise funds to start a few of these schools immediately— we should probably do more to solve the labor question, so far as it affects the women than by using any other means we could possibly employ. Let us explain the situation as we may, the fact remains that trades and avocations, which formerly by common consent belonged almost exclusively to our men and women, are gradually slipping from their grasp.

Whom does such a condition of things affect more directly and disastrously than the women of the race? As parents, teachers and guardians, we teach our children to be honest and industrious, to cultivate their minds, to become skilled workmen, to be energetic and then to be hopeful. It is easy enough to impress upon them the necessity of cultivating their minds, and of becoming skilled workmen, of being energetic, honest and industrious, but how difficult it is for colored women to inspire their children with hope, or offer them an incentive for their best endeavor under the existing condition of things in this country.

As a mother of the dominant race looks into the sweet innocent face of her babe, her heart thrills not only with happiness in the present, but also with joyful anticipations of the future. For well she knows that honor, wealth, fame and greatness in any vocation he may choose, are all his, if he but possess the ability and determination to secure them. She knows that if it's in him to be great, all the exterior circumstances which can help him to the goal of his ambition, such as the laws of his country, the public opinion of his countrymen and manifold opportunities, are all his, without the asking. From his birth he is king in his own right, and is no suppliant for justice.

But how bitter is the contrast between the feelings of joy and hope which thrill the heart of the white mother and those which stir the soul of her colored sister. As a mother of the weaker race clasps to her bosom the babe which she loves with an affection as tender and deep as that the white mother bears her child, she cannot thrill with joyful anticipation of the future. For before her babe she sees the thorny path of prejudice and proscription his little feet must tread. She knows that no matter how great his ability, or how lofty his ambition, there are comparatively few trades and avocations in which any one of his race may hope to succeed. She knows that no matter how skillful his hand, how honest his heart, or how great his need, trade unions will close their doors in his face and make his struggle for existence desperate indeed. So rough does the way of her infant appear to many a poor colored mother, as she thinks of the hardships and humiliations to which he will be subjected, when he tries to earn his daily bread, that instead of thrilling with joy and hope, she trembles with apprehension and despair.

This picture, though forbidding to look upon, is not overdrawn, as those who have studied the labor question in its relation to our race can testify. What, then, shall we do? Shall we sit supinely by, with folded hands, drooping heads, and weeping eyes, or shall we be up and doing, determined to smooth out the rough roads of labor over which tiny feet that now patter in play, will soon stumble and fall? To our own youth, to our own tradesmen, we must preach efficiency, reliability, thorough preparation for any work in which they choose to engage. Let us also appeal directly to the large-hearted, broad-minded women of the dominant race, and lay our case clearly before them. In conversing with many of them privately I have discovered that our side of the labor question has never been made a living, breathing, terrible reality to them. In a vague way they know that difficulties do confront colored men and women in their effort to secure employment, but they do not know how almost insurmountable are the obstacles which lie in the path of the rank and file who want to earn an honest living. Let us ask these women both to follow, themselves, and teach their children, the lofty principles of humanity, charity and justice which they profess to observe. Let us ask that they train their children to be just and broad enough to judge men and women by their intrinsic merit, rather than by the adventitious circumstances of race or color or creed. Let the Association of Colored Women ask the white mothers of this country to teach their children that when they grow to be men and women, if they deliberately prevent their fellow creatures from earning their daily bread, by closing the doors of trade against them, the Father of all men will hold them responsible for the crimes which are the result of their injustice, and for the human wrecks which the ruthless crushing of hope and ambition always makes. In the name of our children, let us ask, also, that they do all in their power to secure for our youth opportunities of earning a living and of attaining unto the full stature of manhood and womanhood, which they desire for their own. In the name of justice and humanity, in the name of the innocence and helplessness of childhood, let us appeal to the white mothers of this country to do all in their power to make the future of our boys and girls as bright and promising as should be that of every child, born on this free American soil. It is the women of the country who mould public opinion, and when they say that trades and avocations shall not be closed against men and women on account of race or color, then the day of proscription and prejudice will darken the dawn no more.

As individuals, we have presented our case again and again. Let us now try the efficacy of organized effort; on this, I build great hope. Organization is one of the most potent forces in the world to-day, and the good it is possible for the National Association to accomplish has not yet been approximated by those most sanguine of its success.

And now, I must briefly call your attention to a subject fraught with interest to us all. The health of our race is becoming a matter of deep concern to many who are alarmed by statistics showing how great is the death rate among us as compared with that of the Whites.

There are many reasons why this proportion is so great among us— chief of which are poverty and ignorance of the laws of health. Our children are sent illy clad through inclement weather to school, for instance. Girls just budding into womanhood are allowed to sit all day in wet boots and damp skirts, in both the high and graded schools which they attend. Thus it happens that some of our most promising and gifted young women succumb to diseases, which are the result of carelessness on the part both of parents and teachers. We must call the attention of our mothers to this fact, and urge the school officials to protect the health of our children as far as possible by wise legislation, and thus stop the awful ravages made by the diseases which a little care and precaution might prevent.

I must not neglect to mention another duty which the Association owes the race, and which it must not fail to discharge. Creating a healthful, wholesome public opinion in every community in which we are represented, is one of the greatest services we can render. The duty of setting a high moral standard and living up to it devolves upon us as colored women in a peculiar way. Slanders are circulated against us every day, both in the press and by the direct descendants of those who in years past were responsible for the moral degradation of their female slaves. While these calumnies are not founded in fact, they can nevertheless do us a great deal of harm, if those who represent the intelligence and virtue among us do not, both in our public and private life, avoid even the appearance of evil. In spite of the fateful inheritance left us by slavery, in spite of the manifold temptations and pitfalls to which our young girls are subjected all over the country, and though the safeguards usually thrown around maidenly youth and innocence are in some sections entirely withheld from colored girls, statistics compiled by men not inclined to falsity in favor of my race show that immorality among colored women is not so great as among women in countries like Austria, Italy, Germany, Sweden and France.

If I were called upon to state in a word where I thought the Association should do its most effective work, I should say unhesitatingly, "in the home." The purification of the home must be our first consideration and care. It is in the home where woman is really queen, that she wields her influence with the most telling effect. It is through the home, therefore, that the principles which we wish to promulgate can be most widely circulated and most deeply impressed. In the mind and heart of every good and conscientious woman, the first place is occupied by home. We must always remember in connection with this fact, however, that observation has shown and experience has proved that it is not the narrow-minded, selfish women who think of naught save their families and themselves, who have not time to work for neglected children, the helpless sick and the needy poor—it is not such women, I say, who exert in their homes the most powerful influence for good.

And now, finally, let us be up and doing wherever a word may be spoken for principle, or a hand lifted to aid. We must study carefully and conscientiously the questions which affect us most deeply and directly. Against lynching, the convict lease system, the Jim Crow car laws, and all other barbarities and abuses which degrade and dishearten us, we must agitate with such force of logic and intensity of soul that the oppressor will either be converted to principles of justice or be ashamed to openly violate them. Let loyalty to race, as displayed by employing and patronizing our own, in refusing to hold up our own to public ridicule and scorn, let allegiance to those whose ability, character and general fitness qualify them to lead, be two of the cardinal principles by which each and every member of this Association is guided. If we are to judge the future by the past, as dark as that past has sometimes been since our emancipation, there is no reason why we should view it with despair. Over almost insurmountable obstacles as a race we have forged ahead until today there is hardly a trade, a profession, or an art in which we have not at least one worthy representative. I challenge any other race to show such wonderful progress along all lines in so short a time, under circumstances so discouraging as that made by the ex-slaves of the United States of America. And though today some of us are cast down by the awful barbarities constantly inflicted upon some of our unfortunate race in the South who have been shot and burned to death by mobs which took no pains to establish the guilt of their victims, some of whom were doubtless innocent, we must remember that the darkest hour is just before the dawn.

As an Association, by discharging our duty to the children, by studying the labor question in its relation to our race, by coming into closer touch with the masses of our women, by urging parents and teachers to protect the health of our boys and girls, by creating a wholesome, healthful public sentiment in every community in which we are represented, by setting a high moral stand and living up to it, and purifying the home, we shall render the race a service, whose magnitude and importance it is not in my power to express.

Let us love and cherish our Association with such loyalty and zeal, that it will wax strong and great, that it may soon become that bulwark of strength and source of inspiration to our women that it is destined to be.

> "In spite of rock and tempest's roar,
> In spite of false lights on the shore,
> Sail on, nor fear to breast the sea!
> Our hearts, our hopes are all with Thee,
> Our hearts, our hopes, our prayers, our tears,
> Our faith, triumphant o'er our fears,
> Are all with Thee, are all with Thee."
> —*Mary Church Terrell*

Bibliography

Giddings, Paula. *When and Where I Enter: The Impact of Black Women on Race and Sex in America*. New York: Bantam Books, 1984.

Jones, Beverly Washington. *Quest for Equality: The Life and Writings of Mary Church Terrell*. Brooklyn, New York: Carlson Publishers, 1990.

Sheppard, Gladys B. *Mary Church Terrell—Respectable Person*. Baltimore: Human Relations Press, 1959.

Terrell, Mary Church. *A Colored Woman in a White World*. Washington, D.C.: Randell, 1940. Reprinted. New York: Arno Press, 1980.

Wesley, Charles H. *History of the National Association of Colored Women's Clubs, Inc.: A Legacy of Service*. Washington, D.C.: National Association of Colored Women's Clubs, 1984.

SARAH DUDLEY PETTEY
(c.1870s)

"From environments, contact and association at home, Mrs. Bishop Pettey always had the instruction and advice of intelligent parents. At the age of six she could read and write. She entered the graded school of her native city, and after finishing her course she entered the State Normal School and remained three years; then she entered the famous Scotia Seminary at Concord, N.C., from which institution she graduated with distinction June, 1883. . . .

For several years she [was] General Secretary of the Woman's Home and Foreign Missionary Society of the A.M.E. Zion Church. As wife, mother and Christian worker, Sarah Dudley Pettey [was] a model woman, endeavoring to lead men and women upward and Heaven-ward."[11]

"What Role is the Educated Negro Woman to Play in the Uplifting of Her Race?"[12]

Woman's part in the consummation of any project which had to do with the elevation of mankind is of paramount importance. With her influence eliminated or her work minimized, failure is inevitable. This is true

---

[11]D. W. Culp, *Twentieth-Century Negro Literature* (Atlanta: J. L. Nichols and Co., 1902) [New York: Arno Press and New York Times Reprint, 1969], n.p.

[12]Ibid., 182-185.

regardless of race or nationality. In the civilization and enlightenment of the Negro race its educated women must be potent factors. The difficulties that the Negro must labor under, in his effort to rise, are manifold and peculiar. The critics of the Negro have assaulted him at the most vital point, viz., character. In their onslaught they have assailed the morals of the entire race. To meet this criticism the Negro must establish a character of high morals, which will stand out so conspicuously that even his bitterest foe will acknowledge its reality. In establishing this our women must lead. It must be understood that their virtue is as sacred and as inviolate as the laws of the eternal verities. They must not compromise even with an apparent virtuous endowment; it must be real. Nothing great is accomplished without the shedding of blood. To convince the world of the virtue of the Negro race, Negro blood must be shed freely. Our young women must be taught that gorgeous dress and fine paraphernalia don't make a woman. They should dress modestly, becomingly and economically.

She is a true woman whose honor must not be insulted; who, though poorly paid, pursues her honest labor for bread and would scorn the obtaining of a livelihood any other way, regardless of the magnitude of the inducement. The foundation for this high sentiment finds its initiative in the home. Home life is the citadel and bulwark of every race's moral life. The ruler of home is mother. A faithful, virtuous and intelligent motherhood will elevate any people. The impress of mother follows her children to the grave; when her form is changed and her physical existence extinct the footprints of her noble and pious life live long after her. Womanhood and manhood begin in the cradle and around the fireside; mother's knee is truly the family altar. True patriotism, obedience and respect for law, both divine and civil, the love and yearning for the pure, the sublime and the good, all emanate from mother's personality. If mother be good, all the vices and shortcomings of father will fail to lead the children astray; but if mother is not what she should be, all of the holy influences of angels cannot save the children. I would urge then, as the first prerequisite for our work, a pure, pious and devoted motherhood.

Secondly, a firm stand for right and truth in all things. Woman's power is her love. This pure flame lights up all around her. Her wishes and desires men love to satisfy. There are many things in society, politics and religion that ambitious men would seek to obtain by all hazards, but when woman takes her stand against these things she invariably wins. Our first stand must be for intelligence. No woman of to-day, who is thirty years of age, has the right to be queen of a home, unless she is intelligent. In this advanced day, to rear up a family by an illiterate woman might well be considered a crime. As a race, if we would possess the intelligence desired, our children must be kept in school, and not allowed to roam idly through the streets when the schoolhouse is open. Since, in most of the

Southern states, countless numbers of our people have been disfranchised, our educated women should institute a movement which will bring about compulsory education and a general reform in the educational system of the South. We need better schools and a higher standard of education for the masses. In our homes wholesome literature, periodicals, papers and books must be had. Mother must be acquainted with these herself. She introduces the little ones to them by the story form. This catchy method soon engrosses their attention, and they become wrapped up in them. Great care must be exercised in the selection of reading matter for our girls. Nothing is more hurtful than obscene literature.

When our homes become intelligent, we shall have intelligent states-men, ministers and doctors; in fact, the whole regime that leads will be intelligent. In public affairs woman has her share. She must speak through husband, son, father, brother and lover. Men go from home into the world to execute what woman has decreed. An educated wife formulates the political opinion of husband and son, and though she may remain at home on election day, her views and opinions will find expression in the ballots of the male members of her household. The same thing is true in the church. I shall not dictate what woman should do here or limit her sphere of activ-ity, but this I know she can with propriety—in her auxiliary work to the church she can become a mighty power. Woman's Missionary Societies, Christian Endeavor Societies, Sabbath School work, etc., afford a broad field of labor for our educated women. Her activity in all things pertaining to racial advancement will be the motive power in establishing firmly and intelligently an enlightened racial existence. Thirdly: the educated Negro woman must take her stand among the best and most enlightened women of all races; and in so doing she must seek to be herself. Imitate no one when the imitation destroys the personal identity. Not only in dress are we imitative to the extreme, but in manners and customs. When our boys and girls become redeemed from these evils a great deal will have been accomplished in the elevation of our race.

There are some noble women among other races whom we may imi-tate in virtue, morality and deportment. Those women come not from the giddy and gay streets of London, Paris or New York; but such women as Queen Victoria, Helen Gould, Frances Willard and others. These women have elevated society, given tone and character to governments and other institutions. They ornamented the church and blessed humanity. I can say with pride just here that we have many noble women in our own race whose lives and labors are worthy of emulation. Among them we find Frances Watkins Harper, Sojourner Truth, Phillis Wheatley, Ida Wells-Barnett and others. Our educated women should organize councils, fed-erations, literary organizations, societies of social purity and the like. These would serve as great mediums in reaching the masses.

I cannot refrain from mentioning public or street decorum here. Woman, as she glides through the busy and crowded thoroughfares of our great cities, is eyed and watched by everyone. It is here that she impresses the world of her real worth. She can, by her own acts, surround herself with a wall of protection that the most suspicious character would not dare attempt to scale or she can make it appear otherwise.

Beware then, mothers; accompany your daughters as often as possible in public.

In this advanced age, if the Negro would scale the delectable heights already attained by more highly favored races, our women must unite in their endeavors to uplift the masses. With concentration of thought and unity of action, all things are possible; these can effect victories when formidable armies and navies fail. The role that the educated Negro woman must play in the elevation of her race is of vital importance. There is no sphere into which your activities do not go. Gather, then, your forces; elevate yourself with the habiliments of a successful warrior; raise your voice for God and justice; leave no stone unturned in your endeavor to route the forces of all opposition. There is not height so elevated but what your influence can climb, not depth so low but what your virtuous touch can purify. However dark and foreboding the cloud may be, the effulgent rays from your faithful and consecrated personality will dispel; and ere long Ethiopia's sons and daughters, led by pious, educated women, will be elevated among the enlightened races of the world.

—*Sarah Dudley Pettey*

Bibliography

Walls, William J. *The African Methodist Episcopal Zion Church: Reality of the Black Church*. Charlotte: A.M.E. Zion Publishing House, 1974.

MARY McLEOD BETHUNE
(1875-1955)

Her rise from rural obscurity to national prominence is an amazing chronicle of leadership, political savvy, and destiny. A missionary at heart, Bethune trained to serve in Africa, but God made use of her myriad talents at home. During an extraordinary life, she founded Bethune-Cookman College, founded the National Council of Negro Women, consulted with Eleanor Roosevelt and other national leaders, and worked toward the advancement of black folks as well as the good of the nation.

"My Last Will and Testament"[13]

Sometimes as I sit communing in my study I feel that death is not far off. I am aware that it will overtake me before the greatest of my dreams—full equality for the Negro in our time—is realized. Yet, I face the reality without fear or regrets. I am resigned to death as all humans must be at the proper time. Death neither alarms nor frightens one who has had a long career of fruitful toil. The knowledge that my work has been helpful to many fills me with joy and great satisfaction.

Since my retirement from an active role in educational work and from the affairs of the National Council of Negro Women, I have been living quietly and working at my desk at my home here in Florida. The years have directed a change of pace for me. I am now 76 years old and my activities are no longer so strenuous as they once were. I feel that I must conserve my strength to finish the work at hand.

Already, I have begun working on my autobiography which will record my life journey in detail, together with innumerable side trips which have carried me abroad, into every corner of our country, into homes, both lowly and luxurious, and even into the White House to confer with the Presidents. I have also deeded my home and its contents to the Mary McLeod Bethune Foundation, organized in 1953, for research, interracial activity and sponsorship of wider educational opportunities.

Sometimes I ask myself if I have any other legacy to leave. Truly, my worldly possessions are few. Yet, my experiences have been rich. From them I have distilled principles and policies in which I believe firmly, for they represent the meaning of my life's work. They are the products of much sweat and sorrow. Perhaps, in them there is something of value. So, as my life draws to a close, I will pass them on to Negroes everywhere in the hope that an old woman's philosophy may give them inspiration. Here, then, is my legacy.

Now that the barriers are crumbling everywhere, the Negro in America must be ever vigilant lest his forces be marshalled behind wrong causes and undemocratic movements. He must not lend his support to any group that seeks to subvert democracy. This is why we must select leaders who are wise and courageous, and of great moral stature and ability. We have great leaders among us today. We have had other great men and women in the past: Frederick Douglas, Booker T. Washington, Harriet Tubman, Sojourner Truth, and Mary Church Terrell. We must produce more qualified people like them, who will work not for themselves, but for others.

---

[13]This is excerpted from a mimeographed copy of the original version distributed by the National Council of Negro Women, Inc.

I LEAVE YOU FAITH. Faith is the first factor in life devoted to service. Without faith nothing is possible. With it, nothing is impossible. Faith in God is the greatest power, but great too, is faith in oneself. In 50 years the faith of the American Negro in himself has grown immensely, and is still increasing. The measure of our progress as a race is in precise relation to the depth of the faith in our people held by our leaders. Frederick Douglas, genius though he was, was spurred by a deep conviction that his people would heed his counsel and follow him to freedom. Our greatest Negro figures have been imbued with faith. Their perseverance paid rich dividends. We must never forget their sufferings and their sacrifices, for they were the foundations of the progress of our people.

I LEAVE YOU RACIAL DIGNITY. I want Negroes to maintain their human dignity at all costs. We, as Negroes, must recognize that we are the custodians as well as the heirs of a great civilization. We have given something to the world as a race and for this we are proud and fully conscious of our place in the total picture of mankind's development. We must learn also to share and mix with all men. We must make an effort to be less race conscious and more conscious of individual and human values. I have never been sensitive about my complexion. My color has never destroyed my self respect nor has it ever caused me to conduct myself in such a manner as to merit the disrespect of any person. I have not let my color handicap me. Despite many crushing burdens and handicaps, I have risen from the cotton fields of South Carolina to found a college, administer it during the years of growth, become a public servant in the government and country, and a leader of women. I would not exchange my color for all the wealth in the world, for had I been born white, I might not have been able to do all I have done or yet hope to do.

I LEAVE YOU A DESIRE TO LIVE HARMONIOUSLY WITH YOUR FELLOW MAN. The problem of color is world-wide. It is found in Africa and Asia, Europe and South America. I appeal to American Negroes—both North and South, East and West—to recognize their common problems and unite to solve them.

I LEAVE YOU LOVE. Love builds. It is positive and helpful. It is more beneficial than hate. Injuries quickly forgotten quickly pass away. Personally and racially, our enemies must be forgiven. Our aim must be to create a world of fellowship and justice where no man's skin, color or religion, is held against him. "Love thy neighbor" is a precept which could transform the world if it were universally practiced. It connotes brotherhood and to me, brotherhood of man is the noblest concept in all human relations. Loving your neighbor means being interracial, interreligious, and international.

I LEAVE YOU HOPE. The Negro's growth will be great in the years to come. Yesterday, our ancestors endured the degradation of slavery, yet they retained their dignity. Today, we direct our economic and political strength toward winning a more abundant and secure life. Tomorrow, a new Negro, unhindered by race taboos and shackles, will benefit from more than 330 years of ceaseless striving and struggle. Theirs will be a better world. This I believe with all my heart.

I LEAVE YOU THE CHALLENGE OF DEVELOPING CONFIDENCE IN ONE ANOTHER. As long as Negroes are hemmed into racial blocs of prejudice and pressure, it will be necessary for them to band together for economic betterment. Negro banks, insurance companies and other businesses are examples of successful racial economic enterprises. These institutions were made possible by vision and mutual aid. Confidence was vital in getting them started and keeping them going. Negroes have got to demonstrate still more confidence in each other in business. This kind of confidence will aid the economic rise of the race by bringing together the pennies and dollars of our people and ploughing them into useful channels. Economic separatism cannot be tolerated in this enlightened age, and is not practicable. We must spread out as far and as fast as we can, but must also help each other as we go.

I LEAVE YOU A THIRST FOR EDUCATION. Knowledge is the prime need of the hour. More and more, Negroes are taking full advantage of hard-won opportunities for learning, and the educational level of the Negro population is at its highest point in history. We are making greater use of the privileges inherent in living in democracy. If we continue in this trend, we will be able to rear increasing numbers of strong purposeful men and women, equipped with vision, mental clarity, health and education.

I LEAVE YOU A RESPECT FOR THE USE OF POWER. We live in a world which respects power above all things. Power, intelligently directed, can lead to more freedom. Unwisely directed, it can be a dreadful destructive force. During my lifetime I have seen the power of the Negro grow enormously. It has always been my first concern that this power should be placed on the side of human justice. I pray that we will begin to live harmoniously with the white race. So often, our difficulties have made us supersensitive and truculent. I want to see my people conduct themselves naturally in all relationships, fully conscious of their manly responsibilities and deeply aware of their heritage. I want them to learn to understand whites and influence them for good, for it is advisable for us to do so. We are a minority of fifteen million living side by side with a white majority. We must learn to deal with people positively and on an individual basis.

I LEAVE YOU, FINALLY, A RESPONSIBILITY TO OUR PEOPLE. The world around us really belongs to youth, for youth will take over its future management. Our children must never lose their zeal for building a better world. They must not be discouraged from aspiring toward greatness, for they are to be the leaders of tomorrow. Nor must they forget that the masses of our people are still underprivileged, ill-housed, impoverished and victimized by discrimination. We have powerful potential in our youth, and we must have the courage to change old ideas and practices so that we may direct their power toward good ends.

Faith, courage, brotherhood, dignity, ambition, responsibility—these are needed today as never before. We must cultivate them and use them as tools for our task of completing the establishment of equality for the Negro. We must sharpen these tools in the struggle that faces us and find new ways of using them. The Freedom Gates are half ajar. We must pry them fully open.

If I have a legacy to leave my people, it is my philosophy of living and serving. As I face tomorrow, I am content, for I think I have spent my life well. I pray now that my philosophy may be helpful to those who share my vision of a world of Peace.

—Mary McLeod Bethune

Bibliography

Bethune, Mary McLeod. "NACW Presidential Address." August 2, 1926. Bethune Papers, Amistad Research Center.

———. National Council of Negro Women, Annual Report. October 1941. Bethune Foundation.

Daniel, Sadie Iola. *Women Builders*. Washington, D.C.: Associated Publishers, 1931.

Holt, Rackham. *Mary McLeod Bethune: A Biography*. Garden City, N.Y.: Doubleday, 1964.

Ross, B. Joyce. "Mary McLeod Bethune and the National Youth Administration: A Case Study of Power Relationships in the Black Cabinet of Franklin D. Roosevelt." In *Black Leaders of the Twentieth Century*. Edited by John Hope Franklin and August Meier. Urbana: University of Illinois Press, 1982.

Leffall, Dolores C. and Janet L. Sims. "Mary McLeod Bethune—The Educator; Also Including a Selected Annotated Bibliography." *Journal of Negro Education* 45 (Summer 1976):342-359.

Newsome, Clarence G. "Mary McLeod Bethune and the Methodist Episcopal Church North: In But Out." *Journal of Religious Thought* 49 (Summer-Fall 1992):7-20. Also found in *This Far by Faith: Readings in African-American Women's Religious Autobiography*. Edited by Judith Weisenfel & Richard Newman. New York: Routledge, 1996.

———. "Mary McLeod Bethune as Religionist." In *Women in New Worlds*. Edited by H. Thomas. 1981.

Peare, Owen. *Mary McLeod Bethune*. New York: Vanguard Press, 1951.

Scole, Evan. "Mary McLeod Bethune." In *Something More Than Human*. Edited by C. Cole. 1986.

NANNIE HELEN BURROUGHS
(1879-1961)

At the age of twenty-one, Nannie H. Burroughs's oratorical skills catapulted her out of obscurity and into the midst of the struggle for women's rights in the church. Her speech, "How the Sisters Are Hindered from Helping," was a catalyst for change in the National Baptist Convention and for the formation of the Women's Convention.

She assumed the presidency of the Women's Convention in 1948 and served until her death in 1961. Nannie Helen Burroughs was a club woman who addressed the issues of the day, and she educated her denomination and the church-at-large as to unrecognized resources and gifts of church women.

"Not Color But Character"[14]

Many Negroes have colorphobia as badly as the white folk have Negrophobia.

There is no denying it, Negroes have colorphobia. Some Negro men have it. Some Negro women have it. Whole families have it, and somebody tells me that some Negro churches have it. Saviour, keep us from those churches, please. Some social circles have it, and so the disease is spreading from men to women, from women to families, from families to churches, and from churches to social circles. The idea of Negroes setting up a color standard is preposterous. . . .

I have seen black men have fits about black women associating with white men, and yet these same men see more to admire in a half-white face owned by a characterless, fatherless woman than in a face owned by thoroughbred, legal heirs to the throne, with pure souls and high purposes in life. We do not say that black women are not as virtueless, in many cases, as their fairer sisters, nor that because a woman is fair she has no character, or because she is black she has no character, for character is no respecter of color, for there are thousands on both sides who are worthy of the name woman; but we do mean to say that many black men have not learned this fact any more than many white men have not learned that all virtue, refinement and culture are not locked up in white women. . . .

---

[14]Nannie H. Burroughs, "Not Color But Character," *The Voice of the Negro* 1:7 (July 1904):277-279.

The encroachments we had to tolerate before the war and during the war are pardoned, but we live at the high-noon of the brightest day of liberty of soul and body. God help us to so live that we may raise the standard higher and higher until the name "Negro woman" will be a synonym for uprightness of character and loftiness of purpose. Let character, and not color, be the first requisite to admission into any home, church, or social circle, and a new day will break upon ten million people.

"The Colored Woman and Her Relation to the Domestic Problem"[15]

You ask what is meant by the domestic problem. It is that peculiar condition under which women are living and laboring without the knowledge of the secrets of thrift, or of true scientific methods in which the mind has been awakened, and hands made capable thereby to give the most efficient services. It is a condition of indifference on the part of our working women as to their needs to how we may so dignify labor that our services may become indispensable on the one hand and Negro sentiment will cease to array itself against the "working girls" on the other hand. It is a question as to how we may receive for our services compensation commensurate with the work done. The solution of this problem will be the prime factor in the salvation of Negro womanhood, whose salvation must be attained before the so-called race problem can be solved.

The training of Negro women is absolutely necessary, not only for their own salvation and the salvation of the race, but because the hour in which we live demands it. If we lose sight of the demands of the hour we blight our hope of progress. The subject of domestic science has crowded itself upon us, and unless we receive it, master it and be wise, the next ten years will so revolutionize things that we will find our women without the wherewith to support themselves.

Untrained hands, however willing, will find themselves unwelcome in the humblest homes. We may be careless about this matter of equipping our women for work in the homes, but if we are to judge from the wonderful progress that recent years has brought in the world of domestic labor we must admit that steps must be taken, and that at once, to train the hands of Negro women for better services and their hearts for purer living. All through the North white imported help is taking the place of Negro help. Where we once held forth without a thought of change we find our places filled by those of other races and climes. The people who had to have servants declared that they wanted intelligent, refined, trained help,

---

[15]From *The United Negro: His Problems and Progress*, edited by I. Garland Penn and J.W.E. Bowen (Atlanta: D.E. Luther Publishing Co., 1902). Reprint. New York: Negro Universities Press, 1969.

and in the majority of cases we were not ready to give them what they needed. Our intelligent Negroes, even though they may not have bread to eat, in many cases shun service work, when the fact is evident that ignorant help is not wanted by the best class of people in this country. The more thorough and intelligent the help the better.

What will this crowding from service mean to Negro women? It will mean their degradation. Our women will sink beneath the undermining influences of insidious sloth. Industry is one of the noblest virtues of any race. The people who scorn and frown upon her must die. While little heed may have been paid to the demand for better help and the supplanting of Negro servants by Irish, Dagoes and English may have been unnoticed by all of us, yet it is time for the leaders to sound the alarm, ere we are rooted from the places we have held for over two centuries. The time will come when we will stand as helpless as babes, as dependent as beggars, without the wherewith to sustain life, unless we meet the demands squarely.

Our women have worked as best they could without making any improvements and thus developing the service into a profession, and in that way make the calling more desirable from a standpoint of being lifted from a mere drudgery, as well as from the standpoint of compensation received.

The race whose women have not learned that industry and self-respect are the only guarantees of a true character will find itself bound by ignorance and violence or fettered with chains of poverty.

There is a growing tendency among us to almost abhor women who work at service for a living. If we hold in contempt women who are too honest, industrious and independent, women whose sense of pride is too exalted to be debased by idleness, we will find our women becoming more and more slothful in this matter of supporting themselves. Our "high-toned" notions as to the kind of positions educated people ought to fill have caused many women who cannot get anything to do after they come out of school to loaf rather than work for an honest living, declaring to themselves and acting it before others, that they were not educated to live among pots and pans. None of us may have been educated for that purpose, but educated women without work and the wherewith to support themselves and who have declared in their souls that they will not stoop to toil are not worth an ounce more to the race than ignorant women who have made the same declarations. Educated loafers will bear as much watching as ignorant ones. When the nobility of labor is magnified, and those who do labor respected more because of their real worth to the race, we will find a less number trying to escape the brand, "servant girl." We are not less honorable if we are servants. Fidelity to duty rather than the grade of one's occupation is the true measure of character. Every gentle virtue will go down before a people and their endeavors come to naught when they forget that the foundation stone of prosperity is toil. What matters it if we do rise from pots and pans? They tell us we came from apes and baboons, and we have made it this far. Further, if God could take a crop of apes or baboons and make beings like us He is God indeed, and we can trust Him to raise us from servants to queens. If we did come from these ungainly animals of the four-footed family, we got here nearly as soon as the people who didn't have so far to come.

What matters is if our women, by honest toil, make their way from the kitchen to places of respect and trust in the walks of life. Are they less honorable because they have been servants? Are not the women who by thrift and economy, with everything operating against them in their own race, and low wages, that mighty power before whom the poor of earth must bow, struggling for mastery, work their way to the front, more deserving of praise, more worthy of recognition and respect than scores of "parlor ornaments" who, by methods, have maintained some social standing, and hold in contempt the "unfortunate servant girl?" There are women at service who would eat their meals off the heads of barrels or dress after the fashion of John the Baptist in the wilderness before they would sacrifice their high-toned moral character, simply to shine in the social world by virtue of their idleness and ability to dress well. It is not the depth from which we come, but the heights to which we soar. The incomparable water lily grows out of the slime of black lagoons, and heaven itself consists not in location but in nobility of the character of its population. It matters not where nor how lowly the station, pursue the unswerving way of industry and victory or defeat will decide our fitness for the places we seek.

Again, if we scorn women who have character and are honest enough to work to preserve it and accept into our company women who have no character and will not work to secure it, are we making the race any more moral? This pulling aside of our silken skirts at the approach of the servant women has materially affected the morals of Negro women. How many of them have abandoned honest labor in which they could have given character and tone to the service rendered by our women, and to satisfy their ambitions for social recognition have resorted to idleness in order to gain the smiles of a class among us who will receive any woman who can dress well without working at service to pay for it?

Scorn the servant women? No, never. Rather scorn that class of women who have resolved not to work and hang out of doors and windows, hold up corners, or keep the neighborhood astir with demoralizing gossip. Scorn young Negro women who flirt and loiter about the streets at the sacrifice of their good name and the name of Negro womanhood. But honor and praise to the women who have learned that all labor is just as honorable, just as honest, as the person who is doing it. Have not all of us been servants? God made us all servants the very day He dismissed Adam from Eden. "By the sweat of thy brow shalt thou eat bread." What mean these women who are eating bread and are not sweating, either, by scorning the women who are obeying the divine injunction?

Young women from rural districts flock to great cities like New York, Chicago, Philadelphia, Boston, Baltimore and Washington in search of employment. Not only are they unprepared to serve but are woefully ignorant of the new social conditions into which they must be thrown. The white women in these large cities conduct guilds and other organizations that employ attendants to meet the trains and be on the alert for the white servant class that may be coming in seeking work or homes. Christian homes and churches are pointed out to the new-comers. The strong arms of Christian women are thrown about them, and while they are far from home and loved ones, they have the assurance that they have friends who will be ever mindful of them and their interests.

What are the results of this wholesale abandonment of working women? Nine cases out of ten the girls who come from the country fall into the hands of ill-disposed Negro men or keepers of some "back way boarding house" of the famous "furnished rooms" character. Thousands of our women are to-day in the clutches of men of our own race who are not worth the cost of their existence. They dress well and live on the earnings of servant girls. Negro men can aid us in the solution of the problem by becoming self-supporting rather than live on the earnings of women who often get less than ten dollars per month. Not only does this increase idleness among us but weakens the moral life of women. Negro women can help solve their own problem by applying to these lazy men Horace Greeley's doctrine, "Root hog or die."

The solution of the servant girl problem, then, can only be accomplished—first, by making it possible for these girls to overcome their ignorance, dishonesty and carelessness by establishing training classes and other moral agencies in these large cities and maintaining one or more first-class schools of domestic science. Second, by employers demanding the trained help from these classes or schools and paying wages in keeping with the ability of the servant to the work. Third, by giving to women who work, time for recreation and self-improvement. This constant all-day "go" has made service a drudgery. If servants had hours for rest and improvement, like other laborers, they would come to their work with a freshness and intelligence that is now absent.

Emphasize the importance of preparation for service work. Let Negro women who are idle find work, stick to it and use it as a stepping stone to something better. Let us cease reaching over women who are servants and have character enough for queens to queens who haven't brains and character enough for servants. By becoming exponents of the blessed principles of honesty, cleanliness and industry, Negro women can bring dignity to service life, respect and trust to themselves and honor to the race. Then in deed and in truth we can mount up as with the wings of eagles, soar above the mountains of virtue and hide our heads among the stars. If anybody is to be scorned, scorn those women who will not honestly toil to raise themselves and are pulling us from the throne of honor and virtue.

—*Nannie Helen Burroughs*

Bibliography

Barnett, Evelyn Brooks. "Nannie Burroughs and the Education of Black Women." In *The Afro-American Woman: Struggles and Images*. Edited by Sharon Harley and Rosalyn Terborg-Penn. Port Washington: Kennikat Press, 1978.

Dodson, Jualynne E. and Cheryl Townsend Gilkes. "Something Within: Social Change and Collective Endurance in the Sacred World of Black Christian Women." In *Women and Religion in America, Volume 3: 1900-1968*. Edited by Rosemary Radford Ruether and Rosemary Skinner Keller. 1986.

Higginbotham, Evelyn Brooks. "Religion, Politics, and Gender: The Leadership of Nannie Helen Burroughs." *Journal of Religious Thought* (Winter-Spring 1988). Also found in *This Far by Faith: Readings in African-American Women's Religious Biography*. Edited by Judith Weisenfeld and Richard Newman. New York: Routledge, 1996.

———. "In Politics to Stay: Black Women Leaders and Party Politics During the 1920s." In *Women, Politics and Change*. Edited by Louise Tilly and Patricia Gurin. 1990.

———. *Righteous Discontent: The Women's Movement in the Black Baptist Church, 1880-1920*. Boston: Harvard University Press, 1993.

Proceedings of the Annual Sessions of the National Baptist Convention and Women's Convention, 1900-1925. American Baptist Historical Society. Rochester, New York.

CHARLOTTE HAWKINS BROWN

(1883-1961)

Born Lottie Hawkins, she transformed the rural community of Sedalia, North Carolina, into an educational oasis. She was the founder of the Palmer Memorial Institute and a pioneer in the field of black preparatory education. Her talents were eclectic and creative: she lectured, taught, gave music recitals and published a novel in 1919 entitled, Mammy: An Appeal to the Heart of the South. *In 1983, the site of the Palmer Memorial Institute became the first historic site designated in honor of a black woman. Charlotte Hawkins Brown's life is an inspiration to all who are committed to the educational and spiritual uplifting of the poor.*

"The Christian Teacher: The Hope of Negro America"[16]

It is the teacher who pictures to the child the noble characters who stand out as examples of useful lives. It is the teacher who aids the child in placing his goal. It is the teacher who guides his trembling steps to fame through his own persistency. . . . [T]here is not one to which America may look with as great a hope for future America as to the teacher. This is, too, true of and applicable to that portion of the population known as Negro America. As with the other races, "similar effects require similar causes."

Are the environments of the bulk of Negro teachers similar to those of other races in this country? Are the responsibilities devolving upon the Negro teachers similar? To these questions one of experience would answer emphatically, "No." The Negro with scarcely half a century of freedom cannot present to the teacher a furrowed field in which to sow the grain, as is present to other teachers. The Negro teacher in most cases must create circumstances, make out of a nag a horse, twist the hemp for plow line and make a plow, before he can turn the soil. Therefore, he must have additional qualifications to produce good results.

The Negro teacher who is working for the betterment of the race must work from a principle, to install a principle, to build a character whom the nation will adore. These teachers, patient, loving, whose lives are instruments in God's hands, are they, upon whom depend the destiny of the Negro race. The race needs and must have Christian young men and women who are willing to throw the energy of their young lives into the service for the race. The race needs men and women who are not looking for monied rewards only, but who are working for the good that may be accomplished in elevating the race. They must put on the whole armour of God. It is not sufficient to wear the uniform to ward off the imposition, but the breast-plate, the shield and the sword, each has its specific duty.

—*Charlotte Hawkins Brown*

Bibliography

Brown, Charlotte Hawkins. *Mammy: An Appeal to the Heart of the South*. Boston: The Pilgrim Press, 1919.

————. *The Correct Thing To Do, To Say, To Wear*. Boston: The Christopher Publishing House, 1941.

Daniel, Sadie Iola. *Woman Builders*. Washington, D.C.: Associated Publishers, 1970.

---

[16]I. Garland Pen and J.W.E. Bowen, eds., *The United Negro: His Problems and Progress* (Atlanta: D.E. Luther Publishing Co., 1902; reprint ed. New York: Negro Universities Press, 1969), 428-429.

YVONNE V. DELK

At the time of the publication of the sermon which follows, "Yvonne V. Delk [was] the executive director of the Community Renewal Society of Metropolitan Chicago. She received degrees from Norfolk Virginia State College, Andover Newton Theological School, and New York Theological Seminary. She [was] active on the local level in religious education and parish work and nationally in affirmative action and as an education specialist to Black urban churches. She has studied and traveled extensively and is also a writer."[17]

"Singing the Lord's Song"[18]

In Psalm 137 these words are recorded:

> By the waters of Babylon,
> there we sat down and wept,
>   when we remembered Zion.
> On the willows there
>   we hung up our lyres.
> For there our captors
>   required of us songs,
> and our tormentors, mirth, saying,
>   "Sing us one of the songs of Zion!"
> *How shall we sing the LORD'S song*
>   *in a foreign land?*
>   —vv. 1-4 (RSV, emphasis added)

The Israelites had been removed by force from their homeland, Zion. They were broken, out of touch with their roots, their identity, and their God. They were in a strange land. The psalmist pictured them sitting by the waters of Babylon. While Zion was the city of salvation, Babylon was the city of death. In Zion there were community, reconciliation, freedom, and peace, but in Babylon there were alienation and hardness of heart. Babylon's god was power, greed, materialism, selling, and buying; religion

---

[17]Ella Person Mitchell, ed., *Those Preachin' Women: Sermons by Black Women Preachers, Vol. 1* (Valley Forge: Judson Press, 1985), 51.
[18]Ibid., 51-59.

was instituted to justify and camouflage Babylon's motives. But the people of Zion were not deceived, for when they remembered Zion—their true ground, the source of their being, the place of their wholeness and renewal—they sat down as mourners. They had not heart for music or song.

The cause of this sad scene as the psalmist described it was the heartless request of the Israelites' captors—those who had enslaved them—to sing for them one of the songs of Zion. Perhaps their masters had heard reports of the temple music of Zion, or perhaps they wished, like other conquerors in history, to extract some amusement from the native songs of the captives.

But for the exiles there were no songs of Zion but the Lord's songs. The songs of Zion were not the songs of patriotism or nationalism. They were the songs of the Creator, who alone calls worlds into being and sets before us the ways of life and death. It was this recognition that forced the exiles to cry out, "How shall we sing the Lord's song in a foreign land?"

Over two thousand years have passed since the psalmist gave expression to that question. And yet people of faith still wrestle with the question as they attempt to be faithful witnesses in the midst of the issues of our day. The seventies and eighties have been times of despair for men, women, youth, and children. The experiences of many in our nation can be compared to the Babylonian experience described in Psalm 137. Many people are existing in what can be called a time of "Code Blue." "Code Blue" is a hospital term used to place all hospital personnel on alert. It is a signal of an emergency or a danger of cosmic proportions. It is a signal that alerts staff to the fact that large numbers of persons have been injured and are in life-threatening situations.

We are living in a time of extreme danger and emergency. It is a time when the survival of people is at stake, when millions of people are out of work, and when many members of our community—the poor—are being denied the right to eat. It is a time of "Code Blue" when one million people have been made ineligible for food stamps and the system denies children access to health care and food for their bodies. For instance, tens of thousands of children have lost Medicaid coverage, and hundreds of thousands of poor youngsters no longer receive free or reduced-price lunches. It is a time of "Code Blue" when we deny nutritional and health support systems to women, infants, and children at a time when Black infants are twice as likely as White infants to die within the first year of life. It is a time of "Code Blue" when men, women, and children are sacrificed on the altar of a military god—by those who believe that national security, respect, and pride can be built by creating more and more armaments. It is a time of "Code Blue" when we face the reality of a nuclear war.

People are frightened about the consequences of a nuclear war because they know there would be no winners. Few people would survive. People are marching to protest nuclear arms. People are marching to affirm the right to life for themselves and their children. It is a time of "Code Blue" when violence and injustice become accepted as a part of the daily fabric of life. In this Babylonian-like time of "Code Blue," *how do we sing the Lord's song?* Will the times in which we live wear us down?

I am afraid that we will fall prey to one of four basic evils as anxiety, confusion, and complexity settle in among us.

There is the danger of becoming a private and narcissistic person. That is, we become "I" persons who turn inward, losing a grounding in community, losing the sense of collective responsibility for being good neighbors. What takes the place of this awareness is a moral vacuum; others are forever trapped in private destinies, doomed to whatever befalls them. In that void the traditional measure of justice or good vanishes completely; the self replaces community, relationships, neighbors, or God.

There is the danger of becoming cynical and disillusioned and settling for the status quo. We give up. We are trapped into believing that it doesn't matter what we do, that things will never change. We merely survive; we simply get by with a minimum of effort.

There is the danger of becoming a ritualistic dancer. That is, we become blind to the conditions around us and keep on with our daily petty routines as if nothing matters. We block out the reality of the world with rituals that consume our time and our energy. We join the social clubs to escape; we watch television to escape; we become joggers and runners to escape; we become obsessed with "things" as a way to escape. Our dancing, however, only creates false illusions, meaningless activity, and empty images as we hide behind masks.

There is the danger that we will retreat to simple places and easy answers. "Simple places" means to go back to the "good old days." Gladys Knight reminds us that time has a way of changing things. We glorify the past as a means of escaping from the present. The other retreat is into easy answers. Yet the journey of faith sometimes leads us to the unknown; it leads us away from the simplicity of easy answers, visible enemies, and the assurances that we are right to the complexity of a world where our faith becomes a verb and not simply a noun.

The question we face as Christians is "How do we sing the Lord's song in the midst of the world's evils?" By becoming closed and private? By becoming disillusioned and cynical? By engaging in ritualistic dances? By escaping into a simple place and time? By seeking easy answers? What is it that keeps us anchored and focused in the midst of the "Code Blues" so that we can sing the Lord's song? Permit me to answer with a parable and three affirmations.

During a performance in observance of the birthday of Martin L. King, Jr., I witnessed a ballet performed by children. The ballet was interpreted by a group of choral readers who were reciting a poem by Owen Dodson. In the ballet the children danced out the journey of struggle, survival, despair, and hope as they moved toward the land of the great mountains, a fertile land which held promise and opportunity for all. They moved in their journey through periods of doubt and disbelief. At times they seemed to be lost; they were on unfamiliar ground and the road seemed unchartered. They told stories while on the journey. The stories reminded them of who they were, of the power that surrounded them and the reason they were traveling. After what appeared to be a long and tiresome journey, they finally caught a glimpse of the "promised land"—the land of the great mountains. However, as they came closer to the land of their dreams, they realized that a chasm separated them from the promise. It was clear that if they were to reach the land of the great mountains, they had to cross the chasm.

The more they looked at the chasm, the more anxious and fearful they became. They knew the danger. They needed a word of hope. And so they regrouped. They retold the story, and the story gave them identity, purpose, and power. Suddenly, in an act of faith, one of them positioned herself, took the risk, and leaped into the air. As the child leaped, she reached forward toward the land of the great mountains and she reached back in an act of solidarity and empowerment to grasp the hand of a brother to take with her. He followed her example while holding onto her hand. He reached back and clasped the hand of a sister to take with him, and suddenly, the stage exploded with a human chain leaping over the chasm to the land of the great mountains. It was a triumphant moment.

However, the joy of the moment was interrupted. A crisis occurred. As the last person prepared for the leap, she put down her baby in order to get a firmer grip on her before they moved across the chasm. However, the momentum of the human chain reached her before she was ready. Her hand was grasped, and before she could grasp her child, she was taken over the chasm. Her child was left—alone—on the other side. The child became fearful and anxious. A chasm separated her from her mother, her people, her hope, her future. She wandered in her anxiety toward the edge of the chasm. However, the community called to her. They called her by name. They told her the story. They encouraged her to leap. I watched with a joy I could hardly contain as the child gathered courage and confidence and was empowered by the community. Keeping her eyes on the great mountains, she leaped into the air over the chasm and into the arms of the waiting community.

There was an old man sitting in the audience. Suddenly, it was no longer a play for him. It was real. He rushed to the stage, picked up the child, held her high in the air, and proclaimed with the voice of wisdom and vision, "Thank God almighty! Even our children know how to fly!" We *can* sing the Lord's song if we remember who we are, if we know what we stand for, and if we realize that God's people, God's songs, and God's word are for Babylon as well as for Zion.

We can sing God's song if we remember who we are. Our task as Christians is to keep clearly before all persons who they are and under whose banner they are marching. *We are God's people.* We are authorized, anointed, or given our authority, not by Reagan, Reaganomics, budgets, or events, but by God. Our spirituality is rooted in God. We can sing God's song because we know we are rooted in God. We can sing God's song because we know that Someone who doesn't use star charts, horoscopes, or stock market predictions has a vision in determining who we are and who we shall be.

This blessed assurance keeps us from the danger of hopelessness. It liberates us from the Babylonian experience of racism, sexism, classism, or militarism. In order to sing God's song, we begin by confessing God as our ground, first, foremost, and always. God becomes to us not simply a psychological feeling but the one who authored us, who breathed into us the breath of life, and who calls us daily into community with the Creator and with our sisters and brothers. It is God, not events, who gives us the song that we can sing.

We are a people with a story and a history of experiences; we must keep our story before us as a way of grounding and rooting ourselves. We must keep telling the stories that remind us of who we are. Storytelling is a way of inviting persons to share in a covenanting mission consciousness. The children in the ballet made it over the chasm because they told stories that reminded them of who they were. My family and I made it through the roughest part of our existence because we had support, the nurturing love of a faith community who reminded us every Sunday morning of our identity: "You are children of God." Whenever two or three of us gather together in the name of Jesus Christ, it ought to be the occasion for telling the story of who we are as God's people.

We can sing God's song if we know what we stand for. Telling our story provides us with a standing ground, a mission, and a practical agenda for our lives that we are not free to walk away from. We can sing God's song if we understand that the demand of the gospel is that we struggle with and on behalf of those who are poor and dispossessed.

Jesus' head and heart were finely tuned to those in need. He healed on the sabbath. Because there was a need, he touched people who had leprosy and a woman who had an issue of blood. Rules, rituals, customs, and even the priests of the temple did not prevent him from being God's new Word in an old world that was still held in captivity and bondage by the powers and principalities of rulers and managers.

The radical demand of the gospel is that we take up the cross and follow Christ. The cross always precedes the crown. There is no victory without struggle. We are therefore called to risk our names, our titles, our degrees, our positions, our statuses, and ye, even our faith for the vision of a world where justice, liberty, and wholeness prevail. When we risk in the name of justice, we sing God's song. When we risk in the name of healing for the broken, we sing God's song. To sing God's song in this decade can require no less than a strong commitment against racism, sexism, and classism, shown by our words and actions. We must be cautious about treating any institution as final, defining any idea as infallible, or accepting any system as closed.

We can sing the Lord's song if we understand a simple but very basic truth: The Lord's song was created not only for Zion but for Babylon as well. We are called to sing God's song wherever people feel trapped, wherever they are hurting, oppressed, or struggling under overwhelming life-denying circumstances. The most powerful song that was ever sung was heard from a cross. However, that cross produced a crown and a symbol for life over death. Persons who have struggled and who know something about pain and how to overcome it can sing God's songs. Those who have been in the valley of the shadow of death can sing the songs of Zion with power and meaning.

Black people know about singing God's song in a strange and foreign land because Black Americans' spirituality was born in the context of the struggle for justice. We sang our songs on boats called *Jesus* that brought us to America. We sang our songs on auction blocks—"Over my head I hear music in the air; there must be a God somewhere." We sang our songs on plantations—"Walk together children, don't you get weary; there is a camp meeting in the promised land." We sang our songs on picket lines—"Ain't gonna let nobody turn me around, I'm gonna keep on marching, keep on praying, keep on singing, moving to the freedom land." We have sung our songs as we moved through the past 367 years. At times the journey was like a sojourn in Babylon; however, we kept on moving from the wilderness of our past and present to the promise and hope of our future.

How can you sing God's song in the midst of the "Code Blues" where you live? You can sing it if: you remember that you are God's people; you remember what you are standing for—Liberation and wholeness in our world; you remember that your "song" is needed not only in the halls of a church or for the good times but also in times of darkness and alienation when you feel as if you are in foreign and strange places.

God's song is needed by all who are wrestling with powers and principalities of darkness. When God's songs are sung with power and conviction, lives are changed. "I" people become "we" people; the cynical and disillusioned have hope; the ritualistic dancers become involved with a real world. Biblical visions come into view, and the reign of God begins to take shape. The proud are scattered in the plans of their hearts; the mighty are cast down, and the humble exalted. Swords are beaten into plowshares. The hungry are fed; the naked are clothed; the captive are freed; the blind can see; the deaf can hear; the lame can walk; and the deceitful are exposed. Justice and mercy roll down like a mighty stream. My prayer is that we will continue to sing God's song wherever we are. Amen.

—Yvonne V. Delk

Bibliography

Cannon, Katie Geneva. "Womanist Interpretation and Preaching in the Black Church." In *Katie's Canon: Womanism and the Soul of the Black Community.* New York: Continuum, 1995.

Kelly, Leontine T. C. "Preaching in the Black Tradition." In *Women Ministers.* Edited by Judith L. Weidman. San Francisco: Harper & Row, Publishers, 1981.

Sanders, Cheryl J. "The Woman as Preacher." *Journal of Religious Thought* 32:1 (1975):6-23.

MARSHA WOODARD

At the time of the publication of the sermon which follows: "Marsha Brown Woodard, . . . a graduate of Ottawa University, Ottawa, Kansas (B.A.) and Eden Theological Seminary (M.Div.), [had] served on the staff of the Antioch Baptist Church of St. Louis and in the Division of Church Education of the American Baptist Churches in the U.S.A. at Valley Forge. She [was] serving. . . as associate pastor of the Saints Memorial Baptist Church in Bryn Mawr, Pennsylvania, and working as a freelance consultant for organizational analysis, program development and conference planning."[19]

"No Greater Legacy"[20]

2 Timothy 2:10-11, 14-15 (NEB)

You have followed my teaching, my conduct, and my purpose in life; you have observed my faith, my patience, my love, my endurance, my persecutions, and my sufferings. You know all that happened to me in Antioch, Iconium, and Lystra, the terrible persecutions I endured! But the Lord rescued me from them all. . . .

As for you, continue in the truths that you were taught and firmly believe. You know who your teachers were, and you remember that ever since you were a child, you have known the Holy Scriptures, which are able to give you the wisdom that leads to salvation through faith in Christ Jesus.

Paul, in prison in Rome, possibly thinking that the end of his career

---

[19]Ella Pearson Mitchell, ed., *Those Preachin' Women: More Sermons by Black Women Preachers,* Vol. 2 (Valley Forge: Judson Press, 1988), 35.

[20]Ibid., 35-39.

was near, wrote a letter to Timothy. We don't know his thinking, but probably he thought this might be his last letter to Timothy. He said, in fact, that he had finished his course, the race of life. Thus Paul felt the need to say things that were important. There was so much he wanted to share.

He wrote: "Knowing these things, Timothy, I want you to continue in the truth, in the teaching that you have been taught which I know you believe." Of course, there were likely many more thoughts that didn't find their way into the letter and, thus, into Scripture. He probably thought: "Timothy, I love you like a son, and there's so much I'd like to leave you. I cannot leave you wealth or a lot of material things. I cannot promise that fame will be yours. I cannot promise that your life will be easy—that everyone will like you—that you won't have to face persecution or suffering. But I can leave you something that endures. Timothy, I'm leaving you a legacy of faith! I leave you my faith: the faith you have seen me living . . . the faith of your mother Eunice and your grandmother Lois . . . the faith they first taught you. Timothy, I leave you a legacy of faith."

Today we are faced with the same questions that Paul faced: What shall we leave behind? What legacy shall we leave for those coming after us?

Yes, what will we leave behind? We often think of this in terms of our individual families. It is also important that we think in terms of our church family. What will we leave behind for the next generation? A building? Maybe a new addition? A trust fund? A set of books? These are good things; indeed, they are things we should consider and, as we are able, should work toward. However, is that all we want to leave behind?

Is there not something more we can leave? Buildings can be demolished by tornadoes or destroyed by fire within a few moments. Windows are broken and books are destroyed. Even investments go bad and money is lost. Is there not something we can leave that is enduring? I would suggest for us that in addition to these other things, we, too, need to leave a legacy of faith! A legacy of faithful living! A faith that withstands storms and fires . . . that cannot be destroyed . . . that doesn't wear out . . . that won't go out of style.

Thinking people know that change is always occurring. All of us have lived through many changes just in our short span of years. The world is radically different today from what it was in our earlier years. Remember when cars were a luxury? when ice blocks were purchased for iceboxes? when coal and kerosene stoves heated our homes? when buses and trains were the main forms of transportation? when hand fans and a few electric window fans were all the air conditioning we had? when corner grocery stores were the place to shop and a radio was the source of entertainment as well as news? Today, cars are almost a necessity. We must have refrigerators and freezers. We flick the switches for central heating and cooling. Airplanes take us back home in minutes, and astronauts soar in spaceships. We shop in supermarkets and shopping malls. Television, cable and all, is basic to our normal lifestyles.

As we think back, some of us will remember days of segregation: buses with special seating, hotels where blacks could not go, restaurants in which blacks could not eat. Today, as long as we can meet the cost, we can ride on anything, stay in almost any hotel, eat in almost any public restaurant.

Some of us may remember when Joe Louis won the heavyweight boxing championship, Jesse Owens earned four gold medals at the Berlin Olympics, and Jackie Robinson entered major league baseball. Today athletes in most professional sports earn salaries never dreamed possible. Yet the deaths of two magnificent athletes (Len Bias and Don Rogers) in the space of a few days shocked us into recognizing that these changes are not sufficient for our needs. Yes, the world has been changing and the world will continue to change. Yet most of us have a need that does not change. Like Paul, we find we want to leave behind something that will endure, something that will help the next generation cope with the changing world they must face, something that responds to the unchanging cry that remains in the depths of our souls.

Our challenge is to leave them a faith that will endure through all times. A faith like the prophet Habakkuk spoke about:

> Even though the fig trees have no fruit
> and no grapes grow on the vines,
> even though the olive crop fails
> and the fields produce no grain,
> even though the sheep all die
> and the cattle stalls are empty,
> I will still be joyful and glad,
> because the LORD God is my savior.
> The Sovereign LORD gives me strength.
> He makes me sure-footed as a deer
> and keeps me safe on the mountains.
> —Habakkuk 3:17-19, TEV

Today if he were writing he might say: "Even though my job ends and there's no employment in sight; even though the price of food goes up and I can't buy those things I want; even though my friends turn away; even though the world seems headed for destruction, and we live under a constant threat of nuclear war; even though racism is still alive, and we face more and more subtle discrimination. . . .

"Even though there are government officials who seem unconcerned about human need; even though life sometimes seems hopeless; yet will I be joyful and glad, for God is my Saviour and the keeper of my life . . . yet will I be joyful because God is the strength of my life . . . yet will I be joyful because God is ever with me! Even though today is not all it should be or all I want it to be, yet will I be joyful, for faith tells me tomorrow can be different."

We need to develop our legacy of faith! Our children need to see by our living that we have believed that "faith is the substance of things hoped for, the evidence of things not seen" (Hebrews 11:1, KJV). We need to be careful about where we put our trust. We might do well to recognize that it is not an American Express card or designer clothes or a new house or a new car or our impressive knowledge that will give us the strength to endure. The witness of our lives is in the way we behave in the most severe circumstances. Our children and neighbors will benefit from this heritage only as they see it and are grasped by the powerful contagion of the serene and trusting soul.

Just as Paul sat calmly on the deck of a storm-tossed sailboat and declared God's promise of no lives lost, our young will receive the heritage in the midst of our storms and trials. When we have testified with smiles of confidence in God at the very moments when the sky was most cloudy . . . when our very lives radiate confidence in a caring and provident God, then we can testify with our mouths, as did Paul:

> You have observed my faith, my patience, my love, my endurance, my persecutions, and my sufferings. . . . [You too] will be persecuted [just as I was]. . . . But as for you, continue in the truths that you were taught and firmly believe (2 Timothy 3:10-14, NEB).

Our children will be blessed with a priceless legacy when they can remember hearing us saying and singing from the heart:

> Through it all, through it all
> Oh I've learned to trust in Jesus,
> I've learned to trust in God.
> Through it all, through it all
> Oh I've learned to depend upon His Word.
> —*Marsha Woodard*

Bibliography

Cannon, Katie Geneva. "Womanist Interpretation and Preaching in the Black Church." In *Katie's Canon: Womanism and the Soul of the Black Community*. New York: Continuum, 1995.

Kelly, Leontine T. C. "Preaching in the Black Tradition." In *Women Ministers*. Edited by Judith L. Weidman. San Francisco: Harper & Row, Publishers, 1981.

Sanders, Cheryl J. "The Woman as Preacher." *Journal of Religious Thought* 32:1 (1975):6-23.

Part III

BEARING PROPHETIC WITNESS IN SOCIETY

"To What Ends Do You Witness?"

AN ANONYMOUS BLACK WOMAN
(c. 1870s)

A black woman at the beginning of the twentieth century was seeking to define herself and the struggle for self-determination in the black community. She understood that her individual autonomy was inextricably bound up with communal liberation. She recognized the strictures attending her task were social myths regarding her alleged immorality, limited viable economic opportunities (regardless of her educational credentials), and continuing legal restraints upon an emancipated but disenfranchised people. Therefore, a black woman entering the twentieth century sought to nurture family life and to secure justice for the black community through individual effort and organized social reform movements which addressed race, gender and class oppression.

"On the South's Idea of Justice"[1]

I am a colored woman, wife and mother; I have lived all my life in the south, and have often thought what a peculiar fact it is that the more ignorant Southern whites are of us, the more vehement they are in their denunciation of us. They boast that they have little intercourse with us, never see us in our home, churches or places of amusement, but still they know us thoroughly.

They also admit that they know us in no capacity except as servants, yet they say we are at our best in that single capacity. What philosophers they are! The Southerners say we Negroes are a happy, laughing set of people, with no thought of tomorrow. How mistaken they are! The educated, thinking Negro is just the opposite. There is a feeling of unrest, insecurity, almost panic among the best class of Negroes in the South. In our homes, in our churches, wherever two or three are gathered together, there is a discussion of what is best to do. Must we remain in the south or go elsewhere? Where can we go to feel that security which other people feel? Is it best to go in great numbers or only several families? These and many other things are discussed over and over. . . .

I know of houses occupied by poor Negroes in which a respectable

---

[1]From *The Independent*, September 18, 1902, as found in Milton Meltzer, *The Black Americans: A History in Their Own Words (1619-1983)* (New York: Harper & Row, 1984), 145-148.

farmer would not keep his cattle. It is impossible for them to rent else where. All Southern real estate agents have "white property" and "colored property." In one of the largest Southern cities there is a colored minister, a graduate of Harvard, whose wife is an educated, Christian woman, who lived for weeks in a tumble-down rookery because he could neither rent nor buy in a respectable locality.

Many colored women, who wash, iron, scrub, cook or sew all the week to help pay the rent for these miserable hovels and help fill the many small mouths, would deny themselves some of the necessaries of life if they could take their little children and teething babies on the cars to the parks of a Sunday afternoon and sit under the trees, enjoy the cool breezes and breathe God's pure air for only two or three hours; but this is denied them. Some of the parks have signs, "no Negroes allowed on these grounds except as servants." Pitiful, pitiful customs and laws that make war on women and babes! There is no wonder that we die; the wonder is that we persist in living.

Fourteen years ago I had just married. My husband had saved sufficient money to buy a small home. On account of our limited means we went to the suburbs, on unpaved streets, to look for a home, only asking for a high, healthy locality. Some real estate agents were "sorry, but had nothing to suit," some had "just the thing" for an unhealthy pigsty. Others had no "colored property." One agent said that he had what we wanted, but we should have to go to see the lot after dark, or walk by and give the place a casual look; for, he said, "all the white people in the neighborhood would be down on me." Finally we bought this lot. When the house was being built we went to see it. Consternation reigned. We had ruined this neighborhood of poor people; poor as we, poorer in manners at least. The people who lived next door received the sympathy of their friends. When we walked on the street (there were no sidewalks), we were embarrassed by the stare of many unfriendly eyes.

Two years passed before a single woman spoke to me, and only then because I helped one of them when a little sudden trouble came to her. Such was the reception I, a happy young woman, just married, received from people among whom I wanted to make a home. Fourteen years have now passed, four children have been born to us, and one has died in this same home, among these same neighbors. Although the neighbors speak to us, and occasionally one will send a child to borrow the morning's paper or ask the loan of a pattern, not one woman had ever been inside of my house, not even at the times when a woman would doubly appreciate the slightest attention of a neighbor.

The Southerner boasts that he is our friend; he educates our children, he pays us for work and is most noble and generous to us. Did not the Negro by his labor for over three hundred years help to educate the white man's children? Is thirty equal to three hundred? Does a white man deserve praise for paying a black man for his work?

The Southerner also claims that the Negro gets justice. Not long ago a Negro man was cursed and struck in the face by an electric car conductor. The Negro knocked the conductor down and although it was clearly proven in a court of "justice" that the conductor was in the wrong the Negro had to pay a fine of $10. The judge told him "I fine you that much to teach you that you must respect white folks." The conductor was acquitted. "Most noble judge! A second Daniel!" This is the South's idea of justice.

Whenever a crime is committed in the South, the policemen look for the Negro in the case. A white man with face and hands blackened can commit any crime in the calendar. The first friendly stream soon washes away his guilt and he is ready to join in the hunt to lynch the "big, black burly brute." When a white man in the South does commit a crime, that is simply one white man gone wrong. If his crime is especially brutal he is a freak or temporarily insane. If one low, ignorant black wretch commits a crime, that is different. All of us must bear his guilt. A young white boy's badness is simply the overflowing of young animal spirits; the black boy's badness is badness, pure and simple . . .

Someone will at last arise who will champion our cause and compel the world to see that we deserve justice; as other heroes compelled it to see that we deserved freedom.

—*An Anonymous Black Woman*

Bibliography

Davis, Angela. *Women, Race and Class*. New York: Random House, 1981.
Giddings, Paula. *When and Where I Enter*. New York: William Morrow, 1984.
Jones, Jacqueline. *Labor of Love, Labor of Sorrow*. New York: Basic Books, 1985.

FRANCES ELLEN WATKINS HARPER

(1825-1911)

Frances Ellen Watkins Harper was a nineteenth-century teacher, novelist, poet, public speaker. Her works spoke to all Americans about the need for justice and equality.

Harper was especially uncompromising in her attack upon the institution of slavery and duplicitous white Christians. She appealed to white Christians to do their duty towards African-Americans and was particularly impatient with the silent complicity of white women in the continuing degradation of African-Americans.

Harper's writings reverberate with her Christian convictions which are the means by which she grapples with the realities of slavery, the fight for temperance, and the struggle for suffrage. Religion provided Harper with the moral basis for her social justice stance because it supplied her with images that conveyed hope for the future.

"The Woman's Christian Temperance Union and the Colored Woman"[2]

A woman sat beneath the shadow of her home, while the dark waves of intemperance dashed against human hearts and hearthstones; but, there came an hour when she found that she could do something else besides wring her hands and weep over the ravages of the liquor traffic, which had darkened so many lives and desolated so many homes. Where the enemy spreads his snares for the feet of the unwary, inexperienced and tempted, she, too, could go and strive to stay the tide of ruin which was sending its floods of sorrow, shame and death to the habitations of men; and, 1873 witnessed the strange and wondrous sight of the Woman's Crusade, when the mother-heart was roused up in defense of the home and all that the home held dearest. A Divine impulse seemed to fan into sudden flame and touch with living fire earnest hearts, which rose up to meet the great occasion. Lips that had been silent in the prayer meeting were loosened to take part in the wonderful uprising. Saloons were visited, hardships encountered, insults, violence and even imprisonment endured by women, brave to suffer and strong to endure. Thousands of saloon visits were made, many were closed. Grand enthusiasms were aroused, moral earnestness awakened, and a fire kindled whose beacon lights still stream o'er the gloomy track of our monster evil. Victor Hugo has spoken of the nineteenth century as being woman's era, and among the most noticeable epochs in this era is the uprising of women against the twin evils of slavery and intemperance, which had foisted themselves like leeches upon the civilization of the present age. In the great anti-slavery conflict women had borne a part, but after the storm cloud of battle had rolled away, it was found that an enemy, old and strong and deceptive, was warring against the best interests of society; not simply an enemy to one race, but an enemy to all races—an enemy that had entrenched itself in the strongholds of appetite and avarice, and was upheld by fashion, custom and legislation. To dislodge this enemy, to put prohibition not simply on the statute book, but in the heart and conscience of a nation, embracing within itself such heterogeneous masses, is no child's play, nor the work of a few short moons. Men who were subjects in their own country and legislated for by others, become citizens here, with the power to help legislate for native born Americans. Hundreds of thousands of new citizens have been

---

[2]*A.M.E. Church Review* 4(1888):313-316.

translated from the old oligarchy of slavery into the new commonwealth of freedom, and are numerically strong enough to hold the balance of power in a number of the States, and sway its legislators for good or evil. With all these conditions, something more is needed than grand enthusiasms lighting up a few consecrated lives with hallowed brightness. We need patient, persevering, Christly endeavor, a consecration of the moral earnestness, spiritual power and numerical strength of the nation to grapple with this evil and accomplish its overthrow.

After the knowledge and experience gained by the crusade, women, instead of letting all their pure enthusiasms become dissipated by expending in feeling what they should utilize in action, came together and formed the Woman's Christian Temperance Union. From Miss Willard we learn that women who had been crusading all winter called conventions for consultation in respective States, and that several organizations, called Temperance Leagues, were formed. Another step was the confederation of the States into the National Christian Temperance Union. A circular, aided by an extensive circulation through the press, was sent out to women in different parts of the country, and a convention was called, which met in Cleveland in November, 1874, to which sixteen States responded. A plan of work was adopted, financial arrangements made, and the publishing of an organ resolved upon. Mrs. Whittemyer, of Philadelphia, was elected President, and Miss Willard, of Illinois, Corresponding Secretary. This Union has increased in numbers and territory until at its last convention it embraced thirty-seven States and Territories. For years I knew very little of its proceedings, and was not sure that colored comradeship was very desirable, but having attended a local Union in Philadelphia, I was asked to join and acceded to the request, and was made city and (afterwards) State Superintendent of work among colored people. Since then, for several years I have held the position of National Superintendent of work among the colored people of the North. When I became National Superintendent there were no colored women on the Executive Committee or Board of Superintendents. Now there are two colored women on the Executive Committee and two on the Board of Superintendents. As a matter of course the colored question has come into this work as it has into the Sons of Temperance, Good Templars and elsewhere. Some of the members of different Unions have met the question in a liberal and Christian manner; others have not seemed to have so fully outgrown the old shards and shells of the past as to make the distinction between Christian affiliation and social equality, but still the leaven of more liberal sentiments has been at work in the Union and produced some hopeful results.

One of the pleasantest remembrances of my connection with the Woman's Christian Temperance Union was the kind and hospitable reception I met in the Missouri State Convention, and the memorable words of their President, Mrs. Hoffman, who declared that the color-line was eliminated. A Superintendent was chosen at that meeting for colored work in the State, at whose home in St. Louis the National Superintendent was for some time a guest. The State Superintendent said in one of the meetings to the colored sisters, "You can come with us, or you can go by yourselves." There was self-reliance and ability enough among them to form a Union of their own, which was named after the National Superintendent. Our work is divided into about forty departments, and among them they chose several lines of work, and had departments for parlor meetings, juvenile and evangelistic work, all of which had been in working order. The Union held meetings in Methodist and Baptist churches, and opened in the African Methodist Episcopal Church an industrial school for children, which increased in size until from about a dozen children at the beginning, it closed with about one hundred and fifty, as I understand. Some of the Unions, in their outlook upon society, found that there was no orphan asylum for colored children, except among the Catholics, and took the initiative for founding an asylum for colored children, and in a short time, [they] were successful in raising several hundred dollars for that purpose. This Union has, I have been informed, gathered into its association seventeen school teachers, and I think comprises some of the best brain and heart of the race in the city. From West Virginia a lady informs the National Superintendent that her Union has invited the colored sisters to join with them, and adds, "Praise God, from whom all blessings flow." In a number of places where there are local Unions in the North the doors have been opened to colored women, but in the farther South separate State Unions have been formed. Southern white women, it may be, fail to make in their minds the discrimination between social equality and Christian affiliation. Social equality, if I rightly understand the term, is the outgrowth of social affinities and social conditions, and may be based on talent, ability or wealth, either or all of these conditions. Christian affiliation is the union of Christians to do Christly work, and help build up the kingdom of Christ amid the sin and misery of the world, under the spiritual leadership of the Lord Jesus Christ. At our last National Convention two States were represented by colored representatives. The colored President of an Alabama Union represented a Union composed of white and colored people, and is called No. 2, instead of Colored Union, as it was not composed entirely of colored people, and in making its advent into the National Union brought, as I was informed, more than twice the amount of State dues which was paid by the white Alabama Union, No. 1. The question of admission into the White Ribbon Army was brought before the National President, through a card sent from Atlanta. Twenty-three women had formed a Union, and had written to the National Superintendent of colored work in the North asking in reference to their admission, and if black sheep must climb up some other way to tell them how. I showed the card to Miss Willard, who gave it as her opinion "That the National could not make laws for a State. If the colored women of Georgia will meet and form a Woman's Christian Temperance Union for the State, it is my opinion that their officers and delegates will have the same representation in the National." The President of the Second Alabama was received and recognized in the National as a member of the Executive Committee, and had a place, as I was informed, on the Committee of Resolutions. Believing, as I do, in human solidarity, I hold that the Woman's Christian Temperance Union has in its hands one of the grandest opportunities that God ever pressed into the hands of the womanhood of any country. Its conflict is not the contest of a social club, but a moral warfare for an imperiled civilization. Whether or not the members of the farther South will subordinate the spirit of caste to the spirit of Christ, time will show. Once between them and the Negro were vast disparities, which have been melting and disappearing. The war obliterated the disparity between freedom and slavery. The civil law blotted out the difference between disfranchisement and manhood suffrage. Schools have sprung up like wells in the desert dust, bringing the races nearer together on the intellectual plane, while as a participant in the wealth of society the colored man has, I believe, in some instances, left his former master behind in the race for wealth. With these old landmarks going and gone, one relic remains from the dead past, "Our social customs." In clinging to them let them remember that the most ignorant, vicious and degraded voter outranks politically the purest, best and most cultured woman in the South, and learn to look at the question of Christian affiliation on this subject, not in the shadow of the fashion of this world that fadeth away, but in the light of the face of Jesus Christ. And can any one despise the least of Christ's brethren without despising Him? Is there any path that the slave once trod that Jesus did not tread before him, and leave luminous with the light of His steps? Was the Negro bought and sold? Christ was sold for thirty pieces of silver. Has he been poor? "The birds had nests, the foxes had holes, but the Son of man had no where to lay His head." Were they beaten in the house of bondage? They took Jesus and scourged Him. Have they occupied a low social position? "He made himself of no reputation, and was numbered with the transgressors." Despised and trodden under foot? He was despised and rejected of men; spit upon by the rabble, crucified between thieves, and died as died Rome's meanest criminal slave. Oh, my brothers and sisters, if God chastens every son whom He receiveth, let your past history be a stimulus for the future. Join with the great army who are on the side of God and His Christ. Let your homes be the best places where you may plant your batteries against the rum traffic. Teach your children to hate intoxicating drinks with a deadly hatred. Though scorn may curl her haughty lip, and fashion gather up her dainty robes from social contact, if your lives are in harmony with God and Christly sympathy with man, you belong to the highest nobility in God's universe. Learn to fight the battle for God and man as athletes armed for a glorious strife, encompassed about with a cloud of witnesses who are in sympathy with the highest and holiest endeavors.

—*Frances E. W. Harper*

Bibliography

Boyd, Melba Joyce. *Discarded Legacy: Politics and Poetics in the Life of Frances E. W. Harper (1825-1911)*. Detroit: Wayne State University Press, 1994.

Brown, Hallie Q. *Homespun Heroines and Other Women of Distinction*. Xenia, Ohio: Aldine Publishing Co., 1926.

Burrow, Rufus. "Sexism in the Black Community and the Black Church." *Journal of the Interdenominational Theological Center*. 13(Spring 1986):317-322.

Davis, Arthur P. and J. Saunders Redding, eds. *Cavalcade: Negro American Writing from 1760 to the Present*. Boston: Houghton Mifflin, 1971.

Foster, Frances Smith, ed. *A Brighter Coming Day: A Frances Ellen Watkins Harper Reader*. New York: Feminist Press, 1990.

———. *Minnie's Sacrifice, Sowing and Reaping, Trial and Triump: Three Rediscovered Novels*. Boston: Beacon Press, 1994.

Harper, Frances E. W. *Iola Leroy* [1892]. Boston: Beacon Press, 1987.

Hill, Patricia Liggins. "Frances Watkins Harper's Moses (A story of the Nile): Apologue of the Emancipation Struggle." *AME Zion Quarterly Review*. 95/4(January 1984):11-19.

Sherman, Joan R. *Invisible Poets: Afro-Americans of the Nineteenth Century*. Second Edition. Urbana: University of Illinois Press, 1989.

Shockley, Ann Allen. *Afro-American Women Writers: 1746-1933*. Boston: G.K. Hall, 1988.

FANNIE BARRIER WILLIAMS
(1855-1944)

One of Fannie Barrier Williams's favorite sayings was this: "As it is, there is much to be unlearned as well as to be learned." As a tireless advocate of women's rights, she realized that the struggle for equality would require attentive minds and willing spirits. Williams challenged prevailing views about black women in speeches before the World's Fair of 1893 as well as the World Parliament of Religions, making her case against injustice and gender oppression with insight and clarity.

Williams also sought equal employment and equal access to opportunity. Toward these ends, she broke the "color line" in a private white women's club in Chicago, served as the first black woman on the Chicago Library Board, and supported the founding of the National Association of Colored Women. In sum,

Fannie Barrier Williams integrated and innovated. Her insight and balance are a legacy to future generations.

"The Awakening of Women"[3]

The colored women of America are becoming conscious of their importance in all things that can make for the social betterment of the Negro race.

The distinctive importance of this fact is, perhaps, a sufficient excuse for a woman, at the risk of being trite, to indulge in some generalizations concerning the nature of the problems that we must grasp and the different points of view from which these problems are to be studied.

In the first place, it is important for us to note that the most aggressive forces in the reform movements of the day are those that are outside of and, in many cases, in spite of the institutions and established conservators of human society. It is not the church, nor the school house, nor the political organizations, nor the purely social establishments that are aggressively engaged in much of the best reform work of the day. Taking Chicago as a typical field, what do we find? Here we have statutory laws to meet almost every conceivable wrongdoing and harm of the saloon power, and yet in nearly everything, save the question of license, there is no official enforcement of these statutes. If it should be asked, who it is that is vigilant in prosecuting the saloon for selling liquor to minors and drunkards, and protecting the home from its poisonous encroachments, the answer is that the opposing forces are not the church nor political parties, but a voluntary association of high-minded and public-spirited citizens, known as the Citizen's League, determined that these righteous laws shall, at least in part, be enforced. So it is in other effective resistance to all the social and political evils of the municipality.

The Civic Federation in Chicago, made up of the best men and women of all parties and interests, stands for public morals, for civic conscience and political decency. In this association is found the reflection of civic pride and civic efficiency that overturn corrupt councils, banish to the penitentiary the corruptors of the ballot box, the manipulators of the tax assessments, the bribers of the jury system, and those who grow rich by official complicity in the social evil. If it be asked who it is that protects the minor children from the cruelties of store-keepers and factories, who it is that protects the unfortunate women of the slums from the blackmailing of the police force, the answer is that that protection comes from the women's clubs of the city—voluntary organizations of noble women, whose culture is so broad and hearts so touched with the divine spirit of altru-

---

[3]*A.M.E. Church Review* 13(1896-1897):392-398.

ism, that their nobility is increased by every effort to reach down the helping hand to lift up the helpless and "disinherited."

These things are referred to merely to suggest the importance of the club movement all over this country. The organizations of colored women may mean much or little to the social life of the colored race, according to the amount of heart that is put into them. The organization of the "National Association of Colored Women" in this country bent upon making their goodness felt wherever good influences are needed, is an event of extraordinary importance, because the best elements of womanhood are behind and a part of the movement. Our women, thus organized, have it in their power to supplement the blessed influences of the churches, the molding forces of the schools, and all the restraining powers of the official forces of our cities, to such an extent as to link their efforts with the best results of woman's work in these latter days of the nineteenth century.

The supreme thing is the spirit of duty, the enthusiasm for action, and an untrammelled sympathy. By sympathy is not meant that far-away, kid-gloved and formal something that enables women merely to know of those who need them, but that deeper and more spiritual impulse to helpfulness that will enable them to find delight in working *with*, rather than *for*, (emphasis added) the unfortunate of their sex. In social reforms we must see but one thing, and that is the vivid soul of humanity—that divinity which neither rags, dirt nor immoralities can entirely obscure.

In the Hull House Settlement of Chicago will be found an apt illustration of what is meant by sympathy at short range. Whoever goes into that homelike refuge from the open evidences of degradation that environ it, will be filled with an exalted sense of the beauty of human kindness. Here shines the gentle spirit of Jane Addams, that apostle of the new gospel of "good deeds in a naughty world." Serene, with philosophic penetration into the causes of social evils, beautifully sensitive to every form of human suffering about her, and always sisterly, motherly or friendly, as requirements demand, Jane Addams has taught to women a new conception of sympathy. The women who surround her as assistants in that desert of sin and human depravity belong to the best social life of Chicago. In going from beautiful homes and social refinements into the slum districts, these women have neither lost social prestige or personal dignity. On the contrary, this new work has given a new value to womanly worth. They are teaching the world that personal service is worth more than purchased service. Behind every dollar, accompanying every word of advice, and connected with every precept, is the immediate and personal service of a noble woman. The poor woman who is sick is visited and feels a thrill of personal interest; the child that is neglected and turned into the streets to learn lessons of depravity, feels, perhaps for the first time, the caressing arm, the gentle chiding and personal direction of a superior personality;

the man whose depravity is the result of poverty and misfortune, hopeless and heartless, feels the kindness of the world drawing near to him when these women express a a personal interest in his condition. The whole fabric of social life is thrilled by the sympathetic service of this newer gospel of charity. In short, what the lower half of our social life wants is not money or institutions, but a sense of relationship and fellowship with the upper half. There is no good reason why the mean politician should have a monopoly of interest over the man who is made to sell his vote for a trifle. There is no good reason why the men and women of the church, of the schools and the higher social conditions should not be able to reach and influence the unfortunate masses to a greater extent than do the men whose motives are mercenary and whose influence is degrading. The good people of every community will command this influence just as soon as they begin to recognize the potency of kindness and the helpfulness of "socializing" their charitable efforts. To be more definite, the first thing to be done in our charitable undertakings is to establish some sort of relationship between those who need help and those who can render help. Apparent differences must not be emphasized.

I recognize the fact that to do all this heartily and effectively many of us must unlearn many things that we have already learned as to social questions. It is important that we should learn that sociality is a very different thing from "society" as we ordinarily understand the term. The mystic cord of congeniality that differentiates the world of humanity into infinite groups or companies for social intercourse and the delights of companionship is the very essence of high living. But sociality, that means sisterhood and brotherhood based on something deeper than selfish preferences, is the divine element in human nature. It is the exercise of this larger element of love that gives peculiar value to woman's work. If we can so expand our hearts to this divine energy, we shall discover all the needs of the human heart and be able to apply the remedies to every secret cause of misfortune. Thus do we begin to feel the difference between the old and new philosophy of social relationships. It has been, and to a considerable extent, still is our misfortune to be regarded and estimated as suited to no other purpose in life than to make the world gay with our vivacity, laughter and social attributes. But when intelligence and that larger love referred to begins to lift women out of a state of social dependency into the larger world of social independence, duties, and responsibilities the very foundations of civilization begin to shake and move forward toward better ideals of life and living. Woman free, woman educated in the academies of experience as well as the academies of science, literature and art, is to-day abroad. By her finer heart and intrinsic sympathy she is helping to give a new and better meaning to religion, more power to education and more preciousness to home, society, and life itself.

Colored women are fortunate to live in this era of freedom and interest in womankind. Never before has the world been so interested in woman and woman's work, and never before in our history have the people of this country been so much interested in colored women as it is today. Public interest in us has grown to such an extent that the press is as eager for every item of news concerning our work and achievement as they are for that of more favored races. The relentlessness of prejudice seems more likely to yield to the winsome voice of our women than to the effort of many of our more less pretentious brothers. Yet it is not in a spirit of boastfulness that these evidences of growing popular interest are referred to, but rather as an encouragement and inspiration to our further efforts along the higher lines of womanly endeavor. It is said that this is "woman's era," and with just as much distinctiveness is it the colored woman's era. Today is our blessed opportunity to stimulate all the spiritual and social forces towards standards that are higher, sweeter and purer and more beautiful, because a greater love and diviner motive have made it so.

As a further word, I should like to urge the necessity of study and preparation in entering upon the work of social reform. To accomplish anything in this kind of work there is needed not only aroused hearts, but an aroused and penetrating intelligence. Human nature is a very much involved and never a solved problem. When we begin to study it in its social connections we find that all other lessons of an academic sort are but superficialities. When we have gone out into the world of misfortune and have graciously lifted some poor woman from a bed of sickness, rescued some precious child from a life of wasted energy, or stayed some miserable man from further degradation, we shall find that in most cases our kindness has been only a remedy, not a cure. Back of the poverty, disease and depravity which we have alleviated is the cause that breeds these conditions. You will not be able to escape the conclusion that those who are worth relieving are worth saving, and when we begin to push the inquiry as to the cause of the disease and poverty we are sure to be overwhelmed with confusion, unless to our kindness we add some special intelligence. What the social world wants today in its minor and larger distresses is not more charity or relief, but cures and the permanent tonic of an upward spirit.

As colored women we can but feel that the requirements and opportunities of the hour challenge us not only to organize, but to organize with high standards. We must not be timid; we must not be narrow or faint-hearted. The standard of life in the aggregate amongst us is not high; it is our blessed privilege to elevate it. There are precious interests close to us that have too long been neglected and it is our golden opportunity to make these interests important. Thus shall we have a conscious share in whatever is true, beautiful and good in the destiny of this republic.

"The Club Movement Among Colored Women of America"[4]

Afro-American women of the United States have never had the benefit of a discriminating judgment concerning their worth as women made up of the good and bad of human nature. What they have been made to be and not what they are, seldom enters into the best or worst opinion concerning them.

In studying the status of Afro-American women as revealed in their club organizations, it ought to be borne in mind that such social differentiations as "women's interests, children's interests, and men's interests" that are so finely worked out in the social development of the more favored races are but recent recognitions in the progressive life of the negro race. Such specializing had no economic value in slavery days, and the degrading habit of regarding the negro race as an unclassified people has not yet wholly faded into a memory.

The negro as an "alien" race, as a "problem," as an "industrial factor," as "ex-slaves," as "ignorant" etc., are well known and instantly recognized; but colored women as mothers, as home-makers, as the center and source of the social life of the race have received little or no attention. These women have been left to grope their way unassisted toward a realization of those domestic virtues, moral impulses and standards of family and social life that are the badges of race respectability. They have had no special teachers to instruct them. No conventions of distinguished women of the more favored race have met to consider their peculiar needs. There has been no fixed public opinion to which they could appeal; no protection against the libelous attacks upon their characters and no chivalry generous enough to guarantee their safety against man's inhumanity to woman. Certainly it is that colored women have been the least known, and the most ill-favored class of women in this country.

Thirty-five years ago they were unsocialized, unclassed and unrecognized as either maids or matrons. They were simply women whose character and personality excited no interest. If within thirty-five years they have become sufficiently important to be studied apart from the general race problem and have come to be recognized as an integral part of the general womanhood of American civilization, that fact is a gratifying evidence of real progress.

In considering the social advancement of these women, it is important to keep in mind the point from which progress began, and the fact that they have been mainly self-taught in all those precious things that make

---

[4]*A New Negro for a New Century*, reprint of 1900 edition (New York: Arno Press, 1969), pp. 379-428.

for social order, purity and character. They have gradually become conscious of the fact that progress includes a great deal more than what is generally meant by the terms culture, education and contact.

The club movement among colored women reaches into the sub-social condition of the entire race. Among white women clubs mean the forward movement of the best women in the interest of the best womanhood. Among colored women the club is the effort of the few competent in behalf of the many incompetent; that is to say that the club is only one of many means for the social uplift of a race. Among white women the club is the onward movement of the already uplifted.

The consciousness of being fully free has not yet come to the great masses of the colored women in this country. The emancipation of the mind and spirit of the race could not be accomplished by legislation. More time, more patience, more suffering and more charity are still needed to complete the work of emancipation.

The training which first enabled colored women to organize and successfully carry on club work was originally obtained in church work. These churches have been and still are the great preparatory schools in which the primary lessons of social order, mutual trustfulness and united effort have been taught. The churches have been sustained, enlarged and beautified principally through the organized efforts of their women members. The meaning of unity of effort for the common good, the development of social sympathies grew into women's consciousness through the privileges of church work.

Still another school of preparation for colored women has been their secret societies. "The ritual of these secret societies is not without a certain social value." They demand a higher order of intelligence than is required for church membership. Care for the sick, provisions for the decent burial of the indigent dead, the care for orphans and the enlarging sense of sisterhood all contributed to the development of the very conditions of heart that qualify women for the more inclusive work of those social reforms that are the aim of women's clubs. The churches and secret societies have helped to make colored women acquainted with the general social condition of the race and the possibilities of social improvement.

With this training the more intelligent women of the race could not fail to follow the example and be inspired by the larger club movement of the white women. The need of social reconstruction became more and more apparent as they studied the results of women's organizations. Better homes, better schools, better protection for girls of scant home training, better sanitary conditions, better opportunities for competent young women to gain employment, and the need of being better known to the American people appealed to the conscience of progressive colored women from many communities.

The clubs and leagues organized among colored women have all been more or less in direct response to these appeals. Seriousness of purpose has thus been the main characteristic of all these organizations. While the National Federation of Woman's Clubs has served as a guide and inspiration to colored women, the club movement among them is something deeper than a mere imitation of white women. It is nothing less than the organized anxiety of women who have become intelligent enough to recognize their own low social condition and strong enough to initiate the forces of reform.

The club movement as a race influence among the colored women of the country may be fittingly said to date from July, 1895, when the first national conference of colored women was held in Boston, Mass. Prior to this time there were a number of strong clubs in some of the larger cities of the country, but they were not affiliated and the larger idea of effecting the social regeneration of the race was scarcely conceived of.

Among the earlier clubs the Woman's League of Washington, D.C., organized in 1892, and the Woman's Era Club of Boston, organized in January, 1893, were and are still the most thorough and influential organizations of the kind in the country.

The kind of work carried on by the Washington League since its organization is best indicated by its standing committees, as follows:

Committee on Education
Committee on Industries
Committee on Mending and Sewing
Committee on Free Class Instruction
Committee on Day Nursery
Committee on Building Fund.

These various activities include sewing schools, kindergartens, well-conducted night schools, and mother's meetings, all of which have been developed and made a prominent part of the educational and social forces of the colored people of the capital. The league has made itself the recognized champion of every cause in which colored women and children have any special interests in the District of Columbia.

The league is also especially strong in the personnel of its membership, being made up largely of teachers, many of whom are recognized as among the most cultured and influential women of the negro race in this country.

Mrs. Helen Cook, of Washington, was the first president elected by the league, and still holds that position. Mrs. Cook belongs to one of the oldest and best-established colored families in the country. She has had all the advantages of culture, contact, and experience to make her an ideal leader of the leading women's organization of the colored race.

The Woman's League claims to have originated the idea of a national organization of colored women's clubs. In its annual report for 1895 there occurs the following language:

"The idea of national organization has been embodied in the Woman's

League of Washington from its formation. It existed fully developed in the minds of the original members even before they united themselves into an association which has national union for its central thought, its inspiring motive, its avowed purpose—its very reason for being."

Having assumed a national character by gaining the affiliations of such clubs as the Kansas City League, the Denver League, and associations in Virginia, South Carolina and Pennsylvania, the Washington League was admitted into the membership of the National Council of Women of the United States.

The league is very tenacious of its name and claim as the originator of the idea of nationalizing the colored women's clubs of America, but its claim has always been challenged with more or less spirit by some of the clubs composing the National Association.

The New Era Club of Boston was organized in the month of February, 1893. The desire of the cultured and public-spirited colored women of that city to do something in the way of promoting a more favorable public opinion in behalf of the negro race was the immediate incentive to this organization. The club began its work of agitation by collecting data and issuing leaflets and tracts containing well-edited matter in reference to Afro-American progress. Its most conspicuous work has been the publication of the *Woman's Era*, the first newspaper ever published by colored women in this country. This paper gained a wide circulation and did more than any other single agency to nationalize the club idea among the colored women of the country. The New Era Club has sustained its reputation as the most representative organization of colored people in New England. It has taken the initiative in many reforms and helpful movements that have had a wide influence on race development. This club has been especially useful and influential in all local affairs that in any way affect the colored people. Deserving young men and women struggling to obtain an education, and defenseless young women in distress have always been able to find substantial assistance in the New Era Club.

This Boston organization embraces a membership of about one hundred women, many of whom are prominent in the ranks of New England's strongest women.

Mrs. Josephine St. Pierre Ruffin has been the president of the Era Club all the time since its organization. She is an active member in any of the influential women's organizations in Massachusetts. She is a woman of rare force of character, mental alertness and of generous impulses. She has played a leading part in every movement that has tended to the emancipation of colored women from the thraldom of past conditions. Her husband, the late Judge Ruffin, held the first position of a judicial character ever held by a colored man in New England.

These two clubs, located respectively in Washington and Boston, were worthy beginnings of the many local efforts that were destined to grow and spread until there should be such a thing in the United States as a national uprising of the colored women of the country pledged to the serious work of a social reconstruction of the negro race.

But these two clubs were not the only examples of the colored woman's capacity for organization. The following clubs were thoroughly organized and actively engaged in the work of reform contemporaneously with the clubs of Boston and Washington:

The Harper Women's Club of Jefferson City, Mo., was formed in 1890 and had established a training school for instruction in sewing; a temperance department and mothers' meetings were also carried on. The Loyal Union of Brooklyn and New York was organized in December, 1892. It has a membership of seventy-five women and was engaged largely in agitating for better schools and better opportunities for young women seeking honorable employment; the I.B.W. Club of Chicago, Ill., organized in 1893; the Woman's Club of Omaha, Neb., organized February, 1895; the Belle Phoebe League of Pittsburgh, Pa., organized November, 1894; the Woman's League of Denver; the Phyllis Wheatley Club of New Orleans; the Sojourner Club of Providence, R.I.; and the Woman's Mutual Improvement Club of Knoxville, Tenn., organized in 1894.

It will thus be seen that from 1890 to 1895 the character of Afro-American womanhood began to assert itself in definite purposes and efforts in club work. Many of these clubs came into being all unconscious of the influences of the larger club movement among white women. The incentive in most cases was quite simple and direct. How to help and protect some defenseless and tempted young woman; how to aid some poor boy to complete a much-coveted education; how to lengthen the short school term in some impoverished school district; how to instruct and interest deficient mothers in the difficulties of child training are some of the motives that led to the formation of the great majority of these clubs. These were the first out-reachings of sympathy and fellowship felt by women whose lives had been narrowed by the petty concerns of the struggle for existence and removed by human cruelty from all the harmonies of freedom, love and aspirations.

Many of these organizations so humble in their beginnings and meager in membership clearly needed behind them the force and favor of some larger sanction to save them from timidity and pettiness of effort. Many of them clearly needed the inspirations, the wider vision and supporting strength that come from a national unity. The club in Mississippi could have a better understanding of its own possibilities by feeling the kinship of the club in New England or Chicago, and the womanhood sympathy of these northern clubs must remain narrow and inefficient if isolated in interest from the self-emancipating struggles of southern clubs.

As already noted some of the more progressive clubs had already conceived the idea of a National organization. The Woman's Era journal of Boston began to agitate the matter in the summer of 1894, and requested the clubs to express themselves through its columns on the question of holding a National convention. Colored women everywhere were quick to see the possible benefits to be derived from a National conference of representative women. It was everywhere believed that such a convention, conducted with decorum, and along the lines of serious purpose might help in a decided manner to change public opinion concerning the character and worth of colored women. This agitation had the effect of committing most of the clubs to the proposal for a call in the summer of 1895. While public-spirited Afro-American women everywhere were thus aroused to this larger vision in plans for race amelioration, there occurred an incident of aggravation that swept away all timidity and doubt as to the necessity of a National conference. Some obscure editor in a Missouri town sought to gain notoriety by publishing a libelous article in which the colored women of the country were described as having no sense of virtue and altogether without character. The article in question was in the form of an open letter addressed to Miss Florence Belgarnie of England, who had manifested a kindly interest in behalf of the American negro as a result of Miss Ida B. Wells' agitation. This letter is too foul for reprint, but the effect of its publication stirred the intelligent colored women of America as nothing else had ever done. The letter, in spite of its wanton meanness, was not without some value in showing to what extent the sensitiveness of colored women had grown. Twenty years prior to this time a similar publication would scarcely have been noticed, beyond the small circles of the few who could read, and were public-spirited. In 1895 this open and vulgar attack on the character of a whole race of women was instantly and vehemently resented, in every possible way, by a whole race of women conscious of being slandered. Mass meetings were held in every part of the country to denounce the editor and refute the charges.

The calling of a National convention of colored women was hastened by this coarse assault upon their character. The Woman's Era Club of Boston took the initiative in concentrating the widespread anxiety to do something large and effective, by calling a National conference of representative colored women. The conference was appointed to meet in Berkeley Hall, Boston, for a three days' session, July 29, 30 and 31, 1895.

In pursuance to this call the 29th day of July, 1895, witnessed in Berkeley Hall the first National convention of colored women ever held in America. About one hundred delegates were present from ten States and representatives of about twenty-five different clubs.

The convention afforded a fine exhibition of capable women. There was nothing amateurish, uncertain or timid in the proceedings. Every subject of peculiar interest to colored women was discussed and acted upon as if by women disciplined in thinking out large and serious problems. The following named women were elected as officers of the conference:

Mrs. Josephine St. P. Ruffin, president; vice-presidents, Mrs. Helen Cook, of Washington, and Mrs. Booker T. Washington; secretary, Miss Eliza Carter.

The sanity of these colored women in their first National association was shown in the fact that but little time was spent in complaints and fault-finding about conditions that were inevitable. Almost for the first time in the history of negro gatherings, this Boston conference frankly studied the status of their own race and pointed out their own shortcomings. They set for themselves large and serious tasks in suggestions of plans and work to redeem the unredeemed among them. The convention did credit to itself by sending far and wide a warning note that the race must begin to help itself to live better, strive for a higher standard of social purity, to exercise a more helpful sympathy with the many of the race who are without guides and enlightenment in the ways of social righteousness.

Of course the Missouri editor was roundly scored in resolutions that lacked nothing of the elements of resentment, but the slanderous article against colored women that was the immediate incentive to the calling of the conference, became of the least importance when the women came together and realized the responsibility of larger considerations. They very soon felt that a National convention of responsible women would be a misplacement of moral force, if it merely exhausted itself in replying to a slanderous publication. The convention, therefore, easily shaped itself toward the consideration of themes and policies more in keeping with its responsibilities to the thousands of women and interests represented.

The chief work of the convention was the formation of National organization. The name adopted was "The National Association of Colored Women." . . .

The importance of this Boston conference to the club movement among colored women can scarcely be overestimated. The bracing effect of its vigorous proceedings and stirring addresses to the public gave a certain inspiration to the women throughout the whole country. The clubs that already existed became stronger and more positive and aggressive in their helpful work.

The National Association has steadily grown in power and influence as an organized body, composed of the best moral and social forces of the negro race. It has held three National conventions since its organization in 1895: At Washington, D.C., in 1896; Nashville, Tenn., in 1897; and Chicago, in 1899. At the Chicago convention one hundred and fifty delegates were present, representing clubs from thirty States of the Union. The growing importance of the National organization was evidenced by the generous notices and editorial comments in the press of the country. Fraternal greetings were extended to the Chicago convention from many of the prominent white clubs of the city. It is not too much to say that no National convention of colored people held in the country ever made such a deep impression upon the public and told a more thrilling story of the social progress of the race than the Chicago convention. The interest awakened in colored women, and their peculiar interests, was evidenced in many ways. The National Association has made it possible for many bright colored women to enjoy the fellowship and helpfulness of many of the best organizations of American women. It has certainly helped to emancipate the white women from the fear and uncertainty of contact or association with women of the darker race. In other words the National Association of Colored Women's Clubs is helping to give respect and character to a race of women who had no place in the classification of progressive womanhood in America. The terms good and bad, bright and dull, plain and beautiful are now as applicable to colored women as to women of other races. There has been created such a thing as public faith in the sustained virtue and social standards of the women who have spoken and acted so well in these representative organizations. The National body has also been felt in giving a new importance and a larger relationship to the purposes and activities of local clubs throughout the country. Colored women everywhere in this club work began to feel themselves included in a wider and better world than their immediate neighborhood. Women who have always lived and breathed the air of ample freedom and whose range of vision has been world-wide, will scarcely know what it means for women whose lives have been confined and dependent to feel the first consciousness of a relationship to the great social forces that include whole nationalities in the sweep of their influences. To feel that you are something better than a slave, or a descendant of an ex-slave, to feel that you are a unit in the womanhood of a great nation and a great civilization, is the beginning of self-respect and the respect of your race. The National Association of Colored Women's Clubs has certainly meant all this and much more to the women of the ransomed race in the United States.

The National Association has also been useful to an important extent in creating what may be called a race public opinion. When the local clubs of the many States became nationalized, it became possible to reach the whole people with questions and interests that concerned the whole race. For example, when the National Association interested itself in studying such problems as the Convict Lease System of the Southern States, or the necessity of kindergartens, or the evils of the one-room cabin, it was possible to unite and interest the intelligent forces of the entire race. On these and other questions it has become possible to get the cooperation of the colored people in Mississippi and Minnesota and of New York and Florida. Such co-operation is new and belongs to the new order of things brought about by nationalized efforts.

Through the united voice of the representative colored women of the country the interests of the race are heard by the American women with more effect than they were in other days. There is certainly more power to demand respect and righteous treatment since it has become possible to organize the best forces of all the race for such demands.

The influence of the National Association has been especially felt in the rapid increase of women's clubs throughout the country, and especially in the south. There are now about three hundred of such clubs in the United States. There is an average membership of about sixty women to each club. Some have an enrollment of over two hundred women and there are but few with less than twenty-five. Wherever there is a nucleus of intelligent colored women there will be found a woman's club. The following is only a partial list of clubs composing the National Association.

CLUB LIST:
NAMES OF THE CLUBS OF THE NATIONAL ASSOCIATION OF COLORED WOMEN

ALABAMA.
Eufaula Woman's Club.
Greensboro Woman's Mutual Benefit Club.
Montgomery Sojourner Truth Club.
Mt. Meigs Woman's Club.
Selma Woman's Club.
Tuskeegee Woman's Club.
Tuskeegee-Notasulga Woman's Club.
Birmingham Sojourner Truth Club.
Ladies' Auxiliary, Montgomery.
Ten Times One, Montgomery.

ARKANSAS.
Little Rock Branch of National Association.
Woman's Club, Little Rock.

CALIFORNIA.
Los Angeles Woman's Club.

NORTH CAROLINA.
Biddle University Club.

SOUTH CAROLINA.
Charleston Woman's League.
Charleston W.C.T.U.

COLORADO.
Denver, The Woman's League.

CONNECTICUT.
Norwich, Rose of New England League.

FLORIDA.
Jacksonville Women's Christian Industrial and Protective Union.
The Phyllis Wheatley Chautauqua Circle, Jacksonville.
The Afro-American Woman's Club, Jacksonville.

GEORGIA.
Atlanta Woman's Club.
Harriet Beecher Stowe, Macon.
Columbus, Douglass Reading Circle.
Augusta, Woman's Protective Club.
Woman's Club of Athens.

INDIANA.
The Booker T. Washington Club, Logansport.

ILLINOIS.
Chicago, Ida B. Wells Club.
Chicago, Phyllis Wheatley Club.
Chicago, Woman's Civic League.
Chicago, Women's Conference.
Chicago, Women's Circle.
Chicago, Progressive Circle of King's Daughters.

KANSAS.
Sierra Leone Club.
Woman's Club, Paola.

TENNESSEE.
Knoxville, Woman's Mutual Improvement Club.
Memphis, Coterie Migratory Assembly.
Memphis, Hook's School Association.
Phyllis Wheatley, Nashville.
Jackson, Woman's Club.
Jackson, W.C.T.U.

TEXAS.
Fort Worth Phyllis Wheatley Club.

VIRGINIA.
Woman's League of Roanoke.
Richmond Woman's League.
Cappahoosic Gloucester A. and I. School.
Urbanna Club.
Lynchburg Woman's League.
Lexington Woman's Club.

DISTRICT OF COLUMBIA.
Washington, D.C., Ladies' Auxiliary Committee.
Washington League.

Washington, Lucy Thurman W.C.T.U.
Woman's Protective Union, Washington, D.C.

WEST VIRGINIA.
Wheeling, Woman's Fortnightly Club.

There are of course hundreds of clubs that are not yet members of the National Association, but these outside clubs have all been brought into being by the influence of the National body, and have received their inspiration and direction from the same source.

A study of the plans and purpose of these clubs reveals an interesting similarity. They show that the wants, needs, limitations and aspirations of the Afro-American are about the same everywhere—North, South, East and West.

If the question be asked: "What do these clubs do; what do they stand for in their respective communities, and what have they actually accomplished?" Satisfactory answer will be found by studying them a little at a short range.

The first thing to be noted is that these club women are students of their own social condition, and the clubs themselves are schools in which are taught and learned, more or less thoroughly, the near lessons of life and living. All these clubs have a program for study. In some of the more ambitious clubs, literature, music and art are studied more or less seriously, but in *all* (emphasis added) of them race problems and sociologic questions directly related to the condition of the negro race in America are the principal subjects for study and discussion.

Many of the clubs, in their programs for study, plan to invite from time to time prominent men and women to address them on questions of vital interest. In this way club members not only become wide awake and interested in questions of importance to themselves and their community, but men and women who help to make and shape public opinion have an opportunity to see and know the better side of the colored race.

Race prejudice yields more readily to this interchange of service and helpfulness than to any other force in the relationship of races.

The lessons learned in these women's organizations of the country all have a direct bearing on the social conditions of the negro race. They are such lessons that are not taught in the schools or preached from the pulpits. Home-making has been new business to the great majority of the women whom the women's clubs aim to reach and influence. For this reason the principal object of club studies is to teach that homes are something better and dearer than rooms, furniture, comforts and food. How to make the homes of the race the shrines of all the domestic virtues rather than a mere shelter, is the important thing that colored women are trying to learn and teach through their club organizations.

Take for example one club in Chicago, known as the "Colored Woman's Conference," and it will be found that its aims and efforts are typical of the best purposes of club life among colored women. The special activities and aims of this particular club are the establishment of kindergartens, mothers' meetings, sewing schools for girls, day nurseries, employment bureau; promoting the cause of education by establishing a direct line of interest between the teacher and the home life of every child; friendly visiting and protection to friendless and homeless girls; and a penny savings bank as a practical lesson in frugality and economy. The special thing to be noted in this program is that colored women are not afraid to set for themselves hard and serious tasks and to make whatever sacrifices necessary to realize their high purposes.

A lack of kindergarten teachers more than a lack of money has retarded the work of establishing kindergartens, especially in the South, where they are specially needed. The progressive woman feels that an increased number of kindergartens would have a determining influence in shaping and molding the character of thousands of colored children whose home lives are scant and meager.

The success of the kindergarten work in St. Louis, Mo., under the direction of Mrs. Haydee Campbell and her able assistant, Miss Helene Abbott, is a happy justification of the wisdom and anxiety of the colored club woman to extend these schools wherever it is possible to do so.

The mothers' meetings established in connection with almost every club have probably had a more direct and beneficial influence on the everyday problems of motherhood and home-making than any other activity. Meetings of this sort have been the chief feature of the women's clubs organized by the Tuskegee teachers among the women of the hard plantation life, within reach of the Tuskeegee Institute. Thousands of these women in the rural life of the South continue to live under the shadow of bondaged conditions. There has come to them scarcely a ray of light as to a better way of how to live for themselves and their offspring.

It is to the credit of the high usefulness of the colored club woman that she has taken the initiative in doing something to reach and help a class of women who have lived isolated from all the regenerating and uplifting influences of freedom and education. It is the first touch of sympathy that has connected the progressive colored woman with her neglected and unprogressive sister.

In this connection especial word ought to be said in behalf of these clubs as agencies of rescue and protection to the many unprotected and defenseless colored girls to be found in every large city. No race of young women in this country have so little done for them as the young colored woman. She is unknown, she is not believed in, and in respect to favors that direct and uplift, she is an alien, and unheeded. They have been literally shut out from the love, favor and protection that chivalry and a common pride have built up around the personality and character of the young women of almost every other race. The colored women's clubs have had heart enough and intelligence enough to recognize their opportunity and duty toward their own young women, and in numerous instances have been the very salvation of unfortunate colored girls.

An interesting example of the usefulness of these clubs in this rescue work was recently shown by the success of the Colored Woman's Conference, above mentioned, in saving a girl, friendless, and a victim of unfortunate circumstances, from the stain of the penitentiary by pledging to take her in charge and to save her to herself and society by placing her under good and redeeming influences.

These women's clubs have never failed to champion the cause of every worthy applicant for advice and assistance. They have made the cause of the neglected young colored woman one of commanding interest, and are interested in her behalf in every possible means of education, and are endeavoring to create for her a kindlier feeling and a better degree of respect, and to improve her standing among young women generally. The clubs have entered upon this department of their work with great heartiness and have enlisted in behalf of young women new influences of helpfulness and encouragement. Colored girls with poor homes and no homes are many. Thousands of them are the poor, weak and misguided daughters of ill-starred mothers. To reach out for and save them from a bitter fate, to lift them into a higher sphere of hopefulness and opportunity is a task altogether worthy of the best efforts of club women.

What has been said of the earnestness and practical aim of colored women's clubs in behalf of kindergartens for the children and salvation for the girls may also be said of the practical way in which they have established and sustained sewing schools, mending schools and friendly visitations in behalf of neighborhood respectability and decency, and of their various committees that visit reformatory institutions and jails in search of opportunities to be useful. Numerous and interesting instances might be given to show to what extent these women are realizing their desire to be useful in the social regeneration of their race.

This chapter on the club movement among colored women would be incomplete without some notice of the leaders of the movement. Nothing that these club women have done or aimed to do is more interesting than themselves. What a variety of accomplishments, talents, successes and ambitions have been brought into view and notice by these hitherto obscure women of a ransomed race! Educated? Yes, besides the thousands educated in the common schools, hundreds of them have been trained in the best colleges and universities in the country, and some of them have spent several years in the noted schools of Europe.

The women thus trained and educated are busily pursuing every kind of vocation not prohibited by American prejudices. As educators, fully twenty thousand of them are at work in the schools, colleges and universities of the country, and some of them teach everything required to be taught from the kindergarten to the university. Among these educators and leaders of Afro-American womanhood are to be found linguists, mathematicians, musicians, artists, authors, newspaper writers, lecturers and reform agitators, with varying degrees of excellence and success. There are women in the professions of law, medicine, dentistry, preaching, trained nursing, managers of successful business enterprises, and women of small independent fortunes made and saved within the past twenty-five years.

There are women plain, beautiful, charming, bright conversationalists, fluent, resourceful in ideas, forceful in execution, and women of all sorts of temperament and idiosyncrasies and force and delicacy of character.

All this of course is simply amazing to people trained in the habit of rating colored women too low and knowing only the menial type. To such people she is a revelation.

The woman thus portrayed is the real new woman in American life. This woman, as if by magic, has succeeded in lifting herself as completely from the stain and meanness of slavery as if a century had elapsed since the day of emancipation. This new woman, with club behind her and the club service in her heart and mind, has come to the front in an opportune time. She is needed to change the old idea of things implanted in the minds of the white race and there sustained and hardened into a national habit by the debasing influence of slavery estimates. This woman is needed as an educator of public opinion. She is a happy refutation of the idle insinuations and common skepticism as to the womanly worth and promise of the whole race of women. She has come to enrich American life with finer sympathies, and to enlarge the boundary of fraternity and the democracy of love among American women. She has come to join her talents, her virtues, her intelligence, her sacrifices and her love in the work of redeeming the unredeemed from stagnation, from cheapness and from narrowness.

Quite as important as all this she has come to bring new hope and fresh assurances to the hapless young women of her own race. Life is not a failure. All avenues are not closed. Womanly worth of whatever race or complexion is appreciated. Love, sympathy, opportunity and helpfulness are within the reach of those who can derive them. The world is still yearning for pure hearts, willing hands, and bright minds. This and much more is the message brought by this new woman to the hearts of thousands of discouraged and hopeless young colored women.

It is a real message of courage, a real inspiration that has touched more sides of the Afro-American race than any other message or thing since the dawn of freedom.

This is not exaggeration or fancy. Demonstration of it can be seen, heard and felt in the widespread renewal of hope and effort among the present generation of young Afro-American women.

These young women, thus aroused to courage, to hope and self-assertion toward better things, can find inspiring examples of success and achievements in the women of their own race. They have begun to feel something of the exaltation of race pride and race ideals. They have been brought face to face with standards of living that are high and ennobling, and have been made conscious of the severe penalties of social misdoings.

Around them has been created a sentiment of care, pride, protection and chivalry that is every day deepening and widening the distinctions between right and wrong in woman's relationship to man, child and society.

The glow of optimism has coursed so easily through this chapter concerning the work done and attempted by colored women that the importance of it all may seem somewhat exaggerated.

It, perhaps, should be confessed that in spite of the actual good already realized, the club movement is more of a prophecy than a thing accomplished. Colored women organized have succeeded in touching the heart of the race, and for the first time the thrill of unity has been felt. They have set in motion moral forces that are beginning to socialize interests that have been kept apart by ignorance and the spirit of dependence.

They have begun to make the virtues as well as the wants of the colored women known to the American people. They are striving to put a new social value on themselves. Yet their work has just begun. It takes more than five or ten years to effect the social uplift of a whole race of people.

The club movement is well purposed. There is in it a strong faith, an enthusiasm born of love and sympathy, and an ever-increasing intelligence in the ways and means of affecting noble results. It is not a fad. It is not an imitation. It is not a passing sentiment. It is not an expedient, or an experiment. It is rather the force of a new intelligence against the old ignorance. The struggle of an enlightened conscience against the whole brood of social miseries born out of the stress and pain of a hated past.

—*Fannie Barrier Williams*

Bibliography

Fischel, Leslie H., Jr. "Fannie Barrier Williams." *Notable American Women 1607-1950.* Vol. 3. Cambridge: Harvard University Press, 1971.

Loewenberg, Bert James and Ruth Bogin, eds. *Black Women in Nineteenth-Century American Life.* University Park, PA: Pennsylvania State University Press, 1976.

Logan, Rayford W. "Fannie Barrier Williams." *Dictionary of Negro Biography.* Edited by Rayford W. Logan and Michael R. Winston. New York: Norton, 1982.

Mossell, Mrs. N. F. *Work of the Afro-American Woman.* Reprint Edition. New York: Oxford University Press, 1988.

Spear, Allan H. *Black Chicago: The Making of a Negro Elite 1890-1920.* Chicago: University of Chicago Press, 1967.

Williams, Fannie Barrier. "A Northern Woman's Autobiography." *Independent.* July 14, 1904.

———. "What can religion further do to advance the condition of the American Negro?" In *The Dawn of Religious Pluralism.* Edited by R. Seager. 1993.

ANNA JULIA HAYWOOD COOPER
(1858-1964)

Born to a slave woman and her master, Cooper had the enviable opportunity to get an education. She became an activist, scholar, educator, and clubwoman who fought for equality in church (i.e. the Episcopal Church) and society. At the age of sixty-six, she became the fourth African American woman to earn a Ph.D. Because of her extensive teaching and lecturing career, Cooper was the only woman elected into the American Negro Academy. A committed teacher and writer, Dr. Cooper was also appointed the second president of Frelinghuysen University in Washington, D.C.

"The Ethics of the Negro Question"[5]

Where there is no vision, the people perish. Proverbs 29:18.

A nation's greatness is not dependent upon the things it makes and uses. Things without thoughts are mere vulgarities. America can boast her expanse of territory, her gilded domes, her paving stones of silver dollars; but the question of deepest moment in this nation today is its span of the circle of brotherhood, the moral stature of its men and its women, the elevation at which it receives its "vision" into the firmament of eternal truth.

I walked not long since through the national library at Washington. I confess that my heart swelled and my soul was satisfied; for however overpowering to a subdued individual taste the loud scream of color in the grand hallway may be, one cannot but feel that the magnificence of that pile, the loftiness of sentiment and grandeur of execution here adequately and artistically express the best in American life and aspiration. I often sat silent in the gallery under the great dome contemplating the massive pillars that support the encircling arches and musing on the texts traced above the head of each heroic figure: Science, holding in her hand an instrument for the study of Astronomy, proclaims, "The heavens declare the glory of God and the firmament showeth His handiwork." Law

---

[5]Anna J. Cooper, "The Ethics of the Negro Question," an address delivered at the biennial session of the Friends General Conference, Asbury Park, N.J., 5 September 1902. Anna J. Cooper Papers, Manuscript Division, Moorland-Spingard Research Center, Howard University, Washington, D.C.

bears the equal scales with the text: "Of Law there can be no less acknowledged than that her voice is the harmony of the world." Religion stands with firm feet and fearless mien, unequivocally summing up the whole matter: "What doth the Lord require of thee but to do justly, to love mercy and to walk humbly with thy God."

Surely if American civilization should one day have to be guessed from a few broken columns and mutilated statues like the present grandeur of Egypt, Greece and Rome, the antiquarian or the historian who shall in future ages, dig from the dust of centuries this single masterpiece, this artistic expression of a people's aspiration and achievement, will yield ready homage to the greatness of the nation which planned and executed such a monument of architectural genius. "Surely here was a Nation," they must conclude, "whose God was the Lord! A nation whose vision was direct from the Mount of God!"

Whether such an estimate is just, it is our deepest concern to examine. Where there is no vision, the people perish. A nation cannot long survive the shattering of its own ideals. Its doom is already sounded when it begins to write one law on its wall and lives another in its halls. Weighed in the balance and found wanting was not more terribly signed and sealed for the trembling Belshazzar than for us by these handwritings on our walls if they have lost their hold on the thought and conduct of the people.

The civilizations that have flowered and failed in the past did not harvest their fruit and die of old age. A worm was eating at the core even in the heyday of their splendor and magnificence so soon as the grand truths which they professed had ceased to vitalize and vivify their national life.

Rome's religion was pagan, it is true, but for all that it was because Rome had departed from the integrity of her own ideal and was laughing in her sleeve at the gods of her fathers that she found herself emasculated and effete before the virile hordes that plundered and finally superseded her. Thor and Woden had not become to the barbarians a figure to paint a wall or adorn a fountain. Let America beware how she writes on her walls to be seen of men the lofty sentiment *"Give instruction to those who cannot procure it for themselves,"* while she tips a wink at those communities which propose to give for instruction to the poor only that which is wrung from their penury. The vision as pictured on our walls is divine. The American ideal is perfect. A weak or undeveloped race apparently might ask no better fate than the opportunity for maturing under the great wing of this nation and of becoming christianized under its spiritual ministrations.

It is no fault of the Negro that he stands in the United States of America today as the passive and silent rebuke to the Nation's Christianity, the great gulf between its professions and its practices, furnishing the chief ethical element in its politics, constantly pointing with dumb but inexorable fingers to those ideals of our civilization which embody the Nation's highest, truest, and best thought, its noblest and grandest purposes and aspirations.

Amid all the deafening and maddening clamor of expediency and availability among politicians and parties, from tariffs and trusts to free coinage and 16 to 1, from microscopic questions of local sovereignty to the telescopic ones of expansion and imperialism, the Negro question furnishes the one issue that says *ought*. Not what will the party gain by this measure or that, not will this or that experiment bring in larger percentages and cash balances; but who, where, what is my neighbor? Am I my brother's keeper? Are there any limitations or special adaptations of the Golden Rule? If Jesus were among men today, is there a type of manhood veiled wherein, the Divinity whom our civilization calls Captain, would again, coming to His own, be again despised, rejected, because of narrow prejudices and blinding pride of race?

Uprooted from the sunny land of his forefathers by the white man's cupidity and selfishness, ruthlessly torn from all the ties of clan and tribe, dragged against his will over thousands of miles of unknown waters to a strange land among strange peoples, the Negro was transplanted to this continent in order to produce chattels and beasts of burden for a nation "conceived in liberty and dedicated to the proposition that all men are created equal." A nation worshipping as God one who came not to be ministered unto, but to minister; a nation believing in a Savior meek and lowly of heart who, having no where to lay His head, was eyes to the blind, hearing to the deaf, a gospel of hope and joy to the poor and outcast, a friend to all who travail and are heavy laden.

The whites of America revolted against the mother country for a trifling tax on tea, because they were not represented in the body that laid the tax. They drew up their Declaration of Independence, a Magna Carta of human rights, embodying principles of universal justice and equality.

Professing a religion of sublime altruism, a political faith in the inalienable rights of man as man, these jugglers with reason and conscience were at the same moment stealing heathen from their far away homes, forcing them with lash and gun to unrequited toil, making it a penal offense to teach them to read the Word of God, —nay, more were even begetting and breeding mongrels of their own flesh among these helpless creatures and pocketing the guilty increase, the price of their own blood in unholy dollars and cents. Accursed hunger for gold!

To what dost thou not drive mortal breasts! But God did not ordain this nation to reenact the tragedy of Midas and transmute its very heart's core into yellow gold. America has a conscience as well as a pocket-book, and it comes like a pledge of perpetuity to the nation that she has never yet lost the seed of the prophets, men of inner light and unfaltering courage, who would cry aloud and spare not, against the sin of the nation. The best brain and heart of this country have always rung true, and it is our hope today that the petrifying spirit of commercialism which grows so impatient at the Negro question or any other question calculated to weaken the money getting nerve by pulling at the heart and the conscience may still find a worthy protagonist in the reawakened ethical sense of the nation which can take no step backward and which must eventually settle, and settle right this and every question involving the nation's honor and integrity.

It gives me great pleasure to record the historians' testimony to the clear vision and courageous action of the Society of Friends who persisted in keeping alive this ethical sense in some dark days of the past.

"The Quakers have the honor," says Von Holtz of having begun the agitation of the Slavery Question from the moral standpoint earliest and most radically. Thanks to the fiery zeal of some members of this Society, the religious and moral instruction of the slaves and the struggle against any further importation of the Negroes were begun by the close of the 17th Century. By the middle of the 18th Century the emancipation of slaves had gradually become a matter of action by the whole Quaker body. By a resolution of 1774 all members concerned in importing, selling, purchasing, giving or transferring Negroes or other slaves were directed to be excluded from membership or disowned. Two years later this resolution was extended to cover cases of those who delayed to set their slaves free. In February 1790 the Quaker meeting in Philadelphia and the Quakers in New York sent addresses to Congress requesting it to abolish the African slave trade. Certain representatives from the North urged that the petitions of so respectable a body as that of the Quakers in relation to so great a moral evil, were deserving of special consideration. The representatives of the South replied with provoking irony and mercilessly castigated the Quakers. Year after year the Friends came indefatigably with new petitions each time, and each time had to undergo the same scornful treatment. In 1797 the yearly meeting at Philadelphia set forth some special wrongs in a petition, a prominent place in which was occupied by a complaint against the law of North Carolina condemning freed slaves to be sold again. Many Southern delegates in Congress expressed in a bullying fashion their scorn for the tenacity with which these men of earnest faith ever constantly came back again and again to their fruitless struggle. Not in America alone, England also witnessed the faith and works of this body of consistent Christians of unimpaired vision and unwavering determination. The first petition to the House of Commons for the abolition of the Slave Trade and Slavery went up from the Friends, and throughout the long agitation which ensued before that prayer was granted, the Society of Friends took an active and prominent part. Their own dear Whittier has sounded the keynote both of their struggle and its reward:

> "Whatever in love's name is truly done
> To free the bound and lift the fallen one
> Is done to Christ."

And the Master Himself: Inasmuch as ye did it unto one of the least of these my brethren ye did it unto Me.

The colored people of America find themselves today in the most trying period of all their trying history in this land of their trial and bondage. As the trials and responsibilities of the man weigh more heavily than do those of the infant, so the Negro under free labor and cut throat competition today has to vindicate his fitness to survive in face of a colorphobia that heeds neither reason nor religion and a prejudice that shows no guarantor and allows no mitigating circumstances.

In the darkest days of slavery, there were always at the North friends of the oppressed and devoted champions of freedom who would go all lengths to wipe out the accursed stain of human slavery from their country's scutcheon; while in the South the slave's close contact with the master class, mothering them in infancy, caring for them in sickness, sorrow and death, resulted as pulsing touch of humanity must never result, in many warm sympathies and a total destruction of that repulsion to mere color which betokens narrow and exclusive intercourse among provincials.

Today all this is changed. White and black meet as strangers with cold, distant or avowed hostility. The colored domestic who is no longer specially trained for her job or taught to look on it with dignity and appreciation, is barely tolerated in the home till she can do up the supper dishes and get away—when she can go—to the devil if he will have her. The mistress who bemoans her shiftlessness and untidiness does not think of offering her a comfortable room, providing for her social needs and teaching her in the long evenings at home the simple household arts and virtues which our grandmothers found time for. Her vices are set down to the debit account of her freedom, especially if she has attended a public school and learned enough to spell her way through a street ballad. So generally is this the case that if a reform were attempted suddenly, the girl herself of the average type would misunderstand and probably resent it. The condition of the male laborer is even more hopeless. Receiving 50 cents a day or less for unskilled but laborious toil from which wage he boards himself and is expected to keep a family in something better than a "one room cabin," the Negro workman receives neither sympathy nor recognition from his white fellow laborers. Scandinavians, Poles and Hungarians can tie up the entire country by a strike paralyzing not only industry but existence itself, when they are already getting a wage that sounds like affluence to the hungry black man. The union means war to the death against him and the worst of it is he can never be lost in the crowd and have his opprobrium forgotten. A foreigner can learn the language and out-American the American on his own soil. A white man can apply burnt cork and impute his meanness to the colored race as his appointed scapegoat. But the Ethiopian cannot change his skin. On him is laid the iniquity of his whole race and his character is prejudged by formula. Even charity does not study his needs as an individual person but the good that love has planned for him must be labeled and basketed "special" for the Negro. Special kinds of education, special forms of industry, special churches and special places of amusement, special sections of cities during life and special burying grounds in death. White America had created a *terra incognita* in its midst, a strange dark unexplored waste of human souls from which if one essay to speak out an intelligible utterance, so well known is the place of preferment accorded the mirroring of preconceived notions, that instead of being the revelation of a personality and the voice of a truth, the speaker becomes a phonograph and merely talks back what is talked into him. It is no popular task today to voice the black man's woe. It is far easier and safer to say that the wrong is all in him. The American conscience would like a rest from the black man's ghost. It was always an unpalatable subject but preeminently now is the era of good feeling, and self complacency, of commercial omnipotence and military glorification. It seems an impertinence as did the boldness of Nathan when he caught the conscience of the great king at the pinnacle of victorious prosperity with the inglorious seizure of the ewe lamb from a man of no importance. Has not the nation done and suffered enough for the Negro? Is he worth the blood and treasure that have been spilled on his account, the heart ache and bitterness that have racked the country in easing him off its shoulders and out of its conscience? Let us have no more of it. If he is a man let him stand up and prove it. Above all let us have peace. Northern capital is newly wed to Southern industry and the honeymoon must not be disturbed. If southern conventions are ingenious enough to invent a device for disfranchising these unwelcome children of the soil, if it will work, what of it?

On the floor of the most august body in the land, a South Carolina senator said: Yes; we bulldozed and terrorized niggers and we are not ashamed of it. If you had been in our place you would have done the same.

During the slavery agitation Garrison was mobbed in the streets of Boston for advocating abolition; but he kept right on and would be heard. In our day the simplest narrative in just recognition of the Negro meets with cold disfavor and the narrator is generally frozen into silence. A lecturer on the Spanish War attempted as an eye witness and with the aid of stereopticon to tell a Richmond audience of the gallant charge up San Juan Hill and the brave part in it by the 10th Cavalry. His words were met by hisses, his lantern slides destroyed and he was obliged to close his entertainment in darkness and confusion.

A professor in a Southern school who in a magazine article condemned the saturnalia of blood and savagery known as lynching arguing that the Negro while inferior, was yet a man and should be accorded the fundamental rights of a man, lost his position for his frankness and fairness. The Negro is being ground to powder between the upper and the nether-millstones. The South, [is] intolerant of interference from either outside or inside, [and] the North too polite or too busy or too gleeful over the promised handshaking to manifest the most distant concern.

But God is not dead neither doth the ruler of the universe slumber and sleep. As a Nation sows so shall it reap. Men do not gather grapes from thorns or figs from thistles. To sow the wind is to reap the whirlwind.

A little over two years ago while the gentlest and kindest of presidents was making a tour of the South bent only on good will to men with a better understanding and the healing of all sectional rancor and ill feeling, there occurred in almost a stone's throw of where he was for the time being domiciled an outburst of diabolism that would shame a tribe of naked savages. A black wretch was to be burned alive. Without court or jury his unshriveled soul was to be ushered into eternity and the prospect furnished a holiday festival for the country side.

Excursion trains with banners flying were run into the place and eager children were heard to exclaim: We have seen a hanging, we are now going to see a burning!

Human creatures with the behavior of hyenas contended with one another for choice bones of their victim as souvenirs of the occasion. So wanton was the cannibalistic thirst for blood that the Negro preacher who offered the last solace of the Christian to the doomed man was caught in the same mad frenzy and made to share his fate. A shiver ran through the nation at such demoniacal lawlessness. But a cool analysis of the situation elicited from the Attorney General of the United States the legal opinion that the case "probably had no Federal aspects!"

Just one year ago the same gentle people loving president was again acting out his instinct of mingling naturally and democratically with his people. Again lawlessness, this time in the form of a single red handed unreasoning ruffian instead of many but the same mad spirit which puts its own will whether swayed by lurid passion or smoldering hate, on the throne of the majesty of law and of duty, made the nation shudder and bleed by striking down unaccused and untried the great head of the nation. A fact may be mentioned here, which was unquestioned at the time by those around, but which was not often repeated afterwards, that it was the burly arm of a Negro that felled the assassin and dealt the first blows in defense of the stricken president.

I will not here undertake an apology for the short comings of the American Negro. It goes without saying that the black [race] is centuries behind the white race in material, mental and moral development. The American Negro is today but 37 years removed from chatteldom, not long enough surely to ripen the century plant of a civilization. After 250 years of a most debasing slavery, inured to toil but not to thrift, without home, without family ties, without those habits of self-reliant industry by which peoples maintain their struggle for existence, poor, naked, weak, ignorant, degraded even below his pristine state as a savage, the American Negro was at the close of the War of the Rebellion "cut loose" as the slang of the day expressed it, and left to fend for himself. The master class, full of resentment and rage at the humiliations and losses of a grinding war, suffered their old time interest to turn into bitterness or cold indifference and Ku Klux

Klan beatings with re-enslaving black codes became the sorry substitute for the overseer's lash and the auction block.

At this juncture the conscience of the Nation asserted itself and the federal constitution was so amended as to bring under the aegis of national protection these helpless babes whom the exigencies of war had suddenly thrown into the maelstrom of remorseless life.

That they are learning to stem the current there is ground for hope; that they have already made encouraging headway even enemies cannot deny. The Negro's productivity as a free laborer is conceded to be greater than formerly as a slave, and the general productivity of the South, where he constitutes the chief labor element, has since his emancipation more than doubled. Not having inherited the "business bump," his acquisitive principles have received some shocks and many times have been paralyzed and stunted by the insecurity of his property and the disregard of his rights shown by his powerful white neighbors. Such was the case in the collapse of the Freedman's Savings Bank and the recent Wilmington massacre when the accumulations of a lifetime were wantonly swept away and home loving, law abiding citizens were forced into exile, their homes and little savings appropriated by others. In spite of this, however, some headway is [being made] in material wealth and the tax lists in former slave states show a credit of several millions to the descendants of the enslaved.

But all his advancement in wealth and education counts for naught, and ought to count for naught, if it be true, as commonly reported in certain quarters, that the Negro is a moral leper and that sexually he is a dangerous animal in any community. It is said that those astounding exhibitions of fury and force which dizzy the head and sicken the heart of civilized people, are necessary to cower his brutish passions and guard the Holy Grail of Saxon civilization. That the sanctity of pure homes, the inviolability of helpless womanhood must be protected at any cost and that nothing short of devastation and war will suffice. That the beast must be kept under a reign of terror to make him know his place and keep his distance. The iteration and reiteration of sharp and swift retribution for the *"usual"* crime is kept up although the "crime" has been again and again proved to be unusual by more than 90 per cent and statistics of lynchings and their causes have been published from year to year showing every cause for a black man's being lynched from "Being impudent to a white man to Preaching the Gospel of Jesus Christ to a doomed convict," and yet we are told that these things have "probably no *Federal aspects*." Don't you think we would find a way to give them Federal aspects if it were poor old Spain lynching her obstreperous islanders?

Says Prof. Shaler of Harvard:

"When we recall the fact that there are now some five million Negro men in the South and that not one in ten thousand is guilty of crimes against womanhood, we see how imperfect is the basis of this judgment.

We have also to remember," he continues, "that this offense when committed by a Negro is through action of the mob widely publicized while if the offender be a white man it is unlikely to be so well known. I therefore hold to the belief that violence to women is not proved to be a crime common among the blacks. I am inclined to believe that on the whole there is less danger to be apprehended from them in this regard than from an equal body of whites of like social grade."

Such is the calm testimony of an expert sociologist who speaks after scientific investigation and careful analysis.

Is it credible that this race which has under freedom caught so eagerly on the rungs of progress in other respects has so shockingly deteriorated in this all important particular as to reverse all claims to humane consideration which they had won by patient service during long years of slavery?

Have a race of men to whom masters not over kind were not afraid to entrust their helpless women and children while faring forth to rivet the fetters more firmly on their dumb driven bodies and who without one single exception demonstrated remarkable fidelity, trustworthiness, reverence for women and kindness toward children, suddenly become such monsters of lust and vindictiveness that a woman is not safe on the same highway with them?

A noble army of Christian workers and helpers have gone to the South ever since the War, have lived with these people on terms of Christian sympathy and perfect social equality. Have you ever heard of one of these pure minded missionaries who was insulted or outraged and her delicate sensibilities shocked by the unconquerable instincts and baser passions of the men they came to help?

You ask what is the need of today.

How can the Negro be best helped?

What can be done by the man who loves his fellowmen and needs not to be convinced of duties but only to be assured of methods? What is the best means of the Negro's uplift and amelioration?

In a word I answer: Christian Education. This is nothing new you say. That experiment has been tried and tried and there are even those whose faith in the efficacy of this expedient is beginning to wane and we are looking around to see if there be not some other, some quicker and surer way of doing the job. Is it not a mistake to suppose that the same old human laws apply to these people? Is there not after all something within that dark skin not yet dreamt of in our philosophy? Can we seriously take the Negro as a man "endowed by his Creator with certain unalienable rights" such as Life, Liberty, Pursuit of Happiness and the right to grow up, to develop, to reason and to live his life? In short can we hope to apply the key that unlocks all other hearts and by a little human sympathy and putting ourselves in his place learn to understand him and let him understand us? Assuredly, yes!

The black man is not a saint, neither can he be reduced to an algebraic formula. His thirty or forty checkered years of freedom have not transfigured *en masse* ten million slaves into experienced, thrifty, provident, law abiding members of society. There are some criminal, some shiftless, some provokingly intractable and seemingly uneducable classes and individuals among blacks as there are still, unless I am misinformed, also among whites. But our philosophy does not balk at this nor do we lose our belief in the efficacy of Christian teaching and preaching. Turn on the light! Light, more light! There will always be some who do not live up to the light they have. But the Master has left us no alternative. Ye are the light of the world.

We cannot draw lines where He recognized none. We cannot falter so long as there is a human soul in need of the light. We owe it, and owe it independently of the worthiness or unworthiness of that soul. Does any one question that Jesus' vision would have pierced to the heart and marrow of our national problem, and what would be His teaching in America today as to *who is my* neighbor?

For after all the Negro Question in America today is the white man's problem—nay, it is humanity's problem. The past, in which the Negro was mostly passive, the white man active, has ordained that they shall be neighbors, permanently and unavoidably. To colonize or repatriate the blacks on African soil or in any other continent is physically impossible even if it were generally desired, and no sane man talks of deportation now except as an exploded chimera. For weal or for woe the lots of these two are united, indissolubly, eternally. Thinking people on both sides are convinced that each race needs the other. The Negro is the most stable and reliable factor today in American industry. Patient and docile as a laborer, conservative, law abiding, totally ignorant of the anarchistic, socialistic radicalism and nihilism of other lands, the American Negro is capable of contributing not only of his brawn and sinew but also from brain and character a much needed element in American civilization, and here is his home. The only home he has ever known. His blood had mingled with the bluest and the truest on every battlefield that checkers his country's history. His sweat and his toil have, more than any others, felled its forest, drained its swamps, plowed its fields and opened up its highways and waterways.

From the beginning was he here, a strong, staunch and unwilling worker and helper. His traditions, his joys, his sorrows are all here. He has imbibed the genius and spirit of its institutions, growing with their growth, gathering hope and strength with their strength and depth. Alien neither in language, religion nor customs, the educated colored American is today the most characteristic growth of the American soil, its only genuinely indigenous development. He is the most American of Americans for he alone has no other civilization than what America has to offer. Its foibles are his foibles. Its youthful weaknesses and pompous self-confidence are all found here imitated or originating, as between sitter and portrait. Here in the warp and woof of his character are photographed and writ large even the grotesque caricatures, the superficial absurdities and social excrescences of "Get-rich-quick" and "Pike's Peak-or-bust" America. Nor is it too much to hope that America's finer possibilities and promise also prefigure his ultimate struggle and achievement in evolving his civilization. As the character of Uncle Tom is rated the most unique in American literature, so the plantation melodies and corn songs form the most original contribution to its music. Homogeneous or not, the national web is incomplete without the African thread that glints and ripples through it from the beginning.

In a description of the Rough Riders' charge on the Block House at El Caney a recent columnist has this to say: "Over against the scene of the Rough Riders set the picture of the 10th U.S. Cavalry—the famous colored regiment side by side with Roosevelt's men they fought—these black men. Scarce used to freedom themselves they are dying that Cuba may be free. Their marksmanship was magnificent, their courage was superb. They bore themselves like veterans and gave proof positive that from nature's congenitally peaceful, carefree and playful, military discipline and an inspiring cause can make soldiers worthy to rank with Caesar's legions or Cromwell's Army."

Mr. Bryce in his study of the American Commonwealth says: "The South is confronted by a peculiar and menacing problem in the presence of a mass of Negroes larger than was the whole population of the union in 1800, persons who though they are legally and industrially members of the nation are still virtually an alien element, unabsorbed and unabsorbable."

A similar judgment was passed by the gifted author of the Bonnie Briar Bush in his "Impressions of America" who thought that the Negroes were like the Chinese in constituting the sole exception to an otherwise homogeneous population. This misapprehension is common. The explanation obvious. Social cleavage in America is strictly along the lines of color only. Jim Crow cars are not for the unwashed of all races, not for the drunken rowdy and the degraded, ignorant, vicious rabble,—not even for the pauper classes who cannot pay for superior comforts in traveling. Quite simply the only question is, "What is the tinge of pigment in your epidermal cells, or in the epidermis of your mother's grandmother?" The colored man or woman of culture and refinement is shoved into the same box with the filthy and the degraded no matter what his ability to pay for and his desire to secure better accommodations. He cannot eat a sandwich in one of the "white" hotels nor set down his luggage in one of their waiting rooms at a railway station. The result is that students of American society like Bryce and Ian McClaren never see or suspect the existence of intelligent aspiring thinking men and women of color in the midst of this social system. Men and women are pondering its adjustment, chafing under its rude and crude incongruities, and gathering strength no doubt to snap asunder one of these days its tissue beltings and couplings.

The American traveler sees and can account for only the black porter and colored boot black, the waiter and barber and scullion. And these only as automatons in a passing show. He cannot know them as human beings capable of human emotions, human aspirations, human suffering, defeats and triumphs. Our traveler is then introduced by design to the criminal records wherein the Negro, because the poorest, weakest, least shielded class in the community figures, of course, at his full strength. Taken for a drive through what would in New York or Philadelphia constitute a slum appealing only to the Christ spirit in good men to send out their light and their love, to start a mission to provide wholesome living conditions for healthy living and clean thinking. But here both the Priest and the Levite pass by on the other side. The missions are to seek and to save the lost who are already fortunate enough to be born white.

Come unto me all ye *whites* who are heavy laden. The Poor (*whites*) have the Gospel preached unto them. Suffer the little *white* children to come unto Me! for of such is the kingdom of heaven. Love the Lord thy God with all thy heart, soul, and strength and thy *white* neighbor as thyself!

But these Negro quarters, these submerged souls, this "darkest America"—Ah, this is our terrible "Problem"! This mass that menaces Anglo Saxon civilization "unabsorbed and unabsorbable!"

But this time our traveler is wholly inoculated. It is truly a *peculiar* problem to be sure. He does not quite see how the question can be solved. He is disposed with Mr. Bryce to trust much to the *vis medicatrix naturae* and to hope that somehow, somewhere, and somewhen the Sphinx will answer its own riddle, and yet I am no pessimist regarding the future of my people in America. God reigns and the good will prevail. It must prevail. While these are times that try men's souls, while a weak and despised people are called upon to vindicate their right to exist in the face of a race of hard, jealous, intolerant, all-subduing instincts, while the iron of their wrath and bitter prejudice cuts into the very bones and marrow of my people, I have faith to believe that God has not made us for naught and He has not ordained to wipe us out from the face of the earth. I believe, moreover, that America is the land of destiny for the descendants of the enslaved race, that here in the house of their bondage are the seeds of promise for their ultimate enfranchisement and development. This I maintain in full knowledge of what at any time may be wrought by a sudden paroxysm of rage caused by the meaningless war whoop of some obscure politicians such as the rally word of "Negro domination" which at times deafens and bemuddles all ears.

Negro domination! Think of it! The great American eagle, soaring majestically sunward, eyes ablaze with conscious power, suddenly screaming and shivering in fear of a little mouse colored starling, which he may crush with the smallest finger of his great claw. Yet this mad shriek is allowed to unbridle the worst passions of wicked men, to stifle and seal up the holiest instincts of good men. In dread of domination by a race whom they outnumber five to one, with every advantage in civilization, wealth, culture, with absolute control of every civil and military nerve center, Anglo Saxon America is in danger of forgetting how to deal justly, to love mercy, to walk humbly with its God.

In the old days, I am told that two or three Negroes gathered together in supplication and prayer, were not allowed to present their petition at the throne of Grace without having it looked over and revised by a white man for fear probably that white supremacy and its "peculiar" system might be endangered at the Court of the Almighty by these faltering lips and uncultured tongues! The same fear cowers the white man's heart to-day. He dare not face his God with a lie on his lips.

These "silent sullen peoples" (so called because sympathetically unknown and unloved) are the touchstone of his conscience. America with all her wealth and power, with her pride of inventions and mastery of the forces of nature, with all her breadth of principles and height of ideals, will never be at peace with herself till this question is settled and settled right. It is the conscience in her throat that is "unabsorbed and unabsorbable!"

The despairing wail of Macbeth's blood that stained the queen in all her gilded misery at the moment of her sickening success, is profoundly and everlastingly true: "Better be that which we destroy!" It is in the power of this mighty nation to turn upon us in a St. Bartholomew's Massacre and in one bloody day reckon us among the extinct races of history. A governor of Georgia is reported to have declared that "a dead Negro in the back yard" was his suggestion for settling this question, and another has recommended that a reward be offered for every one so disposed of.

But the Negro's blood on this great Nation becomes a heavier burden than the Negro's education and Christianization. His extermination will weigh more than all the weight of his uplift and regeneration. A nation's dishonor is a far more serious problem to settle than the extension of a brother's hand and a Christian's grip by a favored race bearing the torch, as a sacred trust from the Source of All light to lead, enlighten and lift. Ye who have the light *owe it* to the least of these my brethren.

> "Is your God a wooden fetish
> To be hidden out of sight,
> That his block eyes may not see you
> Do the thing that is not right?
> But the Destinies think not so;
> To their judgment chamber lone
> Comes no voice of popular clamor
> There Fame's trumpet is not blown

But their silent way they keep.
Where empires towered that were not just,
Lo the skulking wild fox scratches
in a little heap of dust."

Thus it were well for great powers to ponder. The right to rule entails the obligation to rule right. Righteousness and Righteousness only exalteth a nation and the surest guarantee of the perpetuity of our institutions is alliance with God's eternal forces that make for rightness and justness in His world.

As for the Negro there can be no doubt that these trials are God's plan for refinement of the good gold to be found in him. The dross must be purged out. There is no other way than by fire. If the great Refiner sees that a stronger, truer, purer racial character can be evolved from His crucible by heating the furnace seven times, He can mean only good.

With hearty earnestness the million and half colored boys and girls in the public schools South repeat on June 14 the salute to their country's flag: "I pledge allegiance to my flag and to the country for which it stands." I commend these boys and girls to you as staunch and loyal a yeomanry as any country can boast. They are Americans, true and bona fide citizens—not by adoption or naturalization but by birth and blood incontestable.

Whatever may be problematical about us, our citizenship is beyond question. We have owned no other allegiance, have bowed before no other sovereign. Never has a hand of ours been raised either in open rebellion or secret treachery against the Fatherland.

Our proudest aspiration has been but to serve her, the crown of our glory to die for her. We were born here through no choice of our own or of our ancestors; we cannot expatriate ourselves, even if we would. When the wild forces of hate and unholy passion are unleashed to run riot against us, our hearts recoil not more in dread of such a catastrophe for ourselves than in grief and shame at the possibility of such a fall and such a failure for our country's high destiny. It is inconceivable that we should not feel the unnatural prejudice environing us and our children. It is like stones between our teeth and like iron in the marrow of our bones. If at such times we cannot sing America it is not because of any treason lurking in our hearts. Our harps are hung on the willows and in the Babylon of our sorrow we must sit down and weep. But no dynamite plots are hatching amongst us. No vengeful uprising brewing. We are a song loving people and that song of all songs we would love to sing, and we challenge the lustiest singer to sing it more lustily and more eloquently than we. But when the wound is festering and the heart is so sore we can only suffer and be silent, [we] pray God to change the hearts of our misguided countrymen and help them to see the things that make for righteousness. . . .

—*Anna Julia Cooper*

Bibliography

Baker-Fletcher, Karen. *A Singing Something: Womanist Reflections on Anna Julia Cooper*. New York: Crossroad Publishing Company, 1994.

Bogin, Ruth and Bert Loewenberg, eds. *Black Women in Nineteenth-Century American Life: Their Words, Their Thoughts, Their Feelings*. University Park: Pennsylvania State University Press, 1985.

Cooper, Anna Julia. *L'Attitude de las France a l' egard de l' esclavage pendant la Revolution*. Paris: Imprimerie de la Cour d'Appel, 1925. This was Cooper's main doctoral thesis. Translated by Frances Richardson Keller as *Slavery and the French Revolutionists (1788-1805)*. Lewiston, N.Y.: Edwin Mellen Press, 1988.

———. *Le Pelerinage de Charlemagne*. Paris: A. Lahure, Imprimeur-Editeur, 1925. Introduction by the Abbe Felix Klein. This is Cooper's secondary thesis for the doctorate at the Sorbonne.

———. *The Third Step (Autobiographical)*. n.p. n.d.

———. *A Voice from the South: By a Black Woman from the South*. New York: Oxford University Press, 1988. Reprint of the original 1892 edition with a foreword by Henry Louis Gates, Jr. and an introduction by Mary Helen Washington.

Gabel, Leona Christine. *From Slavery to the Sorbonne and Beyond: The Life and Writings of Anna J. Cooper*. Northampton, Mass.: Department of History of Smith College, 1982.

Harley, Sharon. "Anna J. Cooper: A Voice for Black Women." In *The Afro-American Woman: Struggles and Images*. Edited by Sharon Harley and Rosalyn Terborg-Penn. Port Washington, N.Y.: Kennikat Press, 1978.

Hutchinson, Louise Daniel. *Anna J. Cooper, A Voice from the South*. Washington, D.C.: Smithsonian Press, 1981.

Sewall, May Wright. *World's Congress of Representative Women*. Chicago, 1893.

Shockley, Ann Allen. *Afro-American Women Writers, 1746-1933*. Boston: G.K. Hall, 1988.

The Anna Julia Cooper Papers. Moorland-Spingarn Research Center. Howard University. Washington, D.C.

Who's Who in Colored America. 6th ed. Brooklyn: Thomas Yenser, 1942.

IDA B. WELLS-BARNETT

(1862-1931)

Wells-Barnett is known for her courageous drive to end lynchings in this nation. She took her protests abroad and to the White House, presenting a petition to demand justice from President McKinley. Her fearless stance through her writings and actions against the heinous mob executions spotlighted the dark underside of a young "democratic" nation and coalesced black outrage into meaningful but peaceful resistance.

"Lynching, Our National Crime"[6]

The lynching record for a quarter of a century merits the thoughtful study of the American people. It presents three salient facts:

First: Lynching is color line murder.

Second: Crimes against women is the excuse, not the cause.

Third: It is a national crime and requires a national remedy.

Proof that lynching follows the color line is to be found in the statistics which have been kept for the past twenty-five years. During the few years preceding this period and while frontier lynch law existed, the executions showed a majority of white victims. Later, however, as law courts and authorized judiciary extended into the far West, lynch law rapidly abated and its white victims became few and far between.

Just as the lynch law regime came to a close in the West, a new mob movement started in the South. This was wholly political, its purpose being to suppress the colored vote by intimidation and murder. Thousands of assassins banded together under the name of Ku Klux Klans, "Midnight Raiders," "Knights of the Golden Circle," etc., spread a reign of terror, by beating, shooting and killing colored people by the thousands. In a few years, the purpose was accomplished and the black vote was suppressed. But mob murder continued.

From 1882, in which year 52 were lynched, down to the present, lynching has been along the color line. Mob murder increased yearly until in 1892 more than 200 victims were lynched and statistics show that 3,284 men, women and children have been put to death in this quarter of a century. During the last ten years, from 1899 to 1908 inclusive, the number lynched was 959. Of this number 102 were white while the colored victims numbered 857. No other nation, civilized or savage, burns its criminals; only under the stars and stripes is the human holocaust possible. Twenty-eight human beings burned at the stake, one of them a woman and two of them children, is the awful indictment against American civilization—the gruesome tribute which the nation pays to the color line.

Why is mob murder permitted by a Christian nation? What is the cause of this awful slaughter? This question is answered almost daily—always the same shameless falsehood that "Negroes are lynched to protect womanhood." Standing before a Chautauqua assemblage, John Temple Graves, at once champion of lynching and apologist for lynchers, said: "The mob stands to-day as the most potent bulwark between the women of the South and such a carnival of crime as would infuriate the world and pre-

---

[6]*Proceedings of the National Negro Conference, 1909* (New York: Arno Press and the *New York Times*, 1969), 174-179.

cipitate the annihilation of the Negro race." This is the never varying answer of lynchers and their apologists. All know that it is untrue. The cowardly lyncher revels in murder, then seeks to shield himself from public execration by claiming devotion to woman. But truth is mighty and the lynching record discloses the hypocrisy of the lyncher as well as his crime.

The Springfield, Illinois, mob rioted for two days, the militia of the entire state was called out, two men were lynched, hundreds of people driven from their homes, all because a white woman said a Negro had assaulted her. A mad mob went to the jail, tried to lynch the victim of her charge and, not being able to find him proceeded to pillage and burn the town and to lynch two innocent men. Later, after the police had found that the woman's charge was false, she published a retraction; the indictment was dismissed and the intended victim discharged. But the lynched victims were dead. Hundreds were homeless and Illinois was disgraced.

As a final and complete refutation of the charge that lynching is occasioned by crimes against women, a partial record of lynchings is cited; 285 persons were lynched for causes as follow:

Unknown cause, 92; no cause, 10; race prejudice, 49; miscegenation, 7; informing, 12; making threats, 11; keeping saloon, 3; practicing fraud, 5; practicing voodooism, 2; bad reputation, 8; unpopularity, 3; mistaken identity, 5; using improper language, 3; violation of contract, 1; writing insulting letter, 2; eloping, 2; poisoning horse, 1; poisoning well, 2; by white caps, 9; vigilantes, 14; Indians, 1; moonshining, 1; refusing evidence, 2; political causes, 5; disputing, 1; disobeying quarantine regulations, 2; slapping a child, 1; turning state's evidence, 3; protecting a Negro, 1; to prevent giving evidence, 1; knowledge of larceny, 1; writing letter to white woman, 1; asking white woman to marry, 1; jilting girl, 1; having smallpox, 1; concealing criminal, 2; threatening political exposure, 1; self-defenses, 6; cruelty, 1; insulting language to woman, 5; quarreling with white man, 2; colonizing Negroes, 1; throwing stones, 1; quarreling, 1; gambling, 1.

Is there a remedy, or will the nation confess that it cannot protect its protectors at home as well as abroad? Various remedies have been suggested to abolish the lynching infamy, but year after year, the butchery of men, women and children continues in spite of plea and protest. Education is suggested as a preventive, but it is as grave a crime to murder an ignorant man as it is a scholar. True, few educated men have been lynched, but the hue and cry once started stops at no bounds, as was clearly shown by the lynchings in Atlanta, and in Springfield, Illinois.

Agitation, though helpful, will not alone stop the crime. Year after year statistics are published, meetings are held, resolutions are adopted and yet lynchings go on. Public sentiment does measurably decrease the sway of mob law, but the irresponsible blood-thirsty criminals who swept through the streets of Springfield, beating an inoffensive law-abiding citizen to death in one part of the town, and in another torturing and shooting to death a man who, for threescore years, had made a reputation for honesty, integrity and sobriety, had raised a family and had accumulated property, were not deterred from their heinous crimes by either education or agitation.

The only certain remedy is an appeal to law. Lawbreakers must be made to know that human life is sacred and that every citizen of this country is first a citizen of the United States and secondly a citizen of the state in which he belongs. This nation must assert itself and defend its federal citizenship at home as well as abroad. The strong arm of the government must reach across state lines whenever unbridled lawlessness defies state laws and must give to the individual citizen under the Stars and Stripes the same measure of protection which it gives to him when he travels in foreign lands.

Federal protection of American citizenship is the remedy for lynching. Foreigners are rarely lynched in America. If, by mistake, one is lynched, the national government quickly pays the damages. The recent agitation in California against the Japanese compelled this nation to recognize that federal power must yet assert itself to protect the nation from the treason of sovereign states. Thousands of American citizens have been put to death and no President has yet raised his hand in effective protest, but a simple insult to a native of Japan was quite sufficient to stir the government at Washington to prevent the threatened wrong. If the government has power to protect a foreigner from insult, certainly it has power to save a citizen's life.

The practical remedy has been more than once suggested in Congress. Senator Gallinger of New Hampshire in a resolution introduced in Congress called for an investigation "with the view of ascertaining whether there is a remedy for lynching which congress may apply." The Senate Committee has under consideration a bill drawn by A.E. Pillsbury, formerly Attorney-General of Massachusetts, providing for federal prosecution of lynchers in cases where the state fails to protect citizens or foreigners. Both of these resolutions indicate that the attention of the nation has been called to this phase of the lynching question.

As a final word, it would be a beginning in the right direction if this conference can see its way clear to establish a bureau for the investigation and publication of the details of every lynching, so that the public could know that an influential body of citizens has made it a duty to give the widest publicity to the facts in each case; that it will make an effort to secure expressions of opinion all over the country against lynching for the sake of the country's fair name; and lastly, but by no means least, to try to influence the daily papers of the country to refuse to become accessory to mobs either before or after the fact. Several of the greatest riots and most brutal burnt offerings of the mobs have been suggested and incited by the daily papers of the offending community. If the newspaper which suggests lynching in its accounts of an alleged crime, could be held legally as well as morally responsible for reporting that "threats of lynching were heard"; or, "It is feared that if the guilty one is caught, he will be lynched"; or, "There were cries of 'lynch him,' and the only reason the threat was not carried out was because no leader appeared," a long step toward a remedy will have been taken.

In a multitude of counsel there is wisdom. Upon the grave question presented by the slaughter of innocent men, women and children there should be an honest, courageous conference of patriotic, law-abiding citizens anxious to punish crime promptly, impartially and by due process of law, also to make life, liberty, and property secure against mob rule.

Time was when lynching appeared to be sectional, but now it is national—a blight upon our nation, mocking our laws and disgracing our Christianity. "With malice toward none but with charity for all" let us undertake the work of making the "law of the land" effective and supreme upon every foot of American soil—a shield to the innocent and to the guilty punishment swift and sure.

—Ida B. Wells-Barnett

Bibliography

Duster, Alfreda M., ed. *Crusade for Justice: The Autobiography of Ida B. Wells*. Chicago: University of Chicago Press, 1970.

Holt, Thomas C. "The Lonely Warrior: Ida B. Wells-Barnett and the Struggle for Black Leadership." In *Black Leaders of the Twentieth Century*. Edited by John Hope Franklin and August Meier. Urbana: University of Illinois Press, 1982.

Lerner, Gerda. "Early Community Work of Black Club Women." *Journal of Negro History*. 59(April 1954):158-167.

Neverdon-Morton, Cynthia. *Afro-American Women of the South and the Advancement of the Race, 1895-1925*. Knoxville: University of Tennessee Press, 1989.

Ochiai, Akiko. "Ida B. Wells and Her Crusade for Justice: An African American Woman's Testimonial Autobiography." *Soundings* 75(Summer-Fall, 1992):365-381.

Sterling, Dorothy. *Black Foremothers: Three Lives*. Old Westbury, N.Y.: Feminist Press, 1979.

Thompson, Mildred. *Ida B. Wells-Barnett: An Exploratory Study of an American Black Woman, 1893-1930*. Vol. 16 of *Black Women in United States History*. Edited by Darlene Clark-Hine. Brooklyn: Carlson Publishing Co., 1990.

Townes, Emilie M. "Because God Gave Her Vision: The Religious Impulse of Ida B. Wells-Barnett." In *Spirituality and Social Responsibility*. Edited by Rosemary Keller. Nashville: Abingdon Press, 1993.

———. "Ida B. Wells-Barnett: An Afro-American Prophet." *Christian Century* 106(March 15, 1989):285-286.

———. *Womanist Justice, Womanist Hope*. Atlanta: Scholars Press, 1993.

Tucker, David M. "Miss Ida B. Wells and Memphis Lynching." *Phylon* 32(Summer 1971).

ADDIE WAITES HUNTON
(1866-1943)

Hunton was a social activist and writer who maximized every opportunity to confront the bastions of sexism and racism. She was a club woman who was committed to the work of the National Association of Colored Women (NACW) and the YWCA. Educated in the United States and Germany, she served the Black troops in France during World War I through the YWCA. Also, Hunton served the NAACP as field secretary, observed and wrote about the injustices of the United States occupation of Haiti, and helped organize the 1927 Pan-African Congress in New York City.

"Negro Womanhood Defended"[7]

Out of the ever vexing and mysterious hydra-headed evil we name the "race problem," there seems to have grown of late a sentiment, if you will, whose particular function it is to magnify the moral weakness of Negro womanhood. While her character had been assailed from without many times, it remained for a Judas Iscariot, in an awful and sinful malediction, to make the assertion that "not only are ninety percent of the Negro women of America unchaste, but the social degradation of our freedwomen is without parallel in all modern civilization." This assertion, which the author himself unconsciously repudiates before he closes his foul tirade, seems to have given this phase of the "problem" a sudden boom, and to have made a delightfully new and inviting theme for our many enemies and harping critics. Unwarned, unasked, with no sense of delicacy for her feelings, the Negro woman has been made the subject of an increasing and unmerciful criticism. To her, at this time, is being charged every weakness of the race, even though this weakness may have been common to humanity since the days of Adam. Everywhere, her moral defects are being portrayed by her enemies; sometimes, veiled in hypocritical pity, and again, in language bitter and unrelenting.

In taking up the gauntlet of defense, we desire to have it understood that we are in no sense an apologist. We are neither unconscious or unmindful of our shortcomings; we are simply asking now that, in the clear light of truth and justice, her case be given a hearing by all who are inter-

---

[7] *Voice of the Negro* 1/7(July 1904):280-282.

ested in moral and social problems, and who value the principles of justice, freedom and fraternity, or even by those who regard all humanity as something above the common clod. This hearing the Negro woman claims as her right upon the basis that whatever is a benefit or injury to one, that he has a right to concern himself about.

When come these base aspersions to blight and dwarf the spirit of the Negro woman? Who in all this land can be so forgetful of her service and servitude as to seek to crush her already wounded and bleeding soul? Wounded by the violence and shame forced upon her in times when she had no voice to speak her woe; bleeding because of the constant irritation of these wounds by those who, while spending their best energies to vilify her to the world, are at the same time ever secretly seeking to make these villifications true; she asks, Whence comes all this talk about the immorality of the Negro woman?

It is a fact to be noted that most of the articles that bear upon this subject are written not by those who have made a systematic and careful study of the question from every point of view, but rather by those whose conclusions are born of their own limited experiences with and observations of one class or kind of Negro women. The statement has been made often of late that there are different classes of Negro women as there are different classes of other women, but it seems so difficult for some to grasp this idea that it will bear further repetition. It is also a fact that there is a wide gulf—which seemingly grows wider—between the white people of the South and the better class of colored people. They are as Jew and Samaritan, so that those who write most about the moral degradation of the Negro woman know little or nothing of the best element of our women who are quietly and unobtrusively working out the salvation of the race. Because the Negro women with whom they come in contact exhibit none of those higher qualities that are based upon virtue, it is assumed that these women are typical of all Negro women, and, upon this assumption, an attempt is made to prove to the shame of all, a wholesale immorality.

But what of the Negro woman herself? Of her condition and environments? Any argument that does not take more than passing note of the heritage of shame with which she found herself burdened when emerging from slavery, or that does not take more than a mere glance at the very peculiar environment, is at best but erroneous.

For two centuries the Negro woman was forced by cruelty too diverse and appalling to mention to submit her body to those who barter for it. She was voiceless, and there was no arm lifted in her defense. And yet, there is hardly a daughter of a slave mother who has not heard of the sublime and heroic soul of some maternal ancestor that went home to the God that gave it rather than live a life of enforced infamy. There is an unwritten and an almost unmentionable history of the burdens of those soul-trying times when, to bring profit to the slave trade and to satisfy the base desires of a stronger hand, the Negro woman was the subject of compulsory immorality. Not only did she emerge from that dark period crushed by an experience more bitter than death, but her teachers had given her a false conception of the marriage vow and its sanctity. That slavery might be made as profitable as possible, masters reserved the right to join or separate their slaves at will. Prostitution was not only encouraged but fostered.

Stepping suddenly out of the darkness of slavery, the Negro woman was bewildered by the temptations and trials awaiting her. In many instances, they were no less intense than those to which she had been subjected in the past. It is not strange that those whose prey she had been for so long should have followed her into her new environments; and, as they had used cruel force when it was their right, now that this is no longer possible, should seek to subvert her with glittering baubles. With a blighted past, no fireside training nor home life, driven to and fro at will in a world of poverty and ignorance, it would have been strange and unusual had she not, in many cases, fallen by the wayside.

The wages paid the Negro laboring woman are so paltry as to scarcely provide for her the necessities of life. One writer has said "the severest poverty is unfavorable to morality." Then, where, as in this case, the tempter stands on every side, it calls for no ordinary strength to resist his allurements. That versatile and soulful writer of the race in "The Souls of Black Folk" has given a chapter entitled "Of the Coming of John." Therein is a picture of the temptation which forces itself upon the average comely Negro servant girl, and therein, too, is portrayed the tragedy that comes when the Negro man dares raise his hand in the defense of his own. And yet in the face of all this ignominy—all this immorality and cruel oppression—she has staggered up through the ages ladened with the double burden of excessive maternal care and physical toil, and she has, while climbing, thrown off much of the dross and become more chastened and purified, conforming herself as fast as possible to the demand for upright Christian living. To all who are fairminded and unprejudiced, it must be certain that nothing can stay the tide of her progress in its onward flow.

It is quite likely that too much attention has hitherto been given to theorizing on this grave question, while real study, friendly fairness and appreciation of her progress have found no place in the arguments. This fact alone might be sufficient to discourage her and blight her hopes did she not inherit that rare faith of her ancestors who trusted so implicitly in God. Let those who desire to write of her from a moral standpoint hereafter realize the justice and wisdom of studying her in her best as well as her worst condition.

Immorality and thrift do not mate very well, and in spite of all accusations, the Negro woman has been the motive power in whatever has been accomplished by the race. She early realized that the moral and conservative qualities of a race reside in its womanhood, and with this realization came a longing and a reaching after a virtuous home-life; hence, we have thousands of homes dotting this Southland, some mere cottages, others more pretentious residences, but all are citadels of purity and virtue, presided over by women of intelligence and housewifely care. The beneficent influence of these homes is felt in every community, and it will be appreciated more largely by coming generations than it is now possible to realize. The Negro woman is rightly making her first effort for purity and truth at her own fireside. By her thrift she has accumulated property, real and personal, to the value of more than $700,000,000. She has helped to raise nearly $14,000,000 for the education of her children. She has educated more than 25,000 teachers of her own race, and all of this, in her hampered condition, in less than a half century. With her deeper interest in her people, her larger knowledge of their needs, with the culture and character that education gives, she is constantly at work for the uplift of her race.

Finally, we are confronting new conditions which make stern demands upon the wisdom and conscience of both races. Let it not be forgotten that the high virtue of the South has its basis on the souls and bodies of Negro women; therefore, it is now time that Southern chivalry, which ever proclaims its right to "keep pure and undefiled the spirit that worships at the family shrine," should extend itself to the protection of the Negro man who seeks to establish the same principle for his home. In the light of Christianity all women must be protected if for no other reason than that they are akin to the Christ-mother. Until this is done, it would, at least, be charitable to leave the discussion of the morality of the Negro woman to those who are earnestly laboring for her uplift.

—Addie Hunton

Bibliography

Dannett, Sylvia G. L. *Profiles of Negro Womanhood*. Vol. 2. Yonkers: Educational Heritage, 1966.

Davis, Elizabeth Lindsay. *Lifting as They Climb*. Washington, D.C.: The National Association of Colored Women, 1933.

Giddings, Paula. *When and Where I Enter*. New York: Morrow, 1984.

Hunton, Addie. *William Alphaeus Hunton*. New York: Association Press, 1938.

———. and Kathryn M. Johnson. *Two Colored Women with the American Expeditionary Forces*. Brooklyn: Brooklyn Eagle Press, [1920].

Hutson, Jean Blackwell. "Addie D. Waites Hunton." *Dictionary of American Negro Biography*. Eds. Rayford W. Logan and Michael R. Winston. New York: Norton, 1982.

———. "Addie D. Waites Hunton." *Notable American Women, 1607-1950*. Vol. 2. Cambridge: Harvard University Press, 1971.

"The Pan African Congress." *Crisis* 17 (April 1919):271-74.

Wesley, Charles Harris. *The History of the National Association of Colored Women*. Washington, D.C.: National Association of Colored Women, 1984.

SEPTIMA POINSETTE CLARK
(1898-1987)

Septima Poinsette Clark was a teacher and advocate of equal rights. She is best known for her ground-breaking work in literacy training in citizenship schools. Septima defied the purveyors of personal and institutional racism as she prepared the black electorate for their emergence upon the political scene. In the decade that preceded the civil rights movement, she taught at the Highlander Folk School, which was an incubator and training center for social change and civil disobedience. Septima's workshops prepared the peaceful warriors who would form the ranks of the protestors of the sixties. One famous student, Rosa Parks, stepped into history when she put her lesson in civil disobedience into use on a segregated bus.

Excerpt from *Echo in My Soul*[8]

And now too quickly has drawn to its last days the year that marked in my life the ending of one important epoch and the beginning of another that I trust will be of even greater significance.

The Highlander at Monteagle as we knew it and loved it, I have no doubt, is finished.[9] In relaxed moments few and far between when I have occa-

---

[8]Septima Poinsette Clark with LeGette Blythe, *Echo in My Soul* (New York: E.P. Dutton & Co., Inc., 1962), chap. 20.

[9]*Echo in My Soul*, 225-226. "Highlander Folk School was chartered by the State of Tennessee as a non-profit corporation without stockholders or owners as such under Tennessee law. There is a Tennessee law that provides for the revoking of the charter of a non-profit corporation in a legal action brought by the state. In the case of Highlander this action to revoke the charter was brought through the local District Attorney General, the lawyers pointed out, at the instigation of the legislative committee which accused the school of operating in violation of Tennessee segregation laws and policies. In this action it was alleged also that Highlander had violated the provisions of its charter by engaging in commercial activities by offering for sale on its premises candies, chewing gum, razor blades and such things and had sold or exchanged these items, including soft drinks and beer, to the school's students. Highlander, let me say here, insisted that it was not selling these things commercially but that since Negroes attending the school were not permitted to go into local establishments to purchase beer, soft drinks and other items, Highlander furnished them on a rotating fund basis. But it was determined that this was commercial activity in violation of the provisions, and so the state that granted the charter judicially revoked it. And when the Tennessee

sion to recall the years spent there and the friends met and appreciated and enjoyed, I too, like Myles and the others, am deeply moved. The hills, the woods, the little lake beside which sits the house that was so unfairly taken from him, the simple but hospitable buildings—I can close my eyes and my ears and instantly I am there in the Cumberlands—are, I am afraid, a turned page in my life's book. I wonder if ever again I shall experience the deep joy of going with some friend along the path through the woods and out into the pasture and over the barbed wire fence to that corner of the campus where suddenly and precipitately the land falls away a thousand feet into a great gorge and one may stand in awe and look upon a billion years of God's own sculpture. Perhaps I would not be welcomed were I to return to Monteagle's Highlander; I don't know, and I do not wish to sound bitter, for I am not. But I do know that no person or sovereign commonwealth will ever be able to take our Highlander from me. Nor will anyone ever be able to erase from the eternal record its accomplishments in the long and uphill struggle toward the fair day of universal brotherhood.

I shall never forget those beloved Highlander folk. I have but to close my eyes and I am in the charming little cottage on the edge of the campus with May Justus, the writer, and Vera McCampbell, the school teacher. In the same way I am instantly with Mom Horton, Myles' mother, and her sister Aunt Arby Hurst. With them I made many a special trip through the woods to see the rhododendrons and the goldenrods, and to pick turnip greens in the pasture. Back we trudged to one of their homes for a cup of tea and cookie or some special delicacy. And the Marlowes, too, J.D. and Mikii, and their two sons, who invited me to a feast of rabbit or squirrel or a mulligan stew. The Cumberlands have need to be proud of J.D., a skilled carpenter and an experienced hunter. The renovated cabins, beautifully shellacked tables and well-built chimneys show his handiwork on the Highlander grounds.

Then there is Mattie Church, a great Christian woman who fashioned with her own hands a lovely quilt for me; there is the Hargiss family with three handsome well mannered boys born and bred on Highlander's acres. And Dosie Church, our cook from 1955 to 1959, I shall always remember too, for though she testified against us for the state, I can never forget the spark of kindness she showed me and my granddaughter during the illness and death of my daughter-in-law. I shared with her the contents of my son's brokenhearted letter after he had been told the truth about his young wife's ailment, but could not reveal the truth to her, and we talked and felt each other's care as we communed there with God and one another.

Supreme Court upheld the lower court's decision and the United States Supreme Court refused to review the action of Tennessee's highest court, the rulings of the lower court, which had ruled that the charter be revoked, were sustained."

These things and these faces I can never forget, and as I pray for the lamp of freedom to burn incessantly, I know that I am not weaving my life's pattern alone. Only one end of the threads do I hold in my hands; the other ends go many ways linking my life with others, my country with others. My pattern and my country's pattern will depend largely upon the awareness, the insights, the skills, the personal goals and incentives of those who hold the other ends of those threads.

But heaven deliver me from committing phrases of purple sentimentality. My life has been devoted to the practical and the specific. For four decades I have taught innumerable school children such definite and precise things as the fact that in the year 1492 Columbus sailed the ocean blue. For more than half another decade I have been teaching with enthusiasm and great enjoyment such other prosaic information as how one goes about qualifying himself for voting in South Carolina or Georgia or Tennessee or Mississippi. I have been trying all my days to solve problems, and problems—bothersome ones, at any rate—are annoyingly specific.

Perhaps that is why I find it difficult—though I think everyone does—to make a very good statement of my own philosophy of life. Really, I wonder if anybody can do it. I wonder if anybody actually knows himself. Can any man read his own face? Can any man judge his own heart? I truly wonder.

For many years, back even to the days of my childhood, it has been an impelling preoccupation of mine as I walk along the streets or jostle in great crowds to try to read the faces of the people I see.

Faces thrill and inspire me, faces frighten and haunt me.

I still remember the faces of the people on my street as I was growing up in Charleston. In their faces I could see revealed the loneliness they were feeling; and I wished that there were some way by which I might see beyond the faces, behind the sockets of those solemn eyes, and draw out from them the yearnings of their souls.

I have seen these faces on many a street, in many a throng, alone, frightened, weary, pained. I have seen them up and down the land. I saw them in California, where once the father of a family said to me, "I do wish I could get for my children in Tennessee the opportunities that I have found here. I love to fish in those Tennessee streams and hunt in those woods." He had left Clinton, Tennessee, during the turmoil of the period in which they were desegregating the public schools there.

Time and again on New York City subways I have looked into frightened lonely faces and seen mouths working tremendously to frame unuttered fearful phrases. O the faces I have seen, and seeing, could never forget!

But one can never really see into the heart, the mind, the impenetrable soul of another. There is no way to know, to understand completely, to share utterly. Yet when I read of the kidnapping of the Lindbergh baby, the suicide of the maid in the Morrow home, the killing of little Bobby Franks, the murder of Emmett Till, the lynching of Charles Mack Parker, the suffering of Strom Thurmond's wife, and quite recently the anguished search of Governor Nelson Rockefeller for his son, I saw faces, white faces, lowly and high born, impoverished, affluent—all merging into one face of infinite pain forged in the crucible of suffering.

I see the faces of young girls fresh from the farms, their city day's work done and weary in every bone and muscle, sitting forlorn and already on the verge of hopelessness in their one-room dingy walk-ups. And the men, too, I see—young men who should be vibrant and enthusiastic and filled with good hopes, and older men who should be serene in accomplishments achieved and satisfactions earned, I see them pouring from factories and construction jobs to trudge on slowing tired legs toward hovels destitute almost of hope.

But I see another face, kindly, loving and to me a lovely brown face out of days long gone; and seeing my father's face and feeling my father's love for all his fellows, I am moved deeply. My heart hurts for those lonely and lost, those frantic to find a future endurable, those who have stood by helpless and watched loved ones being destroyed by merciless power structures and unprincipled individuals who were destined instead in the providence of God to be their brothers.

To me social justice is not a matter of money but of will, not a problem for the economist as much as a task for the patriot; to me its accomplishment requires leadership and community action rather than monetary investment.

It was encouraging to me during the last days of Speaker Sam Rayburn's accomplishing life to listen to radio and television reports and read articles about his work and his philosophy. One statement, I remember, especially impressed me. "Although he came to maturity in another era," it said, "he adapted himself to our present-day life."

To be able to do that, I feel, is most important. We must change with change, or change will defeat and consume us. Change is the very essence of growth, of life. Nothing is so permanent, so certain, as change. Growth requires change and change demands testing. Even our governmental forms never remain static indefinitely; to do so would be to decay. And surely everyone realizes that interpretations of such bedrock things as our American Constitution change through the years.

So as I work among the Negro people, who, we must agree, have the fewest of the democratic freedoms and many of whom have inadequate education or none at all, who live constantly under the fear of intimidation, insult and violence, I am reminded that here is this continuing test of our democratic form of government. In the recent rise of the image of hope for the segregated black man and his deliverance from this state of pseudo-slavery I see clearly the form of challenge. If permanent social patterns are to be created that are truly democratic, I maintain, then the most lowly being must enjoy equally with every other American the fruits of democracy. Only then will the Negro, and particularly the Negro parent, see the glimmer of a light ahead, only then will he see a way out of his dilemma.

The Negro parent's dilemma is fearsome. There is nothing worse, believe me, and *I know* this, than bringing a child into the world and having to teach him that none of the pleasant things of life are for him, or few of them at most. How do you teach a tot where to sit, where to walk, where not to play, and where not to go . . . like the theater, art gallery, city parks and public libraries? A parent has a terrible time explaining why the native soil is such a hard place for the native to grow in.

I have experienced having to teach my son, my nieces and nephews, and the children I taught in public school that these things are not for them. It is a very hard task, I know for a fact; it is no hypothetical question with me. I can testify out of the bitter school of experience.

Segregation, I have no doubt in the world, is the root of this ugly and evil thing. Out of segregation stem the rank weeds of discrimination and injustice. So, to destroy the present crop of weeds and prevent recurrent growth, we must dig out and cast away the roots.

And I feel impelled to observe that to me there seems to be imbalance in the approach to destroying segregation. Conventional social and welfare institutions conform with local custom and habit. Their influence on changing social patterns is extremely minimal in matters of race. Problems of poverty and social injustice are largely the result of segregation, as I have said repeatedly. These institutions, therefore, concern themselves almost entirely with the *results* of racial inequality.

The sit-in and other forms of protest which have been so successful in focusing national and international attention on racial injustice have thus far done little to change the nature or severity of the social problems which bind the impoverished Negro to lack of education, jobs, housing, safety and participating in governmental processes affecting citizenship. Programs must be developed which embrace the lowest socio-economic groups. Leadership which is competent must completely identify itself with the people in the localities where they live, and work with equal emphasis on motivation and education, employing modern techniques.

The greatest need, as I see it, is working with these people. This is where I shall continue to work for the rest of my useful days. This new hope that the Negro feels is offering him emancipation from segregation must be implemented. The motivation made possible by this new hope can change the face of this nation if properly implemented. But unless it reaches to the very grassroots of our nation it will be dissipated and the hopelessness which is too often taken for apathy will settle again over the Negro community. The centuries of indoctrination by racial discrimination in this nation has had its effect. Even when the lunch counter is desegregated, for example, the Negro does not patronize it. Voluntary participation can only be achieved through motivation. Motivation, like prejudice, lives in men's minds.

The school in which the Negro must be educated is the shopping center he is boycotting, the city council chamber where he is demanding justice, the ballot box at which he chooses his political leaders, the hiring office where he demands that he be hired on merit, the meeting hall of the board of education where he insists on equal education. The Negro needs leaders who are also teachers, who are psychologically fit and competently trained to work directly with the problems of life.

I hope that the Southern Christian Leadership Conference will do this job. It has unique advantages which could well be applied to these modern problems. In any event, wherever there are people working in this manner and at this task, there I will be.

And as I look to the beginning of a new year in an old assignment under a new leadership and direction, I do so hopefully and confidently, yes, and eagerly. The last half-decade for the Negro in the South, and for the other pushed aside and less privileged fold, black and white, in other sections of the nation, too, has been a period of unparalleled advancement. But the next five years, I have good reason to believe, will see an even greater improvement in the status of the Negro, a narrowing and a filling of the wide and deep chasm that through the years has been fixed between the races.

The acceleration of this advancement has been due in large part to the determined efforts of the new Negro leadership and its supporters among the white workers in the cause, and I glory in it. Sometimes I am even impatient that the pace forward isn't more swift. But I realize that it requires time and sometimes new generations to bring about momentous changes in the customs and traditions of a vast region. So I face a new year with confidence and even with enthusiasm. I know—and I am happier for knowing it—that not *all* the Negro's improvement of stature during the last recent years has been accomplished through his own struggling, his own determination, his own demanding. I know that the white South is changing, too, and changing fast; I know that countless good southern white persons have helped, some through the active championing of our struggle, many others through the quiet acceptance of the fact not only that a new day and a new way must come but also that they are already here.

In March at Monteagle we put out a little booklet titled *Songs for Freedom*.

A song is to be sung,
a little foreword declares.

If it remains on the page, it is the same as a new automobile that is bought, placed in the garage and kept there.

A song is to be sung. One's musical abilities may be limited, but there are no limitations to one's spirit. A musical note is a guide, but it alone does not make a song.

A song is to be sung. One's musical abilities may be good for citizenship schools, mass meetings, etc. Some of the songs are to be shouted. Others are to be sung quietly, lived with and allowed to grow within you and with you. A song is to be sung.

I believe that throughout our southland, and in other sections of the nation, too, we have been singing a song.

Sitting here this evening in my old house on Henrietta Street in Charleston, where I'm home for a short holiday season, I have been glancing through this little booklet of twenty-two songs. There are old slave songs, Negro spirituals—*Didn't My Lord Deliver Daniel?*, *Keep Your Lamp Trimmed and A-Burning*—and folk songs; songs from other lands, such as *Shri Ram*, one of Gandhi's prayers in song; martial songs, with modern words set to familiar tunes; calm, hopeful prayerful songs.

I notice words of the last verse in *Shri Ram*:

Gandhi spoke of freedom one night. I said, "Man we gotta fight." He said, "Yes, but love's the weapon we should use, for with killing, no one wins; it's with love that peace begins." It takes courage, when we're only passing through.

Here's one whose modernity cannot be disputed. It is called *Black and White*.

> The ink is black, the page is white, together we learn
>   to read and write, to read and write;
> And now a child can understand this is the law of all
>   the land;
> The ink is black, the page is white, together we learn
>   to read and write, to read and write.

Here's another verse:

> Their robes were black, their heads were white, the
>   school house doors were closed so tight, were
>   closed so tight;
> Nine judges all set down their names to end the
>   years and years of shame, years of shame;
> Their robes were black, their heads were white, the
>   school house doors were closed so tight, were
>   closed so tight.

And a more martial one:

> So let's all sing it loud and clear
> Oh yes oh . . .
> We will not wait another year
> Jim Crow has got to go.

Another verse of the same:

> Sat right down in Woolworth's store
> Oh yes oh . . .
> Told everyone coming through the door
> Jim Crow has got to go.

And:

> Went down to register the other night
> Oh yes oh . . .
> They said you can't vote if you're not white
> Jim Crow has got to go.

There are several other swinging, fighting songs. But I like best a very old song, born long before the days of Governor Faubus and Woolworth sit-ins and Montgomery bus strikes and freedom riders. It's an early Quaker hymn that originated long ago when George Fox and other founders of the Society of Friends were being imprisoned for their beliefs, but it is relevant today:

> My life flows on in endless song above earth's
>   lamentation;
> I hear the real though far-off hymn that hails a new
>   creation;
> Through all the tumult and the strife I hear the
>   music ringing.
> It sounds an echo in my soul; how can I keep from
>   singing!

Indeed, I hear the music ringing. Soon now, for both hands of my mantle clock are reaching for the top of the dial, the bells of old St. Philip's and old St. Michael's will be ringing a glad song and the sirens ashore and the ships in the harbor will be greeting with raucous bedlam the new year. And my heart will be singing. The last year, the last several years, have been wonderful years of accomplishment, of advancement into understanding, of progress toward the realm of universal brotherhood.

Yes, but the new year will be better. And the years after it better, and better. I so desperately hope that they will be, I so earnestly pray that they will be, I have complete and utter faith if we falter and faint not, if we continue in goodwill and outreaching love the good fight, the truth some early day if not tomorrow will make us free. This then is how *I* define my philosophy.

> Indeed, we *will* overcome.
> The Lord will see us through,
> The Lord will see us through,
> The Lord will see us through some day;
> Deep down in my heart I do believe
> The Lord will see us through.
> —*Septima Clark*

Bibliography

Branch, Taylor. *Parting the Waters: America in the King Years 1954-1963*. New York: Simon and Schuster, 1989.

Brown, Cynthia S., ed. *Ready from Within: Septima Clark and the Civil Rights Movement*. Navarro, CA: Wild Tress Press, 1986.

Crawford, Vicki L., Anne Rouse, and Barbara Woods. *Women in the Civil Rights Movement*. Brooklyn: Carlson Publishing, 1990.

Gallman, Vanessa. "Septima Clark: On Life, Courage, Dedication." *View South*. 1:4 (July/August), 1979.

Glen, John. *Highlander, No Ordinary School*. Lexington, KY: University of Kentucky Press, 1989.

McFadden, Grace Jordan. "Septima P. Clark and the Struggle for Human Rights." In *This Far By Faith: Readings in African-American Women's Religious Biography*. Edited by Judith Weisenfeld & Richard Newman. New York: Routledge, 1996.

ELLA JOSEPHINE BAKER
(1903-1986)

Ella Josephine Baker brought an ethos of self-help and mutuality to an era of unprecedented social change. Throughout her life, she worked with civil rights organizations and influenced them in unexpected ways. Baker challenged the hierarchical structure and tendency toward charismatic leadership in established organizations such as the NAACP and SCLC. In her words, "My theory is, strong people don't need strong leaders."[10] Thus, when the students formed SNCC, she mentored grassroots leadership through a structure of participatory democracy. Her vision of participatory political process and challenge to oppressive leadership models are the enduring legacy of Ella Baker.

"Roots"[11]

Where we lived there was no sense of hierarchy, in terms of those who have, having a right to look down upon, or to evaluate as a lesser breed, those who didn't have. Part of that could have resulted, I think, from two factors. One was the proximity of my maternal grandparents to slavery. They had known what it was to not have. Plus, my grandfather had gone into the Baptist ministry, and that was part of the quote, unquote, Christian concept of sharing with others. I went to a school that went in for Christian training. Then, there were people who "stood for something," as I call it. Your relationship to human beings was more important than your relationship to the amount of money that you made.

There was a deep sense of community that prevailed in this little neck of the woods. It wasn't a town, it was just people. And each of them had their twenty-thirty-forty-fifty acre farms, and if there were emergencies, the farmer next to you would share in something to meet that emergency. For instance, when you thresh wheat, if there was a thresher around, you didn't have each person having his own. So you came to my farm and threshed, then you went to the next one and the next one and the next one. You joined in. Part of the land was on a riverbank, the Roanoke River, and now it has been made into a lake through a dam process. But the river would overflow at times and certain crops might be ruined. So if they took place, and it wrecked havoc with the food supply, I am told that my grandfather would take his horse and wagon and go up to the county seat, which was the only town at that point, and mortgage, if necessary, his land, to see that people ate.

The sense of community was pervasive in the black community as a whole, I mean especially the community that had a sense of roots. This community had been composed to a large extent by relatives. Over the hill was my grandfather's sister who was married to my Uncle Carter, and up the grove was another relative who had a place. So it was a deep sense of community. I think these are the things that helped to strengthen my

---

[10]Ellen Cantarow and Susan Gushee O'Malley, "Ella Baker: Organizing for Civil Rights," in *Black Women in United States History* (Vol. 5), edited by Darlene Clark Hine (Brooklyn: Carlson Publishing, Inc., 1990).

[11]Ibid., 60-61. The excerpts in this section are from an interview with Ms. Baker conducted by the authors.

concept about the need for people to have a sense of their own value, and *their* strengths, and it became accentuated when I began to travel in the forties for the National Association for the Advancement of Colored People. Because during that period, in the forties, racial segregation and discrimination were very harsh. As people moved to towns and cities, the sense of community diminished. A given area was made up of people from various and sundry other areas. They didn't come from the same place. So they had to *learn* each other, and they came into patterns of living that they had not been accustomed to. And so whatever deep sense of community that may have been developed in that little place that I spoke of, didn't always carry over to the city when they migrated. They lost their roots. When you lose that, what will you do next. You *hope* that you begin to think in terms of the *wider* brotherhood.

"The NAACP Years"[12]

The first aspect of being on the field staff was to help. You helped raise money. You conducted membership campaigns in different areas. A new person coming on the field would learn how to campaign, and then you would be sent to smaller territory. I started in Florida. I'd never been there before.

The NAACP had a roster of people who were in contact, who were members. And so when you go out in the field, if they had a bank, say, in Sanford or Clearwater, Florida, you had been in correspondence there. So you make your contact with the person in Tampa who's said to the community, "Miss so-and-so's coming in." And so you go down, and they have provided some space in somebody's church or office or somewhere you had access to a telephone.

Where did people gather? They gathered in churches. In schools. And you'd get permission. You'd call up Reverend Brother so-and-so, and ask if you could appear before the congregation at such-and-such a time. Sometimes they'd give you three minutes, because, after all, many people weren't secure enough to run the risk, as they saw it, of being targeted as ready to challenge the powers that be. And they'd say, "You have three minutes after the church service." And you'd take it. And you'd use it, to the extent to which you can be persuasive. It's the ammunition you have. That's all you have.

---

[12]Cantarow and O'Malley, *Black Women in United States History*, 69-73. The excerpt is from Baker's interview in answer to the following questions: "How does a field organizer begin? When you go to a place you don't know, how do you find people who will introduce you into the community? How do you help the fearful overcome their fear and sign up for work? How do you persuade the well-off that they have kinship with the poor?"

We dealt with what was most pressing for a given section. For instance, Harry T. Moore was one of three black principals in Florida who was fired when they began to talk in terms of equal pay. The differential between black and white teachers was tragic, to say the least. Many times, money had been "appropriated" for black education and it had been diverted to other sources. And, of course, there wasn't headlines on that, they just didn't get there, see.

Harry T. Moore's house was bombed from under him one night. And he was killed as a result. This particular night, I think it was Christmas eve, '46, dynamite was placed under his bedroom. He and his wife were blown to smithereens. There were a lot of people whom Harry T. Moore had benefited. We talked to them. He helped them get their pay when they had worked and didn't get paid. So you could go into that area of Florida and you could talk about the virtue of NAACP, because they knew Harry T. Moore. They hadn't discussed a whole lot of theory. But there was a *man* who served *their* interests and who *identified* with them.

On what basis do you seek to organize people? Do you start to try to organize them on the fact of what *you* think, or what they are first interested in? You start where the *people* are. Identification with people. There's always this problem in the minority group that's escalating up the ladder in this culture, I think. Those who have gotten some training and those who have gotten some material gains, it's always the problem of their not understanding the possibility of being divorced from those who are not in their social classification. Now, there were those who felt they had made it, would be embarrassed by the fact that some people would get drunk and get in jail, and so they would be concerned too much about whether they were brutalized in jail. 'Cause he was a *drunk*! He was a so-and-so. Or she was a streetwalker. We get caught in that bag. And so you have to help break that down without alienating them at the same time. The gal who has been able to buy her minks and whose husband is a professional, they live well. You can't insult her, you never go and tell her she's so-and-so for taking, for not identifying. You try to point out where her interest lies in identifying with that other one across the tracks who doesn't have minks.

How do you do that? You don't always succeed, but you try. You'd point out what had happened, in certain cases, where whole communities were almost destroyed by police brutality on a large scale. They went and burned down the better homes. In Tampa, Florida, I met some of those people whose homes were burned down. These were people I'd call middle class. The men got the guns, and they carried their womenfolk and the children into the woods. And they stood guard. Some stood guard over the people in the woods, and they stood guard over their homes and property, ready to shoot. So what you do is to cite examples that had taken place somewhere else. You had to be persuasive on the basis of fact. You cite it, you see. This can happen to *you*. Sometimes you're able to cite instances of where there's been a little epidemic, or an outbreak of the more devastating kinds of disease. You point out that those of us who live across the railroad track and are in greater filth or lack of sanitation can have an effect on you who live on the other side, 'cause disease doesn't have such a long barrier between us, you see. As long as the violations of the rights of Tom Jones could take place with impunity, you are not secure. So you helped to reestablish a sense of identity of each with the struggle.

Of course, your success depended on both your disposition and your capacity to sort of stimulate people—and how you carried yourself, in terms of not being above people who were. And see, there were more people who were not economically secure than people. I didn't have any mink—I don't have any now—but you don't go into a group where minks are prohibitive in terms of getting them and carry your minks and throw 'em around. Why, they can't get past *that*. They can't get past the fact that you got minks and they don't have minks. And see, I had no problems 'cause I didn't have none. Nor did I have aspirations for these things.

I remember one place I got a contribution for a life membership in the NAACP, which was five-hundred dollars then, was from a longshoremen's union. They remembered somebody who had been there before from the NAACP, with a mink coat. When they gave this five-hundred dollar membership, somebody mentioned it. See, they had resented the mink coat. I don't think it was the mink coat that they really resented. It was the *barrier* they could sense between them and the person in the coat. See, you can have a mink coat on and you can identify with the man who is working on the docks. If you got it, if you *really* identify with him, what you wear won't make a damn bit of difference. But if you talk differently, and somehow talk down to people, they can sense it. They can feel it. And they know whether you are talking *with* them, or talking *at* them, or talking *about* them.

If you feel that you are part of them and they are part of you, you don't say "I'm-a-part-of-you." What you really do is, you point something. Especially the lower-class people, the people who'd felt the heel of oppression, see, they *knew* what you were talking about when you spoke about police brutality. They *knew* what you were speaking about when you talked about working at a job, doing the same work, and getting a differential in pay. And if your sense of being a part of them got over to them, they appreciated that. Somebody would get the point. Somebody would come out and say, "I'm gon' join that darn organization." As an example, I remember in someplace out of St. Petersburg, Florida, the first time I'd ever been to the Holy and Sanctified Church. We had a good response. One lady came out and all she could say was how my dress was the same as hers. Now, she didn't know how to deal with issues. But she identified. And she joined.

And, then you have to recognize what people *can* do. There're some people in my experience, especially "the little people" as some might call them, who never could explain the NAACP as such. But they had the knack of getting money from John Jones or somebody. They might walk up to him: "Gimme a dollar for the NAACP." And maybe because of what they had done in relationship to John Jones, he'd give the dollar. They could never tell anybody what the program of the Association was. So what do you do about that. You don't be demeaning them. You say, well here is Mrs. Jones, Mrs. Susie Jones, and remember last year Sister Susie Jones came in with so much. And Sister Susie Jones would go on *next* year and get this money. Now, somewhere in the process she may learn some other methods, and she may learn to articulate some of the programs of the Association. But whether she does or not, she *feels* it. And she transmits it to those she can talk to. And she might end up just saying, "You ain't doin' nothin' but spendin' your money down at that so-and-so place." She may shame him. Or she may say, "Boy, I know your mama." And so you start talkin' about what the mothers would like for them to do. So you do it because there's mama, mama's callin'. See, somewhere down the line this becomes important to them. At least these are the ways I saw it. And I think they respond.

"Somebody Carries On"[13]

I think a number of things happened. The people endured with more sense about what they were involved in. They at least survived with knowledge, and out of it has come various kinds of—let's call it adequate leadership. People are more easily alerted to whether they are getting unusual oppression, and they'll do something. They're quicker to respond now. They would be much less willing to settle for what they had endured before, and they would be more likely to actually go to the Nth degree in revolt, if the pressure of the past were reinstated.

You see, today, they are living in what we call a normal society. The same kinds of denials that we have up here in the North, to one degree or another they have down there. But the major pressures, the things that they consider the most oppressive, are lifted. I mean, you don't ride Jim Crow. You can even go as far as boycotting the stores, which has gotten the NAACP in deep water. But the people have taken action. They elect the people they want to elect whether they turn out to be good or not. And they can make the usual mistake of feeling that you can trust those in power because they have given you a little power. Whether that's good or bad, I'm not in a position at this stage to talk too pointedly about. It's no worse than it is anywhere else. You see, I have grave reservations about what can be accomplished, anyway, by established political parties.

Maybe there will be a new revolution. I don't think there's going to be

---

[13]Cantarow and O'Malley, *Black Women in United States History*, 91-93. This is Baker's response to the questions: "What happened to others in the civil rights movement? And how do you keep going?"

one any time soon, to be honest—I mean among blacks nor whites in this country. The best country in the world you hear them say. I guess it may be, I haven't lived anywhere else. But it's not good enough as far as I'm concerned. But I'm not good enough for the task.

I keep going because I don't see the productive value of being bitter. What else do you do? Do you get so bitter that you give up, and when young people come and want to talk to me, to hear about the past and learn from it, am I to say, "Oh, forget it, go on about your business, I'm bitter." You can just say, the heck with it. I'll break off and do what I need to do. Those of us who have responsibilities of children and family, somebody's got to provide some food for them, so you might decide to concentrate on getting that. I can stand that. But if people begin to place their values in terms of how high they get in the political world, or how much worldly goods they accumulate, or what kind of cars they have, or how much they have in the bank, that's where I begin to lose respect.

To me, I'm part of the human family. What the human family will accomplish, I can't control. But it isn't impossible that what those who came along with me went through might stimulate others to continue to fight for a society that does not have those kinds of problems. Somewhere down the line the numbers increase, the tribe increases. So how do you keep on? I can't help it. I don't claim to have any corner on an answer, but I believe that the struggle is eternal. Somebody else carries on.

—Ella Baker

Bibliography

Dallard, Shyrlee. *Ella Baker: A Leader Behind the Scenes*. Englewood Cliffs, NJ: Burdett Press, 1990.

Lerner, Gerda. *Black Women in White America: A Documentary History*. New York: Vintage Books, 1973.

Mueller, Carol. "Ella Baker and the Origins of 'Participatory Democracy.'" In *Women in the Civil Rights Movement*. Brooklyn: Carlson Publishing, 1990.

FANNIE LOU HAMER
(1917-1977)

A catalyst for change on many fronts, Fannie Lou exchanged her life as a sharecropper in her home state of Mississippi for the glaring space of public advocacy and the struggle for justice. She championed the cause of human and civil rights despite the constant threat of violence from Mississippians who were unwilling or unable to discern the "signs of the times." With a no-

nonsense, hands-on approach, she registered voters, ran unsuccessfully for Congress, pricked the conscience of the Democratic National Party by facilitating changes in the acknowledgment and seating of segregated delegates, and founded political and economic organizations that addressed the plight of rural Blacks.

"Sick and Tired of Being Sick and Tired"[14]

It is not easy to talk about politics in the fall of 1968. The Democratic Convention in Chicago was a very sad experience, one I shall never forget. But somehow we have got to keep enough faith to keep working to change things in America to make it fit for everyone. I am often asked, "What is the future of black people in America?" And this is a very important question for this political campaign. I think the answer to it will explain *why* black people in Mississippi are going to vote, and *who* they are going to vote for. For what happens about politics in the next few years will have much to do with the future of black people in America. And that means that politics will have much to do with the future of all Americans, for we are in this thing together, white and black, yellow and red, brown and polka dot.

Some people say that we have counted too much on politics to cure America's racism, and to give black people what has been ours since white people began *integration* over three hundred years ago when they unloaded the first slave ships on the Atlantic coast. (They didn't bring *segregation* until about 90 years ago.) And sometimes there does seem to be something about America's politics that can't deal with the problems of what the white man is doing to the black man and the red man and the Mexican-American and the Puerto Rican and other minorities. I want to say something about that later on. But black people in the South in the past ten or fifteen years have spent so much time in politics—in voter registrations, in elections, in trying to work in political parties to influence them—that it does not seem to me that we can turn our backs completely on politics, as bad as it seems in 1968.

We can still use politics to try to make America face the truth about its sickness, its racism, for the truth is the only thing that is going to free all of us in America today. After what happened in Chicago, I do think that black people and white people have got to work harder at politics at the grass roots. This is as important for any of the white people who say that they want a change in the way things are done in politics today. We have got to work harder at the grass roots. We have got to be careful that we don't lose what we have already gained there by what we do in this election.

---

[14]*Katallagete 1*(Fall 1968):19-26.

I believe that we have just got to keep some kind of faith that the people who want to make this country a good place to live can gain and influence politics in this country. I do have faith, as bad as the situation is now, for faith is the substance of things hoped for and evidence of things not seen. If I hadn't had faith four years ago, I wouldn't have gone to Atlantic City, New Jersey, to tell the Democratic Convention why the Mississippi Freedom Democratic Party should be seated in place of the "regular" Democrats from Mississippi. And if I didn't have faith, I wouldn't keep pushing as hard as I am for what my people in the Freedom Democratic Party want. My people are saying that none of the candidates are spotless, but some of them are threatening to do things that would be a disaster to them and to the country, and that we must support the candidate who best related to where we are right now. I have to have some kind of faith to keep up that kind of work. And if I didn't have faith, I wouldn't spend so much of my time talking to ninety percent white audiences all over the country, and going to these ninety percent white political conventions, and writing pieces like this for the magazine of the Southern Churchmen.

I have been brutally beaten and permanently injured by white men while I was in jail for no other crime than trying to get citizens of Mississippi to register and vote. But I do not say that every white man in the country would do the same thing to me that a handful of white men did in Mississippi. And I do not say that everybody in the political area at Chicago was bad. There were some good people there. But we have a question to raise to America today, because America must wake up and learn the truth about itself and its racism. And that is one big thing that politics can do about racism in America today.

But we must begin by saying that the signs are not too hopeful that politics is going to help the black people a whole lot, at least not in the immediate future. Just think about the Kerner Commission Report, as it spoke about the responsibility of "white racism" for the riots in the summer of 1967, and about the billions of dollars needed to deal with the ghettos. But this Report upset the President of the United States very much. So he has done nothing about it. But he did sign the so-called "anti-crime bill" which contains many things directed against urban black people, and he got through an income tax hike to help pay for Vietnam. The Vice-President of the United States, Mr. Humphrey, has publicly disagreed with the "white racism" part of the Kerner Commission's Report. And the Congress is not only hostile to the Report, and to the Poor People's Campaign and to Resurrection City—less than two months after they seemed so sorry that Dr. King had been murdered—but everything they have done lately has shown that they are more interested in more profits and power for the rich and the powerful people, and they have no interest in helping the poor people, and they can still think up plenty of ways to embarrass poor people because they are poor.

Martin Luther King—soon after beginning a more directly political role—

has been murdered. Senator Robert Kennedy—soon after raising once again the hopes of poor minorities, black, red, Mexican-American, in his political campaign—has been murdered, two months after Dr. King was murdered. Can anybody be surprised that we wonder if they were killed because America didn't want to have to face up to the truth? The two most effective political spokesmen for black people and minority groups have been taken from us within two months, at the very time many of us believed was the best and probably the last chance for us to get some political success instead of being on the receiving end of the white racist politics which have dominated politics almost completely since our nation began.

You see, politics today are used by the white people not only to keep down the poor black and poor white and poor red man and others who are poor—for instance the way Senator Eastland, the chairman of the Senate Judiciary Committee does in my county, Sunflower County, Mississippi, and throughout America. Politics today are used by the white man to make the white man more wealthy and more powerful, just because he is already white, and wealthy and powerful—as President Johnson's Department of Agriculture does for Senator Eastland in my county, Sunflower County, Mississippi.

The Department of Agriculture—whose Secretary, Mr. Freeman, owes his political life to the Democratic nominee, Hubert Humphrey—the Department of Agriculture last year gave Senator Eastland $157,930 *not to plant crops* in the area of the county where black men and women and children are starving; and it also paid eight other plantation owners in Sunflower County more than $100,000 *each* last year not to grow crops. All that money going into my county would buy a lot of Food Stamps for the poor and hungry people, black and white, in Mississippi. But that same Agriculture Department that paid Senator Eastland and the other plantation owners so much money for *not* growing crops turns back millions of dollars to the Treasury Department that ought to be used for Food Stamps to feed these starving people. One reason they can turn back the money is because many times the Food Stamp programs are controlled by local and county governments that don't want poor people to have anything to eat, so that they will go away, maybe, to the ghettos and slums of Detroit and Chicago and Newark and New York City. If you find this hard to believe, you can read the Winter issue of *The New South*, "Poverty in the Rural South," or the report "Hunger: USA". No wonder Mr. Freeman was so mad about that TV show about poverty in America. Now some Congressmen and Washington officials are saying that there is no one starving in America. They are only getting "improper diets." But personally I can't see the difference. And I *know* the black children who are sick all the time and have bloated little bellies because of what they can't get to eat do not know the difference.

This is one of the things that politics—that is, white man's politics—

means to black people, and one of the things we black people want to use politics to change. For this sort of thing just isn't right. When you speak of "politics and racial progress" you are asking whether politics is going to help the black people and other people have their rightful share in the future of the good things that America has. But to ask *that* question is to say things do not look good for black people, and for all of America, today.

But I still have some hope. And to explain why, I think I ought to go back and explain how I first became involved in the struggle for freedom and human rights in Mississippi in 1962, and draw the line of my own experiences forward to today. I am from Sunflower County, Mississippi, from the most rural and the poorest area in the U.S.A., the home county of Senator James O. Eastland, the chairman of the Judiciary Committee of the United States Senate. In Sunflower County, we have 38,000 blacks, 17,900 whites. We have 14,000 potential black voters, 8,000 potential white voters. In Sunflower County, we have 150% of the white voters registered, but not quite 50% of the black voters registered. Now the reason I say 150% of the white voters are registered is because in my county they vote who are dead and are not yet born. Anyway, I shall never forget when I attended my first mass meeting, in Ruleville, Mississippi, on the Monday night after the fourth Sunday in August, 1962. The Student Non-violent Coordinating Committee and the Southern Christian Leadership Conference came into Mississippi in August 1962 to get black people to register to vote. I went to their meeting in Ruleville, where the Reverend James Bevel preached a sermon from the 16th Chapter of St. Matthew, the 3rd verse, "discerning the signs of the times," tying it to voter registration. Then Jim Foreman talked about how it was our constitutional right as citizens to register and to vote in Mississippi.

That night they asked us to go down the following Friday, and I agreed to try for the first time in my life to register to vote. On Friday, eighteen of us went to Indianola, the county seat, in an old bus that a Negro man used in the summer to haul cotton-choppers and cotton-pickers, and in the winter took the same bus and many of the same people to Florida to work in the fields there, because there wasn't enough work in Mississippi to keep food on their tables. We went to the Clerk's office in the Courthouse, and he asked us what we wanted there. I told him we had come to try to register. Then he said, "Well, all of you will have to leave this room except *two.*" I was one of the two persons he let stay in his office to take what he called the "literacy test." Now this "literacy test" consisted of twenty-one questions. It began: "What is your full name?" "Write the date of this application." Then it went on to questions such as: "By whom are you employed?" —this meant that you would be fired by the time you got back home. "Where is your place of residence in this district?" —this meant that the Ku Klux Klan and the White Citizen's Council would be given your address. It asked: "If there is more than one person of the same name in this precinct, by what name do you want to be called?" After we answered that kind of question, the Clerk pointed out a section of the Mississippi Constitution, told us to copy it and then give a reasonable interpretation of it—and that was the first time, in August, 1962, that I knew that Mississippi had a constitution! It was a hard thing to do, to stay around there in that Courthouse and work on that "literacy test." It took the eighteen of us until about 4:30 in the afternoon to finish it, and it was a hard thing to do, to stay in that Courthouse all day long. People came in and out of the Courthouse with cowboy boots on, and with rifles and with dogs—some of them looked like Jed Clampett of the "Beverly Hillbillies," but these men weren't kidding.

But we finally did finish this "literacy test" and started back for home, but about two miles out of Indianola, some lawmen stopped us and ordered us all off the bus. We got off, then they told us to get back on. When we did, they carried us back to Indianola, and fined the bus driver $100 for driving a bus painted the wrong color. They said that there was *too much yellow* in the bus that day. They finally agreed to lower the fine to $30, which the eighteen of us made up to pay so we could return to Ruleville. I went back to my home in the rural area, on the land of a man I'd worked for as a sharecropper and timekeeper for eighteen years. As I came up to my house, my oldest daughter and her little cousins came out to meet me, and told me that the man I worked for was blazing mad because I had gone down and tried to register. When I got home my husband told me the same thing. Then, the landowner came and called my husband out of the house and asked him if I had "made it back." He said I had, and then I walked out on the porch, and the owner said, "Did Pap tell you what I said?" and I said, "Yes, sir" (because this was still the pattern in the South in August 1962. It's only been in the last two or three years that this old pattern has been broken, although a lot of black people still say, "Yes, sir" and "No, sir" to a white man, no matter who he is, or how old he is). Anyway, the landowner said to me, "You'll have to go back down there and withdraw that thing, or you'll have to leave." And I told him, "I didn't go down there to register for you, I went down there to register for myself." I had to leave my home that night, the 31st of August, 1962. Then ten days later, sixteen bullets were fired into the home of Mr. and Mrs. Robert Tucker, the people I was staying with in Ruleville after I had to leave my home. And that same night, two Negro girls were shot.

This has been the pattern of harassment we have had in Mississippi simply because we participated in voter registration work and in politics. For example, early in 1963, there was a knock on our door, and when my husband opened it, a policeman came in just to intimidate us. It was S.L. Milam—they called him "the Sundown kid"—he was the brother of J.W. Milam, who some said was involved in the lynching of Emmett Till in 1955. But this sort of thing didn't stop my work in the voter registration in Mississippi. Then on June 9, 1963, I was arrested in Winona, Mississippi, U.S.A., and while I was in jail there I was beaten so badly that one of my kidneys was permanently damaged and I received a bloodclot that almost caused me to lose the sight of my left eye. But we kept at our work, for we knew that we had to have a change, not only for the blacks in Mississippi but for the poor whites as well. We tried very hard to work with the so-called "regular" Democratic party in Mississippi, first by going to work on the precinct level. But that didn't work. When I went to a precinct meeting in Ruleville, my husband, who had just been hired on a new job, was fired from that job the next day.

After failures of that sort, we were convinced that they were not going to let us get into their "regular" Democratic Party in Mississippi. That was when we organized what is called the Mississippi Freedom Democratic Party, at the Masonic Temple in Jackson, Mississippi, in June 1964. I was elected vice-chairman of the delegation that went to the Democratic National Convention in Atlantic City, New Jersey, in August of 1964, to challenge the seating of the "regular" Democrats from Mississippi. Mr. Ed King, a white native-born of Mississippi, was elected chairman. That was the time when we found out what *national* politics was like. That was the time when we found out that the politics in the United States was the same as the politics in Mississippi. I saw and heard people threatening us, and threatening those who took a stand with us in the Mississippi Freedom Democratic Party. I have been told that President Johnson himself decided to hold a "news conference" to be put on television in order to take the television cameras away from me when I was testifying before the Credentials Committee of the Democratic National Convention. It was when I was telling about the beatings I received in jail. So the truth we were trying to tell about politics must have been making it hot for even the highest leaders of the Democratic Party. Another meeting I shall never forget was with the man who is now the Vice President of the United States of America, and the Democratic choice for President this year, but this was at a meeting before he had been nominated for Vice President. Mr. Joseph Rauh, Jr., of the A.D.A. told us at that meeting that if we didn't "cool off" what we were doing, if we didn't stop pressing to take our fight to the floor of the Convention, Senator Humphrey wouldn't be nominated that night for Vice President of the United States. Mr. Humphrey was sitting right there with tears in his eyes, when Mr. Rauh of the A.D.A. was talking like that to us. So I asked: "Is Mr. Humphrey's position more important to him than 400,000 black people who live in Mississippi?" They didn't answer me, but after I asked that question, I wasn't permitted in the meetings with the Democratic leaders any more. But we were told that we should accept a "compromise": two at-large votes in the Convention. But we refused to accept a "compromise." We argued that if something was supposed to be ours 300 years ago, no one has the right to hand us only a *part* of it 300 years later. We argued that we wanted *every bit* of what was ours, and that we wanted it *now*. We argued that we were not ever going to get what was ours by taking a bit now, and bit later, because that would make us forget what it was we had the full right to have!

So we didn't accept a compromise, and we went back home to Mississippi. In Knoxville, Tennessee, we were stopped by the Ku Klux Klan, and it took five cars of patrolmen to guard us from Knoxville to Chattanooga. After we got back to Mississippi we tried unsuccessfully to get on the ballots to run as candidates. So we made up our own ballots with the same candidates as on the regular ballot, only with my name added to run in the Second Congressional District against Jamie Whitten. I received 33,009 votes and Jamie Whitten got only 49 votes. (That was when they saw the political power that black people had in the Second Congressional District in Mississippi: one night I went to bed, and didn't turn over and didn't move, but when I woke up, I woke up in the First Congressional District, which is where I am now.) Mr. King and some of us went to Washington, D.C. on January 4, 1965, to challenge the seating of the five "regular" Democratic representatives from Mississippi. We wanted a study made of the elections, and we wanted depositions and evidence taken so that they could see who really deserved to be seated from Mississippi. They didn't dismiss our challenge at that time. So we asked lawyers to come to Mississippi—over one hundred came—to collect evidence. We were able to get three volumes of evidence—15,000 pages—proving why the five white representatives should not be seated in Congress. But on September 13, 1965, we received a telegram from the Speaker of the House, Mr. John McCormack, saying that they wanted to have a hearing to discuss the dismissal—not of the representatives, but of our *challenge!* So we went to Washington, D.C. again to appear before the Subcommittee on Elections, and the way we were treated that time wasn't any different from the way we had been treated in Mississippi, or in Atlantic City. The hearing was closed to the public. At the hearing what they were saying was: "We won't say you Negroes are not right, but if we let *you* get away with it, they'll be doing the same thing all over the South." So on September 17, 1965, Congressman William Fitts Ryan and Don Edwards and some others escorted us into the Gallery of the House of Representatives until they called for the challenge to come to the Floor of the House. When they called for it, we went out of the Gallery and down to the Floor while they argued and then dismissed our challenge.

Racial progress? Almost a hundred years ago, John R. Lynch placed this same kind of challenge before the House of Representatives. He was a black man from Mississippi, and he succeeded with Yankee white help. But we failed a hundred years later with native white Mississippi help and Yankee opposition. We had all kinds of evidence to prove that these five men should not be seated in the House, starting from the fact that Mississippi was readmitted to the Union in 1870 after agreeing and signing a pledge that they would not disenfranchise any citizens, black or white. In 1968, the five white men from Mississippi still sit in the House of Representatives, but they took the seat away from Adam Clayton Powell, a black man. What America must do is see what is happening: they didn't unseat Powell, they unseated *us*, the black people. And they only "censured" Senator Thomas Dodd, they did not unseat him; they gave him a pat on the back and go-ahead, telling him just don't get caught. So you see, this is not Mississippi's problem, it is America's problem.

All of it is America's problem. Many, many of the threatening letters and telegrams I've received since I was on television in Atlantic City weren't from Mississippi. I've had telegrams from Chicago and other places in the North telling me what we shouldn't have done and what ought to happen to us. In Atlantic City I got a letter with a picture of a heart and dagger through the heart, and reading under it, telling me to go back to Africa. So since that time, whenever I've spoken to an audience with white people in it, I've hoped that the person who sent that message is there, so he can hear my answer to his message. I'd like to tell him, we'll make a deal: after they've sent all the Australians back to Australia, and the Koreans back to Korea, and the Chinese back to China, and the Italians back to Italy, and the Germans back to Germany, and then give the Indians their land back, and then get on the Mayflower from whence they came. . . . then, *we* will go home, too.

Some months ago there was a little poem under a cartoon in *Freedom Ways* magazine that sums up the way that most white politicians have acted toward us:

> This is a story of folks black like me—
> No longer slaves but not yet free.
> Told what they can do,
> And told what they shan't.
> Told what to do,
> And told what to don't.
> Damned if we do, and damned if we don't.

Now this has been the pattern, not only in Mississippi, not only in the South, but through America. We black people are fought in so many petty ways. One of the questions that always comes up in an integrated meeting on "race relations" is to tell the Negroes: "*What about Education?*" "*Give Education a Chance!*" You tell *us*, *we* should integrate the schools! We get three black children in your schools, and you start complaining about *that*. My little daughter is the product of what is called by the white people an "integrated" school. And the suffering that kid is going through . . . why, I wouldn't put her in there to go through that for another year for anything. But then, when I take her out, you'll say, "we've segregated ourselves." Yes, you are right, we need education. And we're going to educate our kids, *somehow*. But white Americans are going to have to deal with black Americans *while our kids are getting this education*. Black people are fed up and sick and tired of white people saying that "we can't stand to hear all this talk about integration." White Americans, *you* started it when you unloaded the ships of black people in your slave ships from Africa. And *you* started that other kind of "integration" you claim you are so scared about: I have cousins as white as any white man or woman in America. They have blue eyes and yellow hair, and I know a black man didn't do *that*. It's time for America to face up to the reality of this matter. You have got to get done with this scapegoat about your son marrying my daughter. We couldn't care less about that. But we do want to be treated as human beings.

One thing I always think about when I hear all this talk about the trouble we black people are causing by demanding integration is a letter I received from one of my friends some months go. He was told by the State Department or Defense Department or some one that his son would soon be home from Vietnam. And the letter went on to say that "if your son jumps up when he hears a telephone ring, and runs out into the street or into the back yard and starts digging a foxhole, just have patience with him. And if your son takes his gravy and pours it on his dessert, just bear with him a little longer." There were some other things that that letter said—I couldn't understand all the language—but they just told my friend to have faith and to be patient with their son, and he *might* speak English again.

This is the product of Vietnam. This is why black Americans are so tired that now they are sick and tired of being *sick* and *tired*. We're sick and tired of our people having to go to Vietnam and other places to fight for something we don't have here, and then come home with such letters as this. What we want to do is to make this a better country, to end the wrongs such as fighting a war in Vietnam and pouring billions over there, while people in Sunflower County, Mississippi, and Harlem and Detroit are starving to death because of something that is not their fault. I know, a lot of people say that our people are sorry, that we don't work or won't do anything, because if we would, we'd not be in the shape we're in now, needing education and everything. But just remember, when the power structure had me and *my* kids and *my* people in the cotton fields, they had *their* people in school. It took us a while to realize what was happening to us, but when we did, the cotton picker caught up with the sack. And we're not going to give up now. We're going to move on up.

Now I want to say a word or two about the churches and this race situation. You see, I travel quite a bit across this country, and a lot of the kids are asking, "Is God alive, or is He dead?" Now they *mean* it when they ask that question. They're not just trying to be smart or something like that. And I think I know what makes them ask that question: it is the hypocrites, the black and white hypocrites, who make them ask that question. The hypocrites who do too much pretending and not enough actual working, the white ministers and the black ministers standing behind a podium and preaching a lie on Sunday. For what the kids are now asking is something like this: "If this is Christianity that is being offered in most of the churches around this land, then we don't want any part of it. Look at what is happening all over the land, and the churches don't seem to pay any attention to it." We have almost driven our young people from God with this big act of hypocrisy. We have to take them seriously—I know I do—when they say that God is not God if He lets all these huge churches pour millions of dollars into buildings for their own people, and let the kids in their own neighborhood go without food and without clothing and without decent shelter.

Everybody knows—whoever said it first—that the most segregated hour in America is the eleven o'clock church service. But there is something worse than that. That is when you see these white and black hypocrites in all of their fine clothes come out of a worship service, and turn up their nose at a kid in rags, or a man drunk on the street, and ask themselves, "Now what's wrong with *him*?" They never ask "*Why* is that kid in rags?" "*Why* is that man drunk?" They never stop to think that it was something that put that kid in rags, just as it was something that drove that man to drink.

Just as it's time for America to wake up, it is long *past* time for the churches to wake up. The churches have got to say that they will have no more talk that "because your skin is a little different, you're better than they are." The churches have got to remember how Christ dealt with the poor people, in the 4th chapter of St. Luke, and the 18th verse, when he said, "The spirit of the Lord is upon me, because he hath anointed me to preach the gospel to the poor; he hath sent me to heal the brokenhearted, to preach deliverance to the captives, and recovering of sight to the blind, to set at liberty them that are bruised." Because Jesus wasn't just talking about black people, or about white people, he was talking about *people*. There's no difference in people, for in the 17th chapter of the Book of Acts, the 26th verse, Paul says, "God hath made of one blood all nations of men for to dwell on all the face of the earth." That means that whether we're white, black, red, yellow, or polka dot, we're made from the same blood.

If Christ were here today, he would be branded a radical, a militant, and would probably be branded as "red." They have even painted *me* as Communist, although I wouldn't know a Communist if I saw one. A few weeks ago the FBI was checking on me, and the agent was telling me all the bad things the Communists would do. I told him, "Well, that *is* something! We've sure got a *lot* of Communists right up there in Washington, don't we, Ed?"

We have to realize just how grave the problem is in the United States today, and I think the 6th chapter of Ephesians, the 11th and 12th verses, helps us to know how grave the problem is, and what it is we are up against. It says: "Put on the whole armor of God, that ye may be able to stand against the wiles of the devil. For we wrestle not against flesh and blood, but against principalities, against powers, against the rulers of the darkness of this world, against spiritual wickedness in high places." This is what I think about when I think of my own work in the fight for freedom, because before 1962, I would have been afraid to have spoken before more than six people. Since that time I have had to speak before thousands in the fight for freedom, and I believe that God gave me the strength to be able to speak in this cause.

So we are faced with a problem that is not flesh and blood, but we are facing principalities, and powers and spiritual wickedness in high places: that's what St. Paul told us. And that's what he meant. America created this problem. And we forgive America, even though we were brought here on the slave ships from Africa. Even though the dignity was taken away from the black men, and even though the black women had to bare not only their own kids but kids for the white slave owners. We forgive America for that. But we're looking for this check now, that's long past due, to let us have our share in political and economic power, so that we can have a great country, together.

It's time for black people to stop being brainwashed with the idea that nobody can be right in this country except Mr. Charlie. Mr. Charlie's days are numbered, anyway. Black people have got to learn that it is time for them to stand up and be counted, because they are as much as anybody else. Black people have got to stop trying to be white. For if we live 400 years, when we wake up we're still going to be black. We have to know this, and go on from there.

Black people have got to wake up.

Dr. King is dead.

It does not make sense now to stage demonstrations, and mass marches and sit-ins and all the rest. At least, not the way we have done during the last ten years. The reason is that we have reached the point where it doesn't make sense any more to *ask* the government for anything by mass protests. We are not going to get *anything* that way. They are not going to give anything to black people any more just because black people ask for it, demonstrate for it. It seems to me that the question John Lewis asked at the March on Washington in 1963 is the question that has to be asked today: "Just what side is the federal government on?" For as hard as this may seem, the time has come now when we are going to have to get what we need for ourselves. We may get a little bit of help, here and there, but in the main, we are going to have to do for ourselves. If what the politicians have done to the poverty program hasn't taught us anything else, it has taught us that we are not going to get much help from the politicians. And it has taught us that we are not going to get any serious useful help from the government to deal with problems we have because we are poor and because we are black.

But I don't think that means we can give up our work in politics, especially right now in the 1968 election. We have got to get something from politics for politics owes us something, and since that is so, we have got to work in this election also. For instance, I know that some black people and white people are saying that we ought not to vote in November because the choices are so bad, and the election is not something that is important to black people anyway. But a lot of people, especially in the North, haven't gone through some of the terrible, almost unbearable things we have had to go through in the South. A lot of them who say they aren't going to vote really do not know what it is like to go hungry, and to know that thousands of people who get little or nothing from the government—welfare or food or anything—are starving to death. A lot of these folk don't know what we in the South know—of what it is like to work for twenty-five or thirty cents a day. By having this experience in the South, and by having gone through what I have just talked about—of what it meant a few years ago to register and vote in Mississippi—you can be sure that we will turn out and vote in November, and we are going to carry carloads of people to the polls.

Now I'm going to be very frank and outspoken about this because it is important to us. We have looked at the three candidates, and we have seen one of them saying something positive about where we are, but some are saying very negative things about where we are. No matter how bad the choices may seem, no matter how better they might have been, some of the candidates have come out against welfare, and have said there are a lot of things like welfare they would "close down" in the North and in the South. But there are plenty of people who just can't work, or won't be able to find work. So we have to ask the question of what will happen to them if they cut out welfare? Anyone who knows anything about the South knows that some are starving right now, and sick and have no money, and need Medicare and Social Security. So if they "closed down" what some of the candidates are talking about, it would be a disaster in the South, for poor white people as well as poor black people. We better be clear about *that*. And some of the candidates are leading this country down the path of hate. If this country goes all the way into hate, it is going to be disastrous for everyone, for hate never created anything, it can only destroy.

Now this is the way our people down here see it. They say that they are going to vote for Vice President Humphrey because they hear what the other candidates are saying. We are going to do what the people at the grass roots want us to do. This is the important thing, as I see it, of working at grass roots politics. We are going to lose our people if they vote one thing, and then we go out and do something else.

The whole matter of voting is a very crucial thing to us. For you see, some of our people have died for the right to vote. Now if there are some people who don't want to vote, that is their business, but they might be sorry for the results. So there is no sense in kidding anyone. We would rather have Vice President Humphrey than the other candidates, and we are going to the polls to vote for him in November. We know what it is like in the South when people don't have anything. And we know that much of this campaign is about trying to keep us black people "in our place." So if

Humphrey doesn't win, we will just have to "keep the faith," because that will be about all we can do.

So in October 1968 it is time for America to wake up and realize that black Americans are not going to tolerate what we've had to put up with in the past 300 years. We're *not* going to say that no more black people are going to die. I'm never sure anymore when I leave home whether I'll get back or not. Sometimes it seems like to tell the truth today is to run the risk of being killed. But if I fall, I'll fall five feet four inches forward in the fight for freedom. I'm not backing off that, and no one will have to cover the ground I walk on as far as freedom is concerned. No man is an island to himself, and until I'm free in Mississippi, you're not free anywhere else. A nation that's divided is definitely on the way out. We have the same problems from coast to coast. The future for black people in America is the same as the future for white people in America. Our chances are the same. If you survive, we will too. If we crumble, you are going to crumble too.

So let's each of us ask ourselves the question in the old hymn:

> *Must I be carried to the sky on flowery beds of ease,*
> *While others fight to win the prize and sail through*
> *bloody seas?*
> *—Fannie Lou Hamer*

Bibliography

Collum, Danny. "Prophet of Hope for the Sick and Tired." *Sojourners* 11(December 1982):3-21.

Derr, Mary Krane. "Letting Everyone's Light Shine: The Life and Work of Fannie Lou Hamer (1917-1977)." *Daughters of Sarah* 20 (Fall 1994):20-22.

Mills, Kay. *This Little Light of Mine: The Life of Fannie Lou Hamer.* New York: Dutton Press, 1993.

SHIRLEY CHISHOLM
(1924-   )

Born Shirley Anita Saint Hill to immigrants from Barbados, she was the first Black woman to be elected to the House of Representatives (12th District of New York). She served in the House for fourteen years as an advocate for the political rights of women and minorities. Her unsuccessful bid for the presidency of the United States in 1972 was a first, and Chisholm's bid revised national conceptualizations about the role of Black women in the political process.

"The Relationship Between Religion and Today's Social Issues"[15]

I

It is exceedingly difficult to explain one's inner feelings and motivations especially when it seems that one's actions defy current policy and standards. Often we remain committed to an individual stance or assume a position that is opposed to the general one simply because we must and not because we feel that we should do so. Love for one's fellowman and love for one's country can only be expressed by action. One cannot claim to love something and then remain passive toward it. Philosophically I remain involved because it is the only way in which I can express my love toward a different America, an America that does not yet exist in time and space.

There is an America that exists in the beliefs and actions of many Americans, an America that will come into being because of the positive actions of myself and other people. It is that which has first claim to my love and allegiance.

In 1st John 3:18 we find the following word: "My little children, let us not love in word, neither in tongue, but in deed and in truth." The concept of love is inextricably interwoven throughout philosophy and religion. And it is in the context of the modern world that faith, love and action based upon one's own personal responsibility to all other men and to the future of all mankind becomes most important.

In James 2:14-17 we find: "What does it profit, my brethren, if a man says he has faith but has not works? Can his faith save him? If a brother or sister is ill-clad and in lack of daily food, and one of you says to them 'go in peace, be warmed and filled' without giving them the things needed for the body, what does it profit? So faith itself, if it has no works, is dead."

For much of my years in politics I had faith. I was one of the "party workers," stuffing envelopes, organizing rallies, writing speeches and answering phones. But, above all, I watched and listened to the behind the scenes "wheeling and dealing" that characterizes American politics and perhaps, all politics. In short, I was in an excellent position to see the need for political people with a different set of values, someone who cared enough for people to put them ahead of political deals aimed at increasing personal and party success and power.

---

[15]*Religious Education* LXIX/2(March-April 1974): 117-123. This was the opening address of the Convention of the Religious Education Association at the Royal York Hotel, Toronto, on November 18, 1973.

People constantly told me of the great necessity to see some one who cared enough about them to challenge the status quo political structure, to challenge the existing priorities, to challenge the now-leaders who controlled in very real ways their destiny but whom they themselves could not control or even successfully influence.

I was constantly faced with the question, can faith alone save us? I finally realized the answer was, "no." I finally had to acquiesce to their wishes, to accept their counsel as the wisest course to run for public office. There was no way to be assured that I would reach my goals nor is there any now. My personal goals have not been reached because the goals of those who support me, the people, have not been reached.

One of the most flagrant causes of confusion across America is predicated upon the plethora of promises that are made to people without any intent to match the promises with performances. Every politician makes wild and woolly commitments to the people whom he is trying to influence to vote for him. He chooses certain glaring issues upon which he focuses his attention to attract the support of the voters. He calls it a platform. The fact is, the politician cannot deliver what he has promised. Because of the precariousness of the whole pattern and system of operating under a cloud of rivalry and the out-and-out ruthless competition going on between the "ins" and "outs," all types of tactics are used to deal some destructive blows to the body politic. Thus, the public becomes damned because the politician is struggling to save his own hide by destroying the opposing party. This sort of carrying on is far from being democratic. Too often it is founded upon a dichotomic, two-party struggle that makes it impossible to receive the total support of those who may be termed liberal or progressive, moderate or conservative. The brazen promises, the lack of performance, and the lack of vision to plan for absorption into America's midstream is even more precarious for the total population of the nation as a whole.

What is wrong with our society? It is sick when the younger generations turn their backs on the preventatives for the maintenance of health and the social equilibrium: to allow the body to go unwashed, to let the hair grow on the head and face without deterrents to disease, to permit clothing to go uncleaned or unwashed. This is not mere revolt, a retreat, a protest: these are symptoms of a severe sickness permeating the society—the symptoms of something that is decaying.

In depicting ancient society, a prophet declared that it was sick, having "putrefying sores from the crown of the head to the sole of the feet." Could this be the state of modern man? A sick society being piloted by a sick generation? Could it not be said of America today that we are like Israel of yesterday? The prophet Isaiah speaks to our contemporary society. He sighs: "Ah, sinful nation, a people laden with iniquity, offspring of evil doers, sons who deal corruptly" (Isaiah 1:4).

Take up any morning or afternoon paper and you will see the glaring headlines depicting the pathological disorders of a sick society. We need leadership with a calmness of soul in the turbulence of conflicting situations. We have to pray for our children that they may come to classrooms with open minds having not been poisoned with the prejudices that warp life. We must be free of the anemic spirit of indifference to wrongs about us. We must rekindle the fires of hope, faith and love administered in an atmosphere of concern and compassion. We must become obsessed with cleaning the cesspools in our society that breed vice and vacillation; we must open up doors for the poor in industry, banking, education, government and all areas where men work. The proud stubbornness that hampers the peace which we seek must be removed, and we must realize that loud boastings may prove futile in the endeavor of peace. The window-dressing of false credentials must be discarded and true unity be exercised and exhibited in our behavior pattern as true seekers after peace.

II

In today's world religious institutions more than ever must minister to the whole of the individual and not only to the religious part of life and neglect the other component parts of the person's whole. Quite often the church gives the distinct impression that it is concerned exclusively with its own self-preservation, but the clergy must assume a strong role in preparing young men and women to function meaningfully as religiously oriented citizens who are able to cope with the economic, social, religious and political problems of the day. The church can no longer remain mute upon such questions and expect the young to be satisfied. The Bible touches upon every phase of life and our lives are supposed to be integrated wholes, for unless religion is all of life, it is none of life. The rights and wrongs of political issues cannot be sidestepped. The clergy throughout the churches have a most challenging endeavor to save society literally and not figuratively.

If we are indeed a people who subscribe to Jewish and Christian ethics and profess to have faith, strength and belief, then why are our communities so Godless? We have not committed ourselves to action but rather to the utterances of our respective creeds. If we are sincerely interested in the quality of the human spirit, in the motives and ideals which dominate personality, we must be interested in the economic and political problems of our day. Religion is a universal human experience and it is ultimately our deeds rather than our creeds that will be used to demonstrate our practical life's philosophy about ourselves and those who live around us.

Everywhere we turn today we find our dearest ideals and hopes entangled in the economic and political life. Do we then keep our hands off the factors that will determine whether our children have a daily meal or a good school to attend? There is no room left in our world today for a narrow individualistic religion. To talk of building a Christ-like character while one is absolutely complacent about an economic and political system that engenders selfishness, greed and power lust—all of this is sheer vanity.

If we have faith, then we must address ourselves seriously to the young people in terms of helping them to have confidence and trust in adults who have genuine concern about them as people. The youth of today are not much different from the youth of yesteryear. What is vastly different is the world in which these children are growing up—atom bombs and atomic power, shifting cultural patterns, the influence of television, more working mothers. These are some of the ingredients in our way of life that strike children with tremendous impact. In this revolution our youth need adults in the church who are *real* persons. This may sound simple and obvious but in a world filled with phonies it is not. The nonconformity of the beatnik or the rebel may cause shudders to be raised on the spine of the socially proper, but it is a valid protest against such in our society that is surface and false. They need to see the values of love and concern, service and commitment in the lives of the adults that they know. No religion is worth anything unless expressed in our life with others. As Edmund Burke, an Englishman, said over 200 years ago: "All that is necessary for the triumph of evil in the world is that good men do nothing."

III

Today we need faith and action more than ever. As we look about us, we still see and hear of the telling sights of poverty, oppression, war, human suffering and anger. Many of us have been involved over the past decade in the movement of civil rights and for world peace. Where are we? Housing is worse than ever. Urban slums are only bigger and worse ghettos; public schools and universities are in chaos; police forces have become occupying armies; the gap between rich and poor, black and white, parents and young people is growing. Our government called off the "war on poverty" at home while its war abroad went on at an enormous cost in lives and resources. But a number of us continued to see that faith, self-determination, community environment, loyalty, hope were the real issues of society, and concepts like maximum feasible participation, no strings attached, community control were introduced into the process. Thus, however, a little progress may have been made. Poor communities were organized, self-conscious leadership emerged, and the voice of the poor broke through the mass media. Welfare clients, the elderly, the Indians, the Chicano, the Blacks were on the move only because they had not yet lost faith completely. Their actions began to force the powers that be to drop their beneficent paternal masks and to show their claws. It revealed for all to see some of the defects and hypocrisies of the "American Dream." The failure of reform has laid bare the fundamental contradictions and inhumanities of the system. This in itself is a major gain. We are living, like it or not, in the midst of a new revolution, and this is our only hope. It is a revolution in values and goals, in attitudes and in human relations. It is a liberation of the heart and mind from the whole complex of hand-me-down conventions, prejudices and social structures which limit our vision, constrict our thinking and paralyze our actions. We must proceed to see that human values and relationships take precedence over the demands of military power. There is something amiss in a society which pours its most creative energies into an insatiable war machine and which allows corporate profits rather than human need to determine decisions which shape our lives and our future.

There are those who claim that the gospel is opposed to the changing of priorities I have described and they stress the inner, individualistic, formalistic aspects of religion and obedience to authority and tradition. But I believe that we must reconcile those who are oppressed, alienated, rebellious not by conditional handouts which perpetuate servile dependency but by giving to them access to the reins of decision making and to the resources needed for growth in freedom and maturity. Only then can they stand on their feet as free men and women and join as full and equal members of a united community.

Today as students revolt against the complacent and hesitant leadership of the respectable leadership, they are involved with the spirit of self-assertion and self-reliance. Our youth is looking closely at its leadership these days, and we must be able to give to them the impetus to realize that neither the mistakes of yesterday nor the fears of tomorrow will spoil today. We as religious men and women must assume the responsibility of saying to the thousands of our young people that there is more to this social revolution than seeking a share. We must tell them that their task is to improve and give to them a sense of personal worth and the fact that they have within themselves the ability to realize their fullest potentials and to achieve great horizons. Much of the trouble today is born of man's failure to think in terms of tomorrow. Poverty or success is a legacy you leave to your children. If we give our children a sense of worth and the knowledge that excellence will reap rewards, then we have freed them for a better tomorrow.

Remember that biblical faith is oriented towards a new future not a static past. When Israel's faith faltered, Christ came to free a new community to carry on God's work in history. Through Moses, God freed his people from the rigid structures of Egypt and led them by faith through a wilderness towards a promised land.

Are we ready to learn to deal with others as God has dealt with us? God gave us life at the risk of our rebellion and paid for reconciliation at the price of the cross.

—*Shirley Chisholm*

Bibliography

Brownmiller, Susan. *Shirley Chisholm: A Biography*. Garden City, New York: Doubleday, 1970.

Chisholm, Shirley. *The Good Fight*. New York: Harper and Row, 1973.

————. *Unbought and Unbossed*. Boston: Houghton Mifflin, 1970.

Christopher, Maurine. *America's Black Congressmen*. New York: Crowell, 1971.

Flynn, James J. *Negroes of Achievement in Modern America*. New York: Dodd, Mead, 1970.

Scheader, Catherine. *Shirley Chisholm: Teacher and Congresswoman*. Hillside, N.J.: Enslow Publishers, 1990.

AFTERWORD

"Will the Circle of Witnesses Be Unbroken?"

In the Introduction to this volume, I described tradition as a worldview that can be discerned over time. Important to this understanding of tradition is its dynamism—its ability to endure and adapt. In this Afterword, I will illustrate the dynamism of this prophetic religious tradition of African American women by disclosing relationships between what we discern from the witnesses gathered in this volume and the writings of womanist scholars today who are listening, interpreting, and creating as witnesses in an unbroken circle of prophetic presence.[1]

The witnesses in Part One hear God's voice and offer their conversion and/or call experiences as testimony to how the working of the Spirit compels them to live as God's emissaries. These experiences earmark spirituality as the heart from which flows the prophetic presence of African American women. In Part Two, the documents show how this spirituality extends itself into communal admonishment, analysis of and instruction for the African American community, so that the community will become self-determined and guided by norms grounded in God's purposes. Finally, in Part Three this spirituality comes full circle as social criticism of the larger society, calling for transformation of that society by requiring the society to live by the values it professes and/or evoking visions of a society built upon structures for liberation. Thus, this prophetic religious tradition has as its core a spirituality with three interrelating dimensions: the personal (Part One), the intracommunal (Part Two), and the intercommunal (Part Three).[2]

The Personal Dimension

Hearing God's voice is for Elizabeth an early childhood experience deriving from the spiritual nurture of her parents: "when I was but five years old, I often felt the overshadowing of the Lord's Spirit . . . ." Advised by her mother to look only to God, Elizabeth is enabled later to withstand the charge of "imprudency" from church authorities because she "applied to the Lord for direction" and waited "for the dictates of his Spirit." This connection between the Lord's claim upon a woman's life and the work she is compelled to do against normative expectations for women, opposition to her work, and/or threats to her life is heard repeatedly in the

189

testimonies: from Jarena Lee's claim, "The Lord gave his handmaiden power to speak for his great name, for he arrested the hearts of the people, and caused a shaking among the multitude, for God was in the midst"; to Harriet Ross Tubman's declaration, "For, I had reasoned dis out in my mind; there was one of two things I had a *right* to, liberty or death; . . . I should fight for my liberty as long as my strength lasted, when de time came for me to go, de Lord would let dem take me"; to Virginia Broughton's experience as a missionary, "In the meantime, while God was providing the way to enter churches, He was also preparing His female servants to enter them with an effectual message from His Word, even as He prepared Peter while on the house top for meeting the committee that came to greet him in behalf of Cornelius, the Gentile, with whom he had had no dealings."

Accordingly, the spirituality of African American women's prophetic presence is as womanist ethicist Emilie Townes describes womanist spirituality today:

> Womanist spirituality is not grounded in the notion that spirituality is a force, a practice separate from who we are moment by moment. It is the deep kneading of humanity and divinity into one breath, one hope, one vision. Womanist spirituality is not only a way of living, it is a style of witness that seeks to cross the yawning chasm of hatreds and prejudices and oppressions into a deeper and richer love of God as we experience Jesus in our lives. This love extends to self and to others. It holds together the individual and the community in a soulful relationship that cannot dwell more on one than the other partner of the relation but holds both in the same frame.
>
> Womanist spirituality is the working out of what it means for each of us to seek compassion, justice, worship, and devotion in our witness. This understanding of spirituality seeks to grow into wholeness of spirit and body, mind and heart—into holiness in God. Such cogent holiness cannot hold its peace in a world so desperately separate from the new earth.[3]

The Intracommunal Dimension

Because "the love" that drives the spirituality of African American women's prophetic presence "holds together the individual and community in a soulful relationship," African American women affirm a responsibility to admonish (analyze and instruct) the African American community. Affirming this responsibility makes them vulnerable to isolation from the community; yet, abiding in the communion of Godself (Creator, Redeemer, Sustainer), they have the courage to be prophets because they have taken to heart these words of Jesus whom they profess and proclaim, "Prophets are not without honor, except in their hometown, among their own kin, and in their own house" (Mark 6:4 NRSV).

Listen to some voices of intracommunal admonishment:

I am a strong advocate for the cause of God and for the cause of freedom. I am not your enemy, but a friend both to you and to your children. Suffer me, then, to express my sentiments but this once, however severe they may appear to be, and then hereafter let me sink into oblivion, and let my name die in forgetfulness.

Had the ministers of the gospel shunned the very appearance of evil; had they faithfully discharged their duty, whether we would have heard them or not; we should have been a very different people from what we now are; but they have kept the truth as it were, hid from our eyes, and have cried, "Peace, Peace!" when there was no peace; they have plastered us with untempered mortar, and have been as it were blind leaders of the blind. (Maria W. Stewart)

If I understand our greatest wants aright, they strike deeper than any want that gold or knowledge can supply. We want more soul, a higher cultivation of all our spiritual faculties. We need more unselfishness, earnestness and integrity. Our greatest need is not gold or silver, talent or genius, but true men and true women. We have millions of our race in the prison house of slavery, but have we yet a single Moses in freedom? And if we had, who among us would be led by him? (Frances E. W. Harper)

A race situated as peculiarly as our own, along with its book-learning calls for instruction for its youth (who are our embryo leaders) adapted to its peculiar needs, and training which will meet existing and not imaginary conditions. . . .

And while devotion to principle or courage of conviction, perseverance and patience, and self-control are the predominating requisites of true leadership, over and above them all—embodying the truest leadership, is a deep abiding love for humanity. (Ida B. Wells-Barnett)

I LEAVE YOU FAITH. Faith is the first factor in life devoted to service. Without faith nothing is possible. With it, nothing is impossible. Faith in God is the greatest power, but great too, is faith in oneself. . . . The measure of our progress as a race is in precise relation to the depth of faith in our people held by our leaders. (Mary McLeod Bethune)

The race whose women have not learned that industry and self-respect are the only guarantees of a true character will find itself bound by ignorance and violence or fettered with chains of poverty. (Nannie Helen Burroughs)

Intracommunal admonishment is thus criticism and correction tempered by encouragement.

It is not surprising, therefore, that, rather than wallow in grief for the collective soul of a people who seem caught in cross-currents of violence that are bringing death to black bodies and minds and souls, womanists too admonish the community. We hear womanist words of admonishment when Delores S. Williams stresses embracing "the black ethical task of revaluing value"[4] and this ethical principle, "survival and a positive quality of life for black women and their families in the presence and care of God"[5] as requisites for becoming "the community [who] will . . . see how a liberation ethic and a survival/quality-of-life ethic work together for the creation of freedom, peace and well-being in the African-American community."[6] We also hear it when Kelly Brown Douglas asserts,

> The African American community faces a crisis, perhaps best described by the word *genocide*. It is our duty as African American women and men doing theology to help to forge a culture of resistance that will promote life and wholeness for the entire community—even as we struggle to dismantle the interlocking system of multidimensional oppression. In so doing, we are called to a womanist way of relating to the community and with each other. The crisis of our community compels us to be to our community the image of God who is life and wholeness.[7]

The Intercommunal Dimension

The prophetic presence of African American woman comes full circle as they are driven by divine impulse to challenge values of domination and structures of oppression in the church and society where they seek to do the work of God's Reign. This divinely initiated response to oppression is heard in the challenge issued anonymously through the newspaper by "a colored woman, wife and mother" who knew that a black family's quest to secure adequate housing was part of a larger struggle which had to be waged against "the South's idea of justice." Or, the challenge arises when one's work with others to overcome social evils that affect the overall health and well-being of society is diminished by prejudicial attitudes and behavior. For example, Frances E. W. Harper had these words of reproach for southern women in the Women's Christian Temperance Union who would not affiliate with colored women to do the work of the Union:

> Southern white women, it may be, fail to make in their minds the discrimination between social equality and Christian affiliation. Social equality, if I rightly understand the term, is the outgrowth of social affinities and social conditions, and may be based on talent, ability or wealth, either or all of these conditions. Christian affiliation is the union of Christians to do Christly work, and help build up the

kingdom of Christ amid the sin and misery of the world, under the spiritual leadership of the Lord Jesus Christ.

Believing, as I do, in human solidarity, I hold that the Women's Christian Temperance Union has in its hand one of the grandest opportunities that God ever pressed into the hands of the womanhood of any country. Its conflict is not the contest of a social club, but a moral warfare for an imperiled civilization. Whether or not the members of the farther South will subordinate the spirit of caste to the spirit of Christ, time will show.

Likewise, Anna Julia Cooper, an educator concerned with the transmission of values and their embodied practice, warns those who would provide moral leadership for the country, "A nation cannot long survive the shattering of its own ideals. Its doom is already sounded when it begins to write one law on its wall and lives another in its halls."

As bearers of prophetic witness in society, African American women took their experiences as points of departure for social analytical discourse about and action against injustice. Septima Clark, Fannie Lou Hamer, and Shirley Chisholm offer prime examples of this discourse and action.

Based on her experience as a parent and in the civil rights movement, Septima Clark spoke about racial injustice and how to eradicate it.

The Negro parent's dilemma is fearsome. There is nothing worse, I believe, and *I know* this, than bringing a child into the world and having to teach him that none of the pleasant things of life are for him, or few of them at most. How do you teach a tot where to sit, where to walk, where not to play, and where not to go . . . like the theater, an art gallery, city parks and public libraries? A parent has a terrible time explaining why the native soil is such a hard place for the native to grow in.

Segregation, I have no doubt in the world, is the root of this ugly and evil thing. Out of segregation stem the rank weeds of discrimination and injustice. So, to destroy the present crop of weeds and prevent recurrent growth, we must dig out and cast away the roots.

Fannie Lou Hamer tells how her civil rights work emerged out of her faith and how this faith gave her the needed perspective to address the problems black people confront.

We have to realize just how grave the problem is in the United States today, and I think the 6th chapter of Ephesians, the 11th and 12th verses helps us to know how grave the problem is, and what it is we are up against. It says: "Put on the whole armor of God, that ye may be able to stand against the wiles of the devil. For we wrestle not against flesh and blood, but against principalities, against powers, against the rulers of the darkness of this world, against spiritual wickedness in high places." This is what I think about when I think of my own work in the fight for freedom, because before 1962, I would have been afraid to have spoken before more than six people. Since that time I have had to speak before thousands in the fight for freedom, and I believe that God gave me the strength to be able to speak in this cause.

So we are faced with a problem that is not flesh and blood, but we are facing principalities, and powers and spiritual wickedness in high places: that's what St. Paul told us. And that's what he meant. America created this problem. And we forgive America, even though we were brought here on the slave ships from Africa. Even though the dignity was taken away from the black men, and even though the black women had to bear not only their own kids but kids for the white slave owners. We forgive America for that. But we're looking for this check now, that's long past due, to let us have our share in political and economic power, so that we can have a great country, together.

Shirley Chisholm, a person of faith who became a politician in order to fulfill her faith claims, spoke to religious leaders of her political experience.

I was constantly faced with the question, can faith alone save us? I finally realized the answer was, "no." I finally had to acquiesce to their [supporters] wishes, to accept their counsel as the wisest course to run for public office. There was no way to be assured that I would reach my goals nor is there any now. My personal goals have not been reached because the goals of those who support me, the people, have not been reached.

In today's world religious institutions more than ever must minister to the whole of the individual and not only to the religious part of life and neglect other component parts of the person's whole. Quite often the church gives the distinct impression that it is concerned exclusively with its own self preservation, but the clergy must assume a strong role in preparing young men and women to function meaningfully as religiously oriented citizens who are able to cope with the economic, social, religious and political problems of the day. The church can no longer remain mute upon such questions and expect the young to be satisfied. The Bible touches upon every phase of life and our lives are supposed to be integrated wholes, for unless religion is all of life, it is none of life. The rights and wrongs of political issues cannot be sidestepped. The clergy throughout the churches have a most challenging endeavor to save society literally and not figuratively.

Such social analytical discourse and calls for transformative change continue in womanist writings in varied ways as womanist scholars are engaged in what Katie Cannon describes as "canon formation, . . . a way of establishing new and larger contexts of experience within which African American women can attend to the disparity between sources of oppression and sources of liberation."[8] In the contexts of church, academy, and society, womanist scholars are doing social analysis and proposing alternative visions for the future on the basis of their best creative impulses, their retrieval of black women's history as sources, and their reinterpretation of methodologies and doctrines.

For example, offering her own "prayer-poems . . . as meditational guides" into descriptive and normative ethical analysis of the present African American reality, Emilie Townes concludes:

> Apocalyptic vision. Eschatological hope. These twin concepts move within womanist spirituality. The apocalyptic vision evolves from crisis and martyrdom. It is a theo-ethical, sociopolitical manifesto that refuses to accept or tolerate injustice. It seeks to overcome the discrepancy (and attendant craziness) between what is and what should be—the discrepancy between empirical reality and legitimate expectations.[9]

In my own work, the retrieval of the collective voice of the black women's club movement leads to this articulation of a socioreligious vision for liberative moral agency:

> From the club women we are admonished that moral vision that does not derive from experience and involve continuous intentional moral agency is deficient. From the club women we find direction toward liberative moral vision for the next century in the cultivation of the virtue of the renunciation of privilege, in striving for inclusivity as value and obligation, and in construing our ethical reflection as mediating process. Moral agency defined as socioreligious praxis is critical.[10]

Likewise, womanists today are presenting us with alternative, constructive ways to analyze and respond to forces of oppression, such as Renita Weems's emergent womanist methodology for reading biblical texts, which emphasizes "examining the *values* of [African American women] readers and the corroboration of those values by the text"[11]; Delores S. Williams's use of African American women's historic experience of surrogacy as a lens to reinterpret the doctrine of atonement in order to focus on life rather than death[12]; Jacquelyn Grant's "self-critical (evaluative)" theological reflection whereby she uses black women's experience to expose the contraditions between servitude and the call to service and servanthood central to Christian theology[13]; and the retrieval of the Anna Julia Cooper's metaphor for God, "a Singing Something," by Karen Baker-Fletcher as a means to reawaken theological imagination.[14]

African American women in the past and today have a spirituality of prophetic presence. We therefore envision ourselves within the biblical story itself and we have visions of what we can become. Above all, we embrace the conviction that we have authority that derives from a God who calls whom God pleases. We acknowledge that we are all subject to the judgment of God and that work for liberation must, therefore, be characterized by self-criticism as we affirm that our liberation is ultimately grounded in God's redemptive work of forgiveness and atonement. Out of our particularity as African American women we strive for dialogue and engagement with others in their particularity. This relationship is premised upon mutual respect, accountability, and responsibility as keys to dismantling the oppressive systems that divide us.

At a point in history African American women heard and acknowledged God's call to be prophetic witnesses. At *this* point in history African American women are listening to those witnesses as well as hearing God's call anew. Thus our prophetic religious tradition lives on.

Notes

[1]The term prophetic presence is derived from Walter Brueggemann's discussion of the prophetic task as that of maintaining "a destabilizing presence." See "The Prophet as a Destabilizing Presence" in *A Social Reading of the Old Testament* (Minneapolis: Fortress Press, 1994).

Prophetic presence refers to the moral agency of African American women who engage in a process of mediating the tensions between what is and what should be as they discern creative responses to lived reality. For a fuller discussion of this mediating process see my book, *Awake, Arise & Act: A Womanist Call for Black Liberation* (Cleveland, OH: The Pilgrim Press, 1994), chap. 5.

[2]It is for the purpose of clarifying what is characteristic of each dimension that I am using each part of this volume to distinguish one dimension from another. However, the understanding that I wish for the reader to maintain is that it is the interrelating of these dimensions that creates the fullness of African American women's prophetic presence.

[3]*In a Blaze of Glory: Womanist Spirituality as Social Witness* (Nashville: Abingdon Press, 1995), 11.

[4]*Sisters in the Wilderness: The Challenge of Womanist God-Talk* (Maryknoll: Orbis Books, 1993), 170. Williams says, "The term *revaluing value* has to do with reassessing and/or renaming social principles, goals, standards, values of a group and/or society. Revaluing value may also have to do with rendering visible what has been invisible and then naming and assigning value to what is rendered visible. This is especially true of women's experience" (fn. p. 271).

[5]Ibid., 175.

[6]Ibid., 177.

[7]Kelly Brown Douglas, "To Reflect the Image of God: A Womanist Perspective on Right Relationship" in *Living the Intersection: Womanism and Afrocentrism in Theology* (Minneapolis: Fortress Press, 1995), 77. See also her book, *The Black Christ* (Maryknoll: Orbis Books, 1994).

[8]Katie Geneva Cannon, *Katie's Canon: Womanism and the Soul of the Black Community* (New York: Continuum, 1995), 76.

[9]*In a Blaze of Glory: Womanist Spirituality as Social Witness* (Nashville: Abingdon Press, 1995), 121. See also by Townes, *Womanist Justice, Womanist Hope* (Atlanta: Scholars Press, 1993).

[10]*Awake, Arise, & Act: A Womanist Call for Black Liberation* (Cleveland, OH: The Pilgrim Press, 1994).

[11]"Reading *Her Way* through the Struggle: African American Women and the Bible" in *Stony the Road We Trod: African American Biblical Interpretation*, edited by Cain Hope Felder (Minneapolis: Fortress Press, 1991), 59. See also by Weems *Just a Sister Away: A Womanist Vision of Women's Relationships in the Bible* (San Diego: LuraMedia, 1988) and "Womanist Reflections on Biblical Hermeneutics" in *Black Theology: A Documentary History, Volume Two: 1980-1992*, edited by James H. Cone and Gayraud S. Wilmore (Maryknoll: Orbis Books, 1993).

[12]*Sisters in the Wilderness: The Challenge of Womanist God-Talk* (Maryknoll: Orbis Books, 1993).

[13]Jacquelyn Grant, "The Sin of Servanthood and the Deliverance of Discipleship" in *A Troubling in My Soul: Womanist Perspectives on Evil and Suffering*, edited by Emilie M. Townes (Maryknoll: Orbis Books, 1993), 199-218. See also by Grant, *White Women's Christ and Black Women's Jesus: Feminist Christology and Womanist Response* (Atlanta: Scholars Press, 1989).

[14]Karen Baker-Fletcher, *A Singing Something: Womanist Reflections on Anna Julia Cooper* (New York: Crossroad Publishing Company, 1994).

Permissions

The publisher gratefully acknowledges the following permissions:

The Feminist Press: Selections by Ella Baker are reprinted by permission, from Ellen Cantarow with Susan Gushee O'Malley and Sharon Hartman Strom, *Moving the Mountain: Women Working for Social Change* (New York: The Feminist Press at The City Univesity of New York, 1980), pp. 60-61, 69-73, and 91-93. © 1980 by Ellen Cantarow, Susan Gushee O'Malley, and Sharon Hartman Strom.

Fisk University: Sister Kelly, "Proud of That 'Ole Time Religion'," *Unwritten History of Slavery: Autobiographical Accounts of Negro Ex-Slaves* (Nashville, Tenn.: Social Science Institute, Fisk University), 1945. © 1968 by Fisk University, Nashville, Tennessee. All Rights Reserved. Published by Microcard Editions, 901 26th Street, N.W., Washington, D.C. 210037, a part of the Industrial Products Division, The National Cash Register Company. Reprinted with permission.

Howard University: Anna J. Cooper Papers, edited and "corrected" with the permission of The Moorland-Spingarn Research Center, Howard University.

Indiana University Press: Maria W. Stewart, "An Address Delivered Before the Afric-American Female Intelligence Society of America," reprinted from *Maria W. Stewart, America's First Black Woman Political Writer*, Marilyn Richardson, ed. (Bloomington: Indiana University Press), 1987. Jarena Lee, "My Call to Preach the Gospel" and "The Subject of My Call to Preach Renewed"; Zilpha Elaw, "Conversion and Call," "Call to Ministry," "On Racial Prejudice," and "Proclaiming the Gospel in the Slave States"; and Julia A. J. Foote, "My Call to Preach," "Heavenly Visitations Again," "Public Effort—Excommunication," and "Women in the Gospel," reprinted from *Sisters of the Spirit*, William L. Andrews, ed. (Bloomington: Indiana University Press), 1987. Reprinted with permission.

Judson Press: Yvonne V. Delk, "Singing the Lord's Song," *Those Preachin' Women, Volume I*, Ella Pearson Mitchell, ed. (Valley Forge, Pa.: Judson Press, 1985), 51-59. Reprinted with permission of Judson Press. Marsha Woodard, "No Greater Legacy," *Those Preaching Women, Volume 2*, Ella Pearson Mitchell, ed. (Valley Forge, Pa.: Judson Press, 1988), 35-39. Reprinted with permission of Judson Press.